BEANS, BUGS AND BOMBS

REMEMBRANCES FROM A LIFE ON THE MOVE

CAREY MCINTOSH

CONTENTS

PUBLISHERS NOTE

**Cover design and interior formatting
for digital and print editions:**
Tosh McIntosh

Print Edition (v2.5.5)
ISBN-13: 978-1-695879-22-5

Digital Edition (v2.5.5)

My eternal thanks go to my husband Eddie, my children, Eirwyn and Marion, and our beloved dog Seamus, for giving me the life that is, if inadequately, described in these pages. They have patiently and not-so-patiently weathered storms both literal and metaphorical, and stood at my side through a great deal of malarkey. Kids, here are those stories I promised you.

All who wander are not lost.

— J.R.R. Tolkien

TIMELINE

- Sep 1992: Carey graduates college and moves to Germany
- Apr 1997: Carey joins Balkan Peace Team and moves to Belgrade, Serbia
- Jul 1997: Carey and Eddie meet in Prishtina, Kosovo
- Apr 1998: Carey takes a job with International Rescue Committee and moves to Prishtina
- Aug 1998: Eddie moves to York to do a master's program
- Feb 1999: Carey moves to York with Eddie
- Mar-Apr 1999: Mass exodus of Kosovars to Albania and Macedonia, NATO starts bombing Belgrade
- Jun 1999: Eddie and Carey get married
- Nov 1999: Eirwyn born
- Sep 2000: Family moves to Nairobi
- Dec 2001: Marion born
- Apr 2001: Family moves to Rwanda
- Sep 2001: Carey starts working at US Embassy
- Apr 2004: Rwanda celebrates 10th anniversary of genocide
- Oct 2004: Carey leaves US Embassy
- Apr 2007: Carey starts to work for Catholic Relief Services and moves to Sarajevo, Bosnia and Herzegovina
- Jul 2007: Eddie, Eirwyn, Marion move to Sarajevo
- Aug 2009: Family moves to Lusaka, Zambia
- Aug 2014: Family moves to Ouagadougou, Burkina Faso
- Oct 2014: Popular insurrection; Blaise Compaore resigns and flees the country

- Sep-Oct 2015: Attempted coup d'état
- Nov 2015: Presidential elections
- Jan 2016: Terror attack on Cappuccino restaurant and Splendid hotel, Ouagadougou
- Aug 2017: Terror attack on Turkish restaurant, Ouagadougou

FOREWORD

This book is a work of fiction. An odd thing to say about a "non-fiction" book, but since I've relied entirely on my own memory going back over 25 years, I'm pretty sure my memories have at times only a passing acquaintance with the truth. I've done the best I can to faithfully reconstruct who did what, but if you're looking for encyclopedic recall, you'd best reach for a history book. What I can promise you is that the *feelings* are all real, and all the events did happen in some form. What I hope is that you take away some measure of why we loved the lifestyle we had. In particular, I hope you gain some respect for the people we lived and worked with. It was a humbling privilege to know many of them, and be blown away by their dedication, generosity, and dignity. At least the good ones were like that. Nevertheless, names have been changed to protect people's privacy and, on occasion, their safety.

While every attempt has been made to accurately represent people and events, any error is mine alone.

— February 2019

1

BUT FIRST

Looking back, the whole thing seems like a fever dream. Did I really walk through a leech-infested jungle in Madagascar, fly in a small plane over the mountains of Lesotho, run from fuzzy caterpillars, and cower behind a couch in a rather ineffectual attempt not to get shot? The answer is yes to all of these, but the real question is, how in the world did I get there from here?

I guess it was a hint that I learned to walk in an airport. They should have strapped me down right then and never let go. But then, I was just a middle-class White girl growing up in Northern California, with nothing pointing to half my life being led overseas, let alone in developing countries most people in the US have never heard of. Did I yearn back then to go abroad? Not particularly. My father had hauled me off to Europe for two weeks when I was ten, part of a work trip for him and cultural education for me. In true kid fashion, what made the biggest impression on me was how much walking we had to do and how my feet hurt, not the grand cultural sights.

Thinking about it, the seeds of my travels were sown in sixth grade thanks to my teacher, Mr. Carey. He called me "cousin" all year, which made me feel special. His superpower was that he'd grown up in China (his father was involved in installing telephone systems) and gone to regular Chinese school, so he spoke fluent Chinese. I thought that was the coolest thing. So I asked him to show me some characters, and I learned how to count to ten, and it was all very harmless until it came time to choose a language for seventh grade. They didn't have Chinese, but they did have Japanese, and not particularly knowing the difference, I signed up for that.

Fast-forward to the end of college, and I'd been to Japan once, and was a Japanese and music major. Having taken one language for so long, I thought I'd try a second for a change of scenery, so I took German for the last two years. I won't lie: I was good at it. And I wanted more. So when I hooked up with a German exchange student, it didn't seem beyond all sanity to head to Germany and study for a year, to work on my German and then come back and satisfy my dream of becoming a linguistics professor.

And that's how it started. See what a harmless beginning that was? And is it my fault that I stayed in Germany for more like five years, and that when I felt it was time to move on, I didn't really think of going back to the US? In short, I had The Bug: I wanted to keep meeting new cultures and languages. Well, I got my wish: from Germany I would move to Serbia, working for a peace organization on the Kosovo conflict. There I would meet Eddie, and follow him to the UK, where we would get married and have our first child, Eirwyn.

Eddie then got a job in Nairobi, working on the conflict in (South) Sudan. This was our first foray into Africa. I have to say neither one of us was particularly keen on the whole Africa thing, in part because of the folks who go misty-eyed when they say the word "Ah-free-kaaahhhh" and things suddenly go all sepia-toned. Also, it was supposed to be dirty and chaotic and dangerous, and here we had a 9-month-old to think of. But everyone said

Nairobi was "not really Africa" (how I hate that—as if by definition "development" and Africa are mutually exclusive), so we figured it was OK to try. Ladies and gentlemen, meet Nairobi, our gateway drug.

Next thing you know we were living in Rwanda, which was a real come-down in many ways. Limited food, mediocre health care, water cuts, power cuts, malaria… it was a different customer. Plus, we had a 3½-month baby on our hands: Marion, born in Nairobi. But we came to have a wonderful time in Rwanda and in many ways, it's the place that most put its stamp on our young family.

Until this point Eddie had had the lead job, and I had followed. Mostly I took care of the kids, though for three of our years in Rwanda I worked part-time as a local hire at the US Embassy. At the end of Rwanda, Eddie declared that he needed a break and he was more than ready to take on the childcare if I wanted to take the lead job. I got absurdly lucky in my job search, and was offered a good job in Bosnia.

Our story then wandered from Bosnia to Zambia, and then on to Burkina Faso, where our adventures overseas finally came to an end. It really was just a case of one thing leading to another, and then suddenly two decades passed and the idea of living in my "home country" scares me witless. I confess we get a bit bleary-eyed when we hear the word "Africa"…

WEDDING RINGS

Summer, ca. 2005

I guess it's not typical for brides to pick out their own engagement ring, but I chose mine. Then again, I wasn't strictly speaking a bride anymore, either. My husband, Eddie, and I had already been married for five or six years at this point; we had two kids and were living in our fourth country together. But they say third time's the charm, so I thought what the hell, for our third set of wedding rings maybe I'll splash out and actually get the full set. And if you're wondering what say the husband got in the matter, well, let's just say his role was largely to encourage conspicuous consumption.

We bought our first rings (white gold, please, not silver) about a week before getting married, which gave us time to have them engraved, but not sized. As a result, they were both a little too big. This didn't seem like a big deal until two days after the wedding, when Eddie was shaking some water off his hand and sent his ring flying off his finger, where it came heart-stoppingly close to falling down a storm drain. From that day forward, as they say, he wore his ring on the middle finger.

A couple of months after the wedding, we found out we were moving to Nairobi—a pretty large city, known among residents of East Africa for its relative strengths as a source of consumer goods and decent health care, but unfortunately also its crime rate (code name: "Nairobbery"). So we decided to entrust our real wedding rings to a third party, and we bought a pair of relatively inexpensive, but still pretty, rings to wear instead.

Sadly, said third party was not quite as reliable as advertised in the keeping-valuables-safe department. Long story short, the rings (and other items we'd left for safe-keeping) were stolen—in that obviously dodgy bastion of corruption and insecurity known as the UK. And yes, there's a story there, but if I told you, I'd have to kill you afterwards (no, really).

Thus were our ersatz rings kind of turned into our only/"real" ones. Which wasn't really a problem; we liked them well enough, and they were un-flashy enough that we felt OK wearing them in everyday life. And yet: I should have taken mine off before I went swimming in Lake Kivu…. I think you get the picture.

And so, the next summer, when we were on home leave in the US, I got to pick out a honking great stone (thereafter known as "The Rock") as well as an actual wedding band. The Rock, it is true, only comes out when we are not on the African continent, because it would be awkward to type with fewer than ten fingers. And to be fair, these rings have lasted over ten years, which in my book really does make the third time the charm. And if, for some reason, these, too, should somehow go missing…. At least I know a good jeweler. Actually, three of them.

HOW EDDIE AND CAREY BECAME EDDIE & CAREY

Kosovo, 1997

People think it's interesting that my husband and I met in Kosovo. Personally, I think the noteworthy thing is that we met at a party. The one party I ever crashed, no less.

I was downstairs, chatting for a bit with our landlady and her family. They lived on the bottom floor, and we (Balkan Peace Team, where I was volunteering) had a simple flat upstairs where we would stay when in Kosovo, rather than our main base, in Belgrade.

The son, who was a driver for one of the few international development or relief agencies active in Kosovo at the time, suggested I come to a party with him. I protested that I didn't know anyone at the party, let alone the host.

"Never mind," said the son, "neither do I."

A quick calculation of my options revealed, behind Door #1, a painfully quiet evening in my flat, trying to read by the weak light of a single bulb, or, behind Door #2, the possibility of Death by Social Awkwardness. Fatefully, not only did I choose Door #2, but in a moment of overexcitement, made a vow to myself that I would *absolutely not* linger by the wall looking by turns desperate and anti-social, but would heroically launch myself into the fray, and act like I was both actually invited and not terrified.

There weren't exactly loads of people there when we arrived, so I fled to the balcony, where I saw a group of people chatting among themselves at the far end. So, true to my vow, I walked over and introduced myself. They were French, and possibly pharmacists. I really don't remember anything we discussed, only that at some point I'd pretty much exhausted their tolerance for strange interlopers in their conversation, so I turned around to look for a new victim.

At that moment a guy came out of the flat and onto the balcony, pulled out a cigarette, and started looking in vain for a light. At which point I, young and probably dumb as I was, strode across the balcony to offer him my lighter. Upon which we chatted for a while, and I learned that he was the head of an international relief agency.

This caught my attention, because while I had pretty extensive contacts among local peace groups and such, I really didn't know any of the international aid types. So I asked if I could set up a work meeting with him at some point. He said sure—but didn't take my number.

Now, to understand the next part, you have to know a couple of key pieces of information. One: I may not have known the guy whose leaving party this was, but Eddie most certainly did—and they had quite a history of going dancing till late, with some of the other NGO types. It wasn't about getting drunk or meeting people, just blowing off steam from a pretty heavy work schedule in what was an increasingly tense atmosphere between the ethnic Albanians and Serbs.

The second thing you need to know about is something called "donated aid". Now, you might think this would be useful things, such as blankets, or food, or water-purification tablets. And while I hasten to reassure you that these practical items were indeed being given to people in need, "donated aid" referred to a fairly random collection of stuff that companies donated to aid agencies in order to benefit from the tax write-off.

It could be that there was a small fault in a batch or lot, or it could just have been a stock overrun. The point was, as soon as the merchandise passed ownership from the manufacturer to the aid agency, the company had fulfilled its obligations. The receiving agency was then free to use the stuff as they saw fit, with no need to report back to anyone.

If the articles were found to be of practical use and good-enough quality, they would be distributed to beneficiaries in the usual way. Some things, though, were better kept back, which is why the party-goers on the fateful evening in question had access to a rather large supply of strawberry-scented, exfoliating shower gel.

Picture, then, if you will, the following scene, as I came upon it while trying to leave the party: about ten people, dancing rather madly (and in the corresponding state of dishevelment), covered in smelly pink goo.

And one of these people was Eddie.

So, I did what anyone would do. I walked up to him, put my business card in his shirt pocket (trying not to touch anything), and probably said something really clever, like "Give me a call when you get a chance, and we'll set something up."

And the rest, as they say, is history.

P.S.: About 15 years later, I accompanied some colleagues to a meeting with the head of UNICEF in Madagascar. Monsieur le Représantant Résident looked vaguely familiar, but I couldn't figure out who he reminded me of. As we got up to leave, he looked at me and said, "Were you in Kosovo back in the '90s? Did you know someone called Eddie?" And it hit me like a lightning bolt: This was not UNICEF Mr le Représantant Résident Steven, but MSF Steven, at whose leaving party… you guessed it. The aid biz is really no different from many other industries: you'd better be as nice as you can to whomever you know, because you're perfectly likely to see them again—and they'll probably be your boss.

4

MISSING IN ACTION

Kosovo, 1999 and Sarajevo, 2007

My first "real" job, i.e. for which I got paid an actual salary, was with the International Refugee Committee in Kosovo. We were doing a "community-building" program on what is nowadays a fairly standard model: offering mixed-ethnic "communities" or villages resources to make concrete improvements to their infrastructure, if they could get together and agree on what their priorities were (of course, only if their "priorities" were something that figured on our menu of possible interventions). It was a long-term development project in a territory that was fast becoming a war zone.

Our staff were a couple of expats, and mostly ethnic-Albanian national staff. Among these, Mahmoud stood out for a number of reasons, not least because he was a good decade or two older than most of our other staff, and he was from the village rather than the capital. An engineer, he was tall and thin, with a weather-beaten face. He was of a generation that had come of age in the old Yugoslavia, and so spoke good enough Serbian for the two of us to be able to communicate without a translator, even though he didn't understand much English and my Albanian was mostly about food.

The thing about Mahmoud was that he had a very unique way of expressing himself. The first words of Albanian my supervisor learned were, "Mahmoud! *Po ose jo?*" "Mahmoud, yes or no?" Because his answer to even the most direct question had a tendency to ramble over hill and dale, and back again, only by a different route the second time.

But for as annoying and seemingly random it could seem to us, he was solid gold when we had to go talk to local communities. Normally, once you've done the same exercise with three or four communities, you kind of know how the spiel is going to go. Even if you got someone to whisper a translation in your ear the first time or two, eventually you can skip it, because you can know what's being said more or less by looking at your watch.

But Mahmoud was different. Every single time that man opened his mouth, no matter what I was thinking he might say next, guaranteed it was something not just different from what I expected, but often practically incomprehensible in terms of what we were trying to accomplish. And yet: looking at the villagers' faces as he talked, hearing them chuckle and seeing their knowing nods of agreement, you had to recognize that he was a genius. He was one of them: a villager talking to his people. And he got shit done.

A lot of the Serbs who worked as local police were also from local villages, and many of them knew Mahmoud. Funny thing, at least in my experience, about people from the Balkans: you put them in groups, where they can feel that their identity group is under threat, and they can very well be at each other's throats. But put two individuals, supposed enemies, in a room together, and chances are they'll be getting drunk and telling off-color jokes by the time you can say "Milošević". So having Mahmoud among our ranks was a little bit of a free pass. On a good day, you'd get to a Serbian checkpoint, and the police would say, "Oh, IRC! You work with Mahmoud? *Hajde*, go then, good luck."

Because Mahmoud was from the village, it was too far (and not really safe) for him to go home from the office every day. So he lived in a little flat under the converted house that was our office. The other resident was our one other staff member from the village: Dejan, a 20-something (closer to 20 than something) Serb, every bit the stereotype of the jolly fat guy. Dejan couldn't stop smiling if you paid him. But make no mistake, he was a pretty courageous dude, working for an American agency and running English classes in ethnic-Serb schools at a time when the West was being vilified by Serbia.

Perhaps unexpectedly, perhaps inevitably, Mahmoud and Dejan became fast friends. United by their village backgrounds, and despite significant differences in age and ethnicity, they were Tweedle Dum and Tweedle Dee, a nearly inseparable pair.

In March 1999, I was just a couple of weeks out of Kosovo, but the proverbial shit had finally hit the proverbial fan. NATO was bombing Belgrade, and my former colleagues were mostly living in refugee camps in Macedonia. This was back when e-mail addresses were rare and usually tied to an institution, and I didn't have phone numbers for most of my friends. So when my friends and colleagues became refugees, I pretty much lost contact with all of them. It was frightening, and frustrating to have been so close to people and to now be away from it all, powerless.

One day I got an e-mail from an expat friend, in which she was notifying people that Mahmoud had been killed. Of all the people, I thought—not that I wanted harm to come to any of my former colleagues, but Mahmoud... it was pretty devastating. And of course I had no way of communicating with my other colleagues, let alone his family, so I was left to process the news pretty much on my own, as best I could.

Eight years later, I was hired by Catholic Relief Services

(CRS) to cover the Balkans region, based in Sarajevo. Having worked (and met each other) in Kosovo, Eddie and I were excited by the prospect of coming back to the Balkans. And I would have the opportunity to travel again to Serbia and Kosovo, which I hadn't seen since leaving in January of 1999.

One person I did sort of keep in touch with from back then was my former supervisor ("*po ose jo!*"). One day I wrote to him, just to say hi and talk a bit about being back in the Balkans. In his reply was the sentence, "How funny, I heard from you and Mahmoud in the same day."

Cue goosepimples on my arms and neck, and a close call with falling out of my chair and straight onto the floor. Um... you mean... "Could you give me his e-mail address?"

A few months later, I managed to organize a work trip to Kosovo with a weekend in the middle, and I took the bus down to meet Mahmoud the ghost. We spent the whole day together. He showed me the factory he managed, and I met a bunch of his friends. Every time he introduced me, he got a great big grin on his face, and said, "This is Carey. She thought I was dead for 10 years!" Yeah, hilarious.

So, I finally asked: what was the scoop? How come I heard he was dead and he wasn't really dead? Here's his story:

When the war started (OK, not technically a war, but it sure quacked like one), Mahmoud's name was on a list, as someone who had been working for an American NGO, so the dudes with guns were looking for him. He's spent some time hiding in the forest, and then holed up in a neighbor's barn. When the dudes with guns showed up at his house, they were not pleased to find him gone—and no one would tell them where he was.

So they hauled the whole family out of the house, and lined them up: kids, grandma, everybody. "Tell us where he is, or we start shooting," they said. Thinking fast, one of the family called out, "He's already dead. He died yesterday. I can show you where he's buried, just over there." Which wasn't exactly true, but one fresh grave looks pretty much like the next one, so he figured he could bluff his way through if he needed to. The guys with the guns considered for a moment, and then said OK, marked him as deceased on their list, and left.

In this way, Mahmoud was officially considered killed in combat, and his name was put on the list that Deutsche Welle broadcast in Macedonia every evening. Which is how the information got to my friend, and then to me.

Some months later, that same friend was walking down the streets of Prizren, a wonderful little very historic town out West, by the Albanian border. Imagine her double-take when she saw Mahmoud coming at her from the opposite direction. He had managed to make himself known to a group of European observers, and showed them his old ID from working with the Westerners. They hooked him up with one of the aid agencies, which gave him work, and that's why he was walking down the streets of Prizren on that particular day.

The American threw her arms around him, crying with relief. She pulled a wad of money out of her pocket. "This," she said, "is the money we collected for your funeral. I was on my way to give it to your wife."

I asked whether Mahmoud had kept in touch with Dejan. "Oh, yes," he said. "Let's go see him." And off we troodled to Dejan's family home. The place was easy to recognize. Most of the office had been there for a family celebration towards the end of my original stay, just a few weeks before everything went crazy.

As we drove in, I had a major flash of déjà vu. I swear they were the same chickens. His parents looked the same, and made all the right noises as if they actually remembered me. But the best was Grandma: a hundred years old if she was a day back in '99, and still ticking, bless 'er. And still as impossible to understand as back then, too. It was the home-spun dialect, coupled with the absence of quite a few teeth. We used to say that being able to understand her was the true test of how well you spoke Serbian. She clasped my hand in hers, and made an endearing show of greeting me. I still couldn't understand most of what she said, but it was very sweet.

Dejan had built himself a room over the garage, where we went to hang out for a bit. We reminisced for a while, and then the conversation quickly turned to cement. What kind was Dejan using, Mahmoud wanted to know, and how much was he paying? Ah, well, if he wanted a better deal, there's a guy he knows, mention his name and Dejan will get a better price.

In short, they were still thick as thieves—and still taking care of each other. When things started to explode, and the Serbs were the dangerous guys, Dejan warned Mahmoud and his family, and told them where they could safely go and where to avoid. When the Albanians came out the victors of the conflict, and declared independence from Serbia, the situation was reversed—and Mahmoud helped Dejan's family stay safe.

And Mahmoud still thought it was hilarious that I'd thought he was dead.

GEORGE

Rwanda, 2002—2005

Mahmoud was not the only person I knew who'd had to hide out when the death squads were passing by.

George was my assistant when I ran the small-grants program for the US Embassy in Rwanda. I should really say "sometimes assistant", because he also worked for my supervisor, the Economics and Consular Officer. I mention that only so you don't think my job was grander than it was. Don't get me wrong: I saw pretty much every corner of the (admittedly tiny) country, and certainly got out a heck of a lot more than any of the "real" diplomats.

George was kind of hard to figure out. He had a good sense of humor, when he felt like it, and could get quite animated—but often also went moody and uncommunicative. We spent a lot (a *lot*) of time in the car together, visiting prospective grantee groups and checking up on the current ones. So we had plenty of time to get to know each other, but it was a very on-again, off-again thing.

One time, George's son came to visit. The son lived with his mother, who had a good job as international staff with a UN body, so he was living the nice expat lifestyle: big house, international school paid by the employer, all that jazz. Which, of course, George couldn't offer. So he saw his son only on the brief occasions when the mother brought him back to Rwanda to visit.

Which was ironic, because all of George's siblings had been killed in the genocide, and he was raising all twelve of their surviving children. Twelve living reminders of his own dead brothers and sisters—and a constant reminder of the son he almost never saw.

One day, George described to me how he had survived the genocide. Like many people, he imagined that he'd find some kind of sanctuary in a church building. He made his way to the Catholic Cathedral, in the center of Kigali, where he lived for several weeks. "Every time the death squads would come to the church, I would run and hide under the rafters," he said, miming someone clinging onto the roof. "The priest would meet them out front and say, 'I have such and such a person staying here.'"

"You mean, he was helping the killers?" I asked.

George tried not to look bored. Of course the church had helped the death squads.

In some ways, I wasn't that surprised. Driving to the field, we regularly passed a church building that had been left as a burned-out ruin, a memorial to the hundreds of men, women and children who crowded in, thinking they would be safe in the holy space. In vain. The death squads barred the doors from the outside, and lit the building on fire. They waited outside with their machetes in case anyone managed to squeeze out the window.

That was just one church, but throughout the country, and indeed throughout Rwanda's history, the Church (better said, some of its representatives) has at times stoked the fires of radicalization and instrumentalized ethnic identity. And unfortunately, there are many documented cases of religious figures failing to do the right thing during the genocide—just as others put their lives on the line to try to prevent violence and death.

One day, UN peacekeepers came to the cathedral where George was hiding. Since he'd previously done a stint with the UNAMIR forces, he ran up to them and showed them his ID. This is how he was able to leave the cathedral, and what would almost certainly have meant death if he'd stayed.

We used to drive by that cathedral all the time. I can't imagine what it must have been like for him to see it like that, just about every day. In 2004, for the 10th anniversary of the genocide, several films were made. *Hotel Rwanda* is probably the most famous to Western audiences, even though that was the only one not actually filmed in Rwanda, and not using Rwandan actors. For one or two others, the film crews recreated the scenes of destruction at some of Kigali's more iconic locations: the Milles Collines hotel (the real "Hotel Rwanda"), for example, and the Cathedral. For those of us who didn't regularly listen to local news, which might have warned us, it was certainly a shock to drive by these buildings and see what looked to be bullet holes and debris lying all over the place. At the Cathedral, there were even people walking around leaking "blood" and trailing bits of bandage behind them. What must have crossed George's mind, seeing that.

SOMETIMES AT THE AMERICAN CLUB

Rwanda, 2004

A round the time of the 10th anniversary of the genocide, probably four or five motion pictures were made depicting actual or quasi-actual events from the time. At least three were shot at pretty much the same time in and around Kigali. And, of course, they needed extras and people to play various bit parts.

The best of these films was probably *Sometimes in April*, which depicted the story of a Tutsi family near Kigali during the genocide, using Rwandan actors (except for the star, Idriss Elba), and shot almost entirely on location. April was the month when the genocide began; it's also the month when the long rains typically start, so there's obviously room for some nifty symbolism there.

Initially I really wasn't all that keen to watch any of the movies, having heard plenty of harrowing stories from various friends and colleagues, not to mention some media and books, from the actual genocide. And no, you can relax—I'm not sharing any of the bad ones here. Suffice it to say, I had no desire to see any of that re-enacted. We've owned a copy of *Hotel Rwanda* for easily 10 years, and I've never watched it.

Sometimes in April, though, was shown at the American Club (not nearly as grand as it sounds, I promise), so a friend and I decided to brave it and go together. In part, we wanted to go because a number of people we knew had been given small parts in the film, so of course we couldn't pass up the opportunity to see them on the silver screen.

As it turned out, I needn't have worried about the horror and violence. I should have known that no film-maker in his or her right mind would put the worst of reality on screen, unless they had slasher-movie fans as their primary target audience.

The other thing that helped break the tension, though, was the cognitive dissonance of seeing people we knew onscreen. Judges at the International Criminal Tribunal for Rwanda, in Arusha, Tanzania? Try Tony the defense attaché from the US embassy, and the girlfriend of another embassy employee. Seeing them in robes, looking terribly serious, was pretty hilarious. And then my personal favorite: during a particularly tense scene, when maybe 15 people are being lined up, about to be killed, my friend leans over and says, "See that the guy, the third from the left? He's my friend's gardener."

IN WHICH I FAIL MISERABLY AT BEING AN ENTREPRENEUR

Rwanda, 2005—2006

After working at the US Embassy for about three years, I decided to call it a day and re-focus my energies toward Very Important Things like watching daytime TV and eating cherry bonbons. Which is not to imply that the work I was doing at the embassy wasn't important; in fact, in some ways it may have been among the most satisfying work I ever did. I certainly got to the field and interacted with "regular" Rwandans more than any other international embassy employee. Secretly they were all jealous, I'm telling you.

Now what you probably need to know about shopping in Kigali at this time is that there kind of wasn't any. I used to bemoan the fact that tourists were leaving Rwanda with quality greenbacks in their pockets, simply for lack of souvenirs that were stylish and well-made enough to be worth schlepping home.

The point of it all is that imported food was pretty much limited to staples, like rice (often from Vietnam) or mustard. Which, I thought, created this great niche for US-style salsa. There was a woman who made tortillas, which we could order with one of the embassy employees and pick up once per week. She actually did white and whole-wheat, and they froze pretty well, so with some local beans and seasoning, it wasn't that hard to produce something vaguely reminiscent of "Mexican" food.

I realized that if I could get my house help to blanch the tomatoes and get rid of the seedy bits inside, the process of cooking up a batch of salsa was pretty easy. We even had jalapeño peppers growing in my husband's thoroughly wonderful garden out back. So I started selling jars here and there to friends and colleagues, not for a lot of money, but it was kind of fun, and very satisfying when my "customers" said they liked it and bought a second and then a third jar.

Was it delusions of grandeur I got from this? Honestly I can't say. But somehow I got this idea, when I left the embassy and was trying to think of ways to fill my time, that I could start a catering business. Now, understand that this was not an actual registered business or anything, just a bit of fun. This type of thing was not at all uncommon; one of the kids' pre-school teachers had a nice little sideline running a very small Thai restaurant out of her home.

My big break came when the US embassy got a permanent Marine presence. This meant two exciting things: an annual Marine Ball, and a regular movie night! The only other cinema at the time in Kigali was defunct, and the days of streaming TV were long in the future, so you can imagine that the opportunity to watch decent-quality movies, in English, was a pretty popular thing in certain crowds.

Somehow I negotiated a gig catering dinner at the movie night, which I probably wound up doing all of three or four times. Here's what I learned: 1) Trying to make any kind of profit on food if you are buying the ingredients retail and selling in low volumes is a really dumb idea. 2) It's really hard to pick meals that will please enough different palates, especially when you are in the process of becoming a vegetarian again, and your customers include hunky Marines who like their meat. 3) If you're going to cook any of your food on-site, make sure the ovens work and can draw enough power to get properly hot. 4) I am probably not cut out to run a catering business, let alone a restaurant—thus killing off a vague dream I'd held for many years.

I did also cater one reception for an exhibition, also at the embassy. Making all those bitty little finger foods nearly killed me, but I remember there was one woman who kept coming back to one thing, a mix of strained yoghurt and avocado wrapped in a bit of crepe (tastes way better than it sounds, I promise), in a kind of help-me-I've-had-too-many-of-these-already-but-can't-stop way. I suspect that was the pinnacle of my success.

It wasn't a total loss, though. I had to buy a bunch of big serving utensils, plastic plates (the paper ones kept collapsing) and serving bowls, which our family used for easily the next ten years, in particular when entertaining involved kids or being outside. And I got one thing I could definitively cross off my list of prospective careers.

IN WHICH I (MIS-)REPRESENT THE USA

Rwanda, 2005

The main work I did for the US Embassy in Rwanda was administer the Ambassador's Special Self-Help Fund. This fairly discretionary pot of money is essentially a way of creating positive feelings toward the US by supporting small, local initiatives that would otherwise pass under the radar of most funders. Embedded in the term "Self-Help" is the idea that the fund will support groups that have already invested in their idea, and perhaps just need a nudge to become viable.

I always appreciated the fact that we kept the guidelines pretty open, meaning that many different types of projects could be eligible. In my view, this gave at least one institution of the US Government the flexibility to respond to the needs that the groups had already decided were important enough to invest in, instead of having to line up with priorities decided in the capital city or even Washington, DC.

Being as open as we were, we looked at proposals from all over the country. Now, Rwanda being 26,000 km2, or roughly the size of Maryland, you could make the argument that "all over the country" isn't actually all that exciting, but I thought it was pretty cool that there wasn't a province or major town that I didn't visit. Thankfully, with some strategic planning and a bit of luck, we managed to make most of our visits in a day, and be back in the capital for dinnertime.

One of the things Rwanda is known for is its high population density. Even in the early 2000s, when we were there, I was told that up north there were rural areas with as many as 1,000 people per km2 (global average for non-ocean space is 50.4). This, of course, has all sorts of implications in terms of the burden on health and education services, and threats to agricultural livelihoods through overgrazing, erosion and the splintering of land holdings into ever tinier pieces (an average of 0.6 km2 per family of 8 when we were there—and if you can't imagine what that means, just know it's really, really small).

I bring this up not to educate you about Rwanda, but for one simple reason: For a woman, it's a rather inconvenient fact that, with very few exceptions, it's impossible to stop anywhere for a quick wee without being observed by at least five people. I swear, you think the coast is clear and then you get out of the car and bam! This can make day trips a bit tricky, to say the least. And here's a bit of life advice for you: if you ever have the choice between using the toilet in a school and pretty much anything else, choose the anything else. (You'll thank me.)

One evening, the phone rang at our house. I nearly hung up on the guy because I initially couldn't understand what he was on about. Eventually I caught the name Francine, which I recognized as the president of an association we were funding up north. They had managed to get their hands on a few knitting machines, and so were able to generate a bit of revenue by knitting things like sweaters for school uniforms. Given that the members all had some kind of physical disability, providing them with a productive activity was all the more important.

I really hate having conversations over the phone in languages I'm not very strong in. It took me an embarrassingly long time to figure out that the man on the phone was saying *Elle est déjà morte* ("she's already dead")—which, frankly, freaked me out a little bit because I had seen her probably two days previously, with her newborn baby, when she came to the embassy to discuss the project. Apparently she'd taken ill after childbirth and never recovered.

The man on the phone was the husband. He was calling to tell me which day the burial was going to be, and it gradually dawned on me that I was going to have to go to this thing. Of course it wasn't in the town where the association was based, which still would have been a good three hours away, no: it was going to be up in the village, way the heck up in the north-east, in spitting distance of Uganda. Not a friendly little day jaunt, but it did seem like the polite thing to do, so I felt obliged to make the trip.

When we arrived at the spot, the terror hit. There weren't 30 or even 100 people there; the crowd was easily 300 or 400 people strong, filling the small clearing around the house and spilling up onto the hillside more or less as far as the eye could see. And I, as the American, was given a seat of honor towards the front. Apparently, as the president of a local association and a member of the rural intelligentsia, Francine had enjoyed pretty high status in the region.

Now, I'd been to funerals, but never a burial, let alone one in a foreign country where I was the face of the US Government. Imagine my joy, then, when I was invited to the head of the line to go view the body, along with the closest relatives. I wasn't particularly squeamish about seeing the corpse of someone I'd known, if not well, but it did feel a little weird to do so while on display myself, and then there was the fact that I'd been talking and joking with her less than a week before.

The husband was also there with the baby, and of course their other children. My kids were still in pre-school at the time, and we'd decided not to have any more of our own, but I'd always said that if another child were to accidentally find its way into our family, well, I could be OK with that.

So the whole car-ride up I'd been vaguely wondering what I would do if the husband tried to hand the baby to someone who could so obviously give her a better life, i.e. moi. Lest you accuse me of parental megalomania, let me just say that it wouldn't have been entirely outside the realm of experience. Suffice it to say I was very relieved, and possibly just a little bit sad, to learn that the husband had immediately identified a woman to serve as nurse and nanny to the wee babe.

After the body viewing, there were the obligatory speeches. Everything was in Kinyarwanda, so my colleague gave me a perfunctory translation of the highlights, such as they were, but it was pretty standard stuff. A few speeches in, I started to realize that *I* was going to have to speak.

Not only had I prepared nothing, but I was going to have to speak in such a way that my long-suffering colleague could knit together a vaguely coherent text, sentence by sentence, in the local language. I'd really never needed to speak off the cuff like this before, and here I was, not even a real diplomat, being expected to say something clever and moving on the part of the US Government regarding someone I barely knew.

I honestly barely remember the actual speech I gave. I know it was the first in a long series through which I perfected the art of the diplomatic blah blah, but what I remember most was giving some kind of firm-sounding pledge that the project with the US Government would continue, because, why would it not?

And so I was thoroughly thrown by the enthusiastic applause that issued from the crowd at this point. I shouldn't have been surprised, really, since I was essentially promising that the money would still flow, and who wouldn't welcome that news? I sat down, relieved and shaking, and tried not to think about how hot it was as I watched them lower the coffin into the prepared hole a few feet in front of me.

As I recall, that was actually one of our better projects. Those school uniforms made it possible for an enormous number of (mostly) women to earn a living as tailors, and the bulk order for sweaters they were able to secure in part with our help was a gold mine for the association. It's strange to think that at the time of this writing, that little baby is 13 or 14 years old.

9

KIGALI

April, 2002 – August, 2007

K igali has changed almost beyond recognition since we left, so if you've been there you could be forgiven for thinking that I'm writing about another city entirely.

Overall, the capital definitely gave credence to the country's "Land of a Thousand Hills" moniker. Each hill had a separate name, so these were in essence the city's neighborhoods. It all worked pretty well for navigation except for the one place where you could decide to drive left or right and you'd eventually get to the same place on the other side. I knew it was circular but that didn't make it any more intuitive.

The one thing even short-term visitors seemed to notice was how clean the streets were. And they *were* clean, probably more so than many a street in the "developed" world. Of course the reasons for that were stiff fines for littering and monthly voluntary-compulsive labor dedicated to picking it up. This attempt to clean up the city also resulted in the famous plastic-bag ban (or "paper-bag ban", if you listen to the locals), and a ban on flip-flops, even for tourists.

Grocery shopping usually involved a circuit of downtown involving two or three different shops, starting with the more "local" place to get the basics, and then something more upscale like La Baguette or the German Butcher for meat, cheese (goats' or gouda? gouda or goats'?), upper-end imported goods, and other gourmet items. That is, unless they just weren't available at all, which wasn't uncommon.

Given the lack of supermarket chains, we went local. I adored Frulex. It had that wonderful feeling of Ali-baba's cave, where this completely unprepossessing exterior opens into a land of plenty. It was pretty much a shed with a tin roof down a rough, dirt path with dead fridges on the left, and an auto-repair shop on the right. But inside, there was a great selection of the basics, including your standard supermarket own-brand stuff from Belgium. This might be considered pretty bottom-of-the-barrel in Europe, but it could go for a pretty penny in tiny, land-locked Rwanda.

What I loved most about Frulex were the fruits and vegetables. Except for the apples and imported oranges (both probably coming from South Africa, the apples showing clear signs of having been frozen), all the produce was super fresh and ridiculously inexpensive. The best thing was that I could put all the produce straight into my carrier bag: they'd give me the top of the weighing scales and let me put what I wanted onto that, where it would be weighed and then tipped straight into my bag. I loved not bringing home an explosion of those wafer-thin, anti-gravity plastic bags.

The cashier would write out the receipt by hand at the rather deliberate pace of someone who really has nowhere else to be, and the total would then be added up, by hand, on a simple calculator—and then checked by repeating exactly the same tallying exercise a second time. So, Frulex: not the place you just dash into for a few items on your way somewhere. But I went often enough that they came to know me, and were terribly sweet. I often spent quite a while just yakking with the staff and heard some very interesting stories.

One thing that I grew to love about living in an under-resourced environment is the simplicity of it all. Water's off? Heat on the stove some from the bucket you have in the kitchen for just such a situation, and have a bucket bath. It's how millions of people wash every day, anyway. Electricity's off? Out come the candles—or we can put the generator on for a while, only that it was purchased to power a sub-office and was so big that is was really loud.

We were pretty much prepared to live off-grid for maybe three days. Now think what would happen if you didn't have running water for three days. People usually worry about the electricity, and it's true that three days is a long time if you don't have any, but believe me, the water is the bigger challenge. I pity the people in Kigali whose water was on a pump, so they lost water when the water cut off *and* when the electricity went—a problem I was most happy not to share.

No public parks to speak of? It's OK; you buy a swing set and someone else has a trampoline and someone else a pool, and so the kids get their entertainment in a serial fashion instead of all at once. No playdough? Make your own! (Though this requires cream of tartar, not something commonly found on shelves outside the US as far as I know. Thankfully it's small and so easy to bring back from homeless leave.)

I once burst out laughing in the car, sitting beside my mother and uncle, who were having a perfectly normal first-world conversation about tomatoes: which types they liked best, when and where you could find the different varieties. I leaned forward and said, "You people are so complicated. In Rwanda, there are tomatoes [Roma, for those who wonder about these things] or there are no tomatoes! Easy!"

In sum, though, let me say that we loved living in Kigali. It was a simple, natural space for the kids to grow up in, with pretty perfect weather; friends all colors of the rainbow; cheap, tasty food and some of the most beautiful scenery I've ever taken in.

That said, every city has a dark side, and Kigali's was particularly threatening to international workers. The basic tenet of Rwandan culture is that you can never trust anyone. Expect that colleague or housekeeper you're friendly with is plotting how they can get you when you're in a weak position. I know this sounds paranoid, but that doesn't change the fact that people really are out to get you.

The situation is further complicated by the fact that people have unlikely connections left over from diaspora and genocide days. One organization I knew of had a driver who was connected to the Minister of the Interior. So you can never entirely know who is connected to whom or might be working with that other guy. People hide their feelings so well that you think you're having a positive conversation and yet you've completely offended the other person.

This became very apparent when the Rwandan government released its report on the Genocide. Suddenly anyone who used the terms "Hutu" or "Tutsi" was criminally liable, and "genocidal ideology" became equal in severity to treason. Ethnic labels were no longer appropriate because they were a "Belgian fabrication" and "we [were] all Rwandans now". An international colleague was accused of genocidal ideology by a national staff with an axe to grind, and had to take a very low profile for a while.

But of course people still wanted to know who they were sitting down with. So any time two Rwandans were introduced, if nothing about the environment suggested ethnic identity, the two people would start putting out feeler questions, such as "where did you go to high school?", that would indicate by proxy who you were. The answer to the high-school question gives information based on whether one was in school at all and then which school or type of school, and high school in Uganda meant part of the Rwandan (Tutsi) diaspora there.

Also, Rwandans who'd grown up in Rwanda and those who'd grown up in the diaspora speak Kinyarwanda differently. It's a very subtle thing, but I've spoken with more than one international who agreed with me on this. I was never able to tell whether the Rwandans heard it, too, though I think they must have.

The sum of all this is that we'd go through perfectly normal times feeling OK and then we'd hear of an inside job on a burglary a couple of houses down, or a rumor of coming war with Uganda, or another rumor of something being cooked up inside the Government, and just feel completely paranoid again.

This was the stuff that made living in Kigali extremely mentally and emotionally tiring, amid all the good stuff. This is why, around the time we were there, all the USG staff who'd taken a bonus for staying three years in their posting gave back the bonus money and left.

Even Rwandans complain about their own culture. They hate the secrecy and the backstabbing, but somehow they just keep doing it. I spent a really long time trying to figure out how Rwandans survive is this atmosphere where you can't trust anyone. Then I realized, each person or family has a small group of relatives and true friends, maybe they know each other from school days, with whom they can share what they really think and who provide mutual protection. Think circling the wagons.

Now, we'd come to understand a lot about Rwandan culture anyway just by being there, and so things had started feeling easier from around year three I always felt sorry for people who left after two years because it was like they got all the bad energy from being a struggling newcomer and never got to feel how things can get more comfortable if you give it time and let yourself learn from people. Anyway, by year four, I realized that we'd been adopted into someone's inner circle. This was the wonderful Denis, who is described more below. The point is that we became like family with another family, and it was a lot easier negotiating the world knowing that no matter what, Denis had our back.

10

TWO MEETINGS, THREE PHONE CALLS, AND ONE E-MAIL

Rwanda, ca. 2004

The first meeting took place outside the consular entrance to the embassy. I was heading in to work, when I recognized Faustin, the head of a school we'd visited, which had applied for the small-grants program I administered. I went up to say hello and chat for a bit, as you do. After a few minutes, he started asking me about how to get a visa to the US. Not surprising, given that I was an embassy employee (I wasn't a diplomat, but played one on TV), and it's not exactly uncommon for people to dream of making the transition to the Land of Plenty.

I told Faustin what I knew about the visa process and the green-card lottery, which wasn't a lot, but at least it was probably mostly accurate. So far, so good. But then he started telling me *why* he wanted to get to the US, and it wasn't because he thought the sidewalks were paved in gold. As a (whisper it) *Hutu*, he might have been a part of the numerical majority, but he gave me to understand that the position of school director was considered too high-status for one of *those people*, and that he was being harassed and threatened as a result.

It didn't surprise me that the position of school director was considered prestigious. In most villages I've known, and not just in Africa, you have one central point, which is the office or house of the mayor/traditional leader/clan leader, and then you have the school. Often the only structure in the village to have solid(-ish) walls and a roof, potentially the only place with electricity, or the host of a borehole that serves the community with water in addition to the schoolkids, the school often functions as a kind of community focal point. No wonder, then, that the director carries some clout.

In this case, though, that clout was apparently working against Faustin and his family. According to him, besides threatening letters and such, someone had actually launched a grenade into the compound immediately in front of his house. I didn't personally know anyone who would be able to intervene in a situation like this, but I knew that Human Rights Watch had opened an office in Kigali, and had at least one permanent staff in-country.

The second meeting, then, took place between Faustin and the HRW representative. I listened, a bit nervously, as Faustin told his story and the HRW rep took notes. To be honest, his story sounded scary to the point that I genuinely wondered whether it was all just made up as a ruse to get himself and his family to the US. I half expected the HRW rep to stand up in a huff afterwards and berate me for wasting her time with such claptrap. "Actually," she said instead, "its's one of the most credible stories I've heard."

Oh.

The first phone call came one morning as I was getting ready for work. It was Faustin.

"I just wanted to let you know that my family and I are fleeing to Uganda in a few days," he said. My first thought was how dumb it was to tell me that over a mobile phone, and I told him as much. But he wanted to thank me for trying to help him. We spoke for a few minutes, and he rang off.

The second phone call was a few weeks later (again, on the mobile—what did I say about that?). Faustin was in trouble. He was in Uganda as advertised, and hadn't been able to get to see the UNHCR yet, and so he and his family had no legal status in the country. They couldn't work, and money was running out.

Worse yet, some guys had attacked him and beaten him up on the street. He was convinced that they were hired by the Rwandan secret police, and it could well have been true. The arm of the Rwandan security forces is notoriously long, and they've been credited with a number of alleged kidnappings and killings of opponents to HEPK's (His Excellency Paul Kagame's) regime. In this case there was *really* nothing I could do, so I made sympathetic noises and hoped he'd be able to get in touch with UNHCR as soon as possible.

A number of months passed, and as I heard nothing more from Faustin, I could only assume that he and his family were still lying low, eking out some kind of existence in Uganda. Then came phone call number three.

"We've done it," he said. "UNHCR has accepted our status as political refugees, and we've been approved for relocation to [Country X]. We're leaving today. I just wanted to say thank you again."

I couldn't believe what I was hearing. Third-country resettlement? That's kind of the Holy Grail for people who really, really don't want to go home ever again. Apparently he had convinced people that he needed to get far away and start a new life. The small part I'd played in his story seemed so insignificant to me in many ways, but then it did feel pretty amazing to think that what felt like a minor blip to me had such a profound impact on someone else's life.

The e-mail came several years later, when we were living in

Zambia. Faustin managed to track me down via a former embassy colleague, and wrote to say that he was working as a bus driver in Country X. He'd found the transition difficult and the people (unsurprisingly) not very friendly, but he and his family were safe. Considering that I'd expected never to hear from him again after we left Rwanda, it felt like an amazing gift to learn that he was still doing OK.

The sting in the tail was that his extended family was all still in Rwanda, and suffering threats and reprisals because he and his immediate family had fled. Faustin of course asked whether there was anything I could do to help them leave, and sadly there wasn't, at least nothing I was prepared to commit to.

People talk about "refugees" and usually think of hundreds or even thousands of people flooding into a neighboring country, or trying by hook or crook to get to Europe or the US. It's easy to see them in practical terms: where will they go? Who will feed them? Where will their kids go to school? Will they take away my job? All of which can be legitimate questions.

But I find it helpful to think of Faustin, who left his job, his home, his parents and friends, the country and village he'd grown up in, everything he'd ever known or cared about, to drive unfriendly people around in a bus and feel cold all the time. Maybe one of his children will grow up to be a school principal.

11

WHY BABIES HAVE FAT THIGHS

Rwanda December, 2013 – January, 2014

The flu started going around some time in late November. Eirwyn (just 4) got it first, then Marion (almost 2), and finally us parents: felled right as Eirwyn, at least, started feeling better and needing active parenting again. Eddie and I did the best we could, and were starting to feel a little better—but Marion was still running a low fever and had a cough, which we thought was just her taking a while to get over this flu.

My mother had given her a set of three plastic rings, little pink things with a heart. Thank goodness they were identical, because we kept losing them, but as long as there was another one in reserve, we were OK. Because Marion *loved* these rings and had to have one on her finger *at all times*. Even while not feeling well.

In early December, I was sitting next to Eirwyn and saw that he had blood coming out of his ear. Now I may be the kind of parent whose kid has to be pretty far gone for me to take him or her to the doctor, but blood in the ear crossed even my threshold.

And given that we were all feeling a bit mealy still, we thought we'd all go.

So off we trundled to the Belgian doctor, who decided that the ear thing was nothing too serious, but put Eirwyn on a course of antibiotics just to prevent infection of the eardrum while it was healing. So far, so good.

Then she turned to Marion, who'd been coughing quietly in the corner. "Let me see this one," she said. Picked up the stethoscope and listened. "Yeah," she said to Eddie and me, "now listen. You go to King Faisal Hospital and get her lungs x-rayed. I'm sending you there because the machine is good, but don't let them interpret it for you. Just come back when you have the films."

Which is how young Marion spent her second birthday not among balloons and chocolate cake, but in a hospital waiting room. And did we wait. Good thing I'd dropped Eddie and Eirwyn at home so they could rest. What seemed like hours later —no, it really *was* hours later—the guy brought out the films for us, and as predicted started spouting something about a healing tuberculosis, and a bunch of other stuff I didn't really try to follow.

Back with the Belgian doctor, she confirmed pneumonia in both lungs. "The antibiotic I want to give her isn't available as a syrup in Rwanda, so you'll have to crush up the pill and put it in honey or jam so that she takes it, until we can fly the other one in from Belgium. Oh—and I'm leaving for the Christmas holiday tonight, so I'm sending you to another doctor, who is actually a pediatrician. Go see her this evening."

The reason, it turned out, that we had to wait until the evening to see Dr. Agnes was that by day she ran the national anti-AIDS program. As you do. (She would go on to become Minister of Health.) But considering how few pediatricians there were in the country, there were plenty of parents who would brave the wait outside her home, swatting away the mosquitoes that came out with the waning light and hoping their child didn't contract malaria while waiting to see the doctor.

And thus you see how brain drain starts inside poorer countries, not to mention from those countries to richer ones. The best doctors are drawn from a very small pool to serve as administrators and government functionaries, thereby often reducing the number of, say, cardiologists (or pediatricians) in a country by a statistically significant number.

Dr. Agnes took one look at Marion and pointed out the two signs of respiratory distress she was showing. "Three," she informed me, "and she would go into the hospital." Oh. She changed the antibiotic and sent us home.

Late that evening, I gave Marion her first dose of the antibiotic Dr. Agnes had described. Ten minutes later, she bought it all back up again. Dr. Agnes had given me her personal mobile number, so I called it and told her what had happened.

"Go to the nearest 24-hour pharmacy (it was like 10 pm), and call me when you get there," she instructed. I did as I was told.

"OK, give the phone to the pharmacist," she ordered. Which I did—and then I understood. Rather than try to explain to me what she wanted me to get, and hope that I explained it correctly to the pharmacist (both times risking seriously garbling the message thanks to my patchy French), she preferred to talk professional to professional.

Thus began what was, for a long time, probably the worst week of our lives as parents. Eirwyn had to get his antibiotic every eight hours, which meant one of us had to stay awake long enough to wake him up at 10:00 pm, and someone had to then be up at oh six hundred. Marion was alternating ibuprofen and acetaminophen (paracetamol for the Brits) in an attempt to keep her fever down, and had to take the first medicine to prevent vomiting and wait 40 minutes before taking the antibiotic.

This might have been when Eddie first started his serious love affair with spreadsheets. Actually, we just had about four pieces of paper going, where we tracked temperatures, drugs given and at what time. Given how exhausted we were, I kind of hate to think what might have happened without them.

And to cap it off, we weren't sleeping through the night, either—because Marion insisted on wearing that little pink ring to bed, where it would inevitably fall off her finger. So once or twice per night, we would hear the now-infamous refrain: "I need da pink ring!" At which point one of us would stumble into her room, dig around a bit in the bed for the ring, and put it back on her finger. Upon which she would happily pop her thumb back in her mouth and go back to sleep.

It's experiences like this that lead to friendships among people who barely know each other, which can become as strong as family, at least for a while. After we'd been lugging ourselves through this medical obstacle course for about a week, our friend Henry came over with all of the really special goodies from his fridge.

He'd gotten a care package from the UK, so I'm talking about *quality* special. Onion confit. Really good cheese. Pâté (hey, I wasn't a veggie then, and it was gooooood....). He made this totally incredible spread, just to give us something a little bit special because we'd had such a rough time of it. Dear Henry is still a good friend.

I learned two things from this experience: First of all, healthy babies have fat thighs because when they get sick and stop eating, that's what keeps them alive. Through all this, Marion essentially didn't eat for the better part of two weeks, and her thighs lost all of the usual chubby cherub-ness we associate with very young children. If she hadn't been well nourished going in to that experience, her reserves would not have been sufficient to keep her going. Which is why I'm not that surprised that respiratory infections generally hover around second or third place as the cause of death in children under five on the African continent. Want to know #1? It's not malaria. Ready? Measles.

The second thing I learned was that all health systems may not be created equal, but there's something to say for the slightly fly-by-night, more personalized touch of the Rwandan way. Imagine, if you will, the following scene: It's 10:00 at night, your kid has a potentially life-threatening infection, and she's just vomited up the medicine you gave her that's supposed to save her life. Do you brave the ER? Or call the advice nurse, navigate your way through an elaborate phone tree, and explain for the fifth time in the same day what your kid has and what you're doing about it? And maybe not get any helpful advice, after all?

Or, imagine being able to call your own pediatrician on her private number, who remembers everything about the case because you saw her that same day, and will walk you through the steps to take until the problem is resolved. Of course the overall picture is mixed; my point is that reality is mixed. Not all of the greener grass is in Developed Land.

12

MY WEST WING MOMENT

Rwanda, 2005

One of the many TV series we liked to watch while we were in Rwanda was *The West Wing*. I got kind of a double thrill out of it, because it coincided with my time working at the US embassy, which I fancied gave me all sorts of privileged insights into what it was like to be part of the cool insider group doing lots of Important Things. Never mind that 1) I've never been cool, and 2) I was pretty much the lowest ranking US citizen in the joint, with a job that nobody really cared about—in the nicest possible way, of course.

My main job was to administer the Ambassador's Special Self-Help Fund, but I was also in charge of the SSH's poorer stepchild: the Democracy and Human Rights Fund. So it wasn't really a surprise that when the embassy needed someone to administer the Ambassador's Girls' Scholarship Fund, somebody clever thought, "Ambassador's this, Ambassador's that," and decided I was their guy. After all, it wasn't huge money by USAID standards, and USAID didn't have an education point person in Rwanda, so there really was no other obvious choice.

I actually really liked the scholarship fund. It seemed like such a straightforward and obvious way to have a huge impact on girls' education: find the girls who show promise but are likely to drop out of secondary school because of money, and cover their costs. Given the very high attrition rates between primary and secondary school, low graduation rates, and the well-documented fact that every year of additional schooling for girls improves not only their lives but their children's, really, it seemed like a no-brainer.

To identify the girls whose school fees should be covered by the fund, we worked with the Rwanda chapter of the Forum of African Women Educationalists. FAWE had the connections with the education ministry to get the school lists and test scores, ran their own "model" school designed to show what girls could achieve if given the proper infrastructure and encouragement, and organized mentoring activities for the AGSF girls, in which they were encouraged to aim high and introduced to successful female role models.

In early 2005, we received notice that there had been a hitch with the process to select the US contracting organization that administered the fund on behalf of the USG in Washington. So they were going to have to repeat the procurement process, meaning a delay of a couple of months before the funds could be sent out to the country offices. Embassies were asked to notify Washington if the delay would somehow damage the reputation of the US, so that alternative arrangements could be made.

Well. Considering that we had already communicated the names of the scholarship recipients to the relevant schools, and requested that they allow the girls to start school in January in anticipation of their fees being paid by the USG…. Um, yeah. It was going to look pretty bad if we suddenly came back with "Just kidding!" and asked them to wait another several months.

So I drafted something or other for Washington, and they

agreed to send the money through the local office of USAID, which was logical because USAID is the people who do aid money, only they aren't part of the Department of State....Still with me? The point is, we had to do some fancy bureaucratic hand-waving to get it all sorted. Thankfully I had a great ally at USAID who understood the administrative stuff waaay better than I did. So between my pushing and her clever finessing, we got it done, and the girls were allowed to stay in their respective schools.

Some months later, a couple of women from Washington came for a visit, and one of the things they wanted to see was the FAWE school. So we obligingly set up the visit, not really knowing what it was all about, but if there's one thing your African recipient of Western largesse knows, it's how to sing for their supper. There were songs, yes, also poetry, a skit on the virtues of girls' education, and a really painful focus group— painful, because the visitors did things like ask all the girls affected by HIV to raise their hands. Confidentiality, anyone?

When we got back in the car, one of the women whipped out her Blackberry and started typing furiously. There was some discussion among the visitors, lots of positive noises, but nothing really clear. Eventually we learned that they were a scouting visit, and that we were about to get a very high-level visitor, indeed: FLOTUS, aka the First Lady of the United States, aka Laura Bush.

Avid diplomacy geeks might remember the G8 Gleneagles summit of 2005. It's OK: I wouldn't, either, except that Africa was on the agenda, and FLOTUS took a two-week tour through the continent on its heels. I really don't remember what else she visited in Rwanda. What mattered to me was that she was going to visit the FAWE school, and make a speech there.

You can imagine the logistics of something like this—actually, you probably can't. Just imagine a cross between a wedding with 250 guests and the invasion at Omaha beach. My role was an extremely modest one: I mostly stood around at the school to help direct people as they got set up, and then stood in the back.

What I didn't know until the day was that, in her speech, she would make specific reference to the AGSF, and to all the girls who had had the opportunity to advance in their schooling because of it. And I knew that, in my own way, I had fought to make it happen. It was one of the most satisfying, and proudest moments of my career.

After the FAWE ceremony, FLOTUS was scheduled to go back to the embassy for the "meet & greet", a (relatively speaking —it's still the First Lady) informal gathering with USG employees, during which the visitor gets to express gratitude on behalf of the government and the American people for the work that the diplomats do overseas. The problem was, everyone was supposed to be in place like 30 minutes before she arrived, which was obviously not going to happen if we were providing support during the whole FAWE gig.

The only answer: as soon as FLOTUS makes her exit stage right, we book it back to the road and jump in the last car of her motorcade, so that we can arrive with her. Yeah, that would be me, riding in the First Lady's motorcade. Did I mention this was all about my West Wing moment?

What I mostly remember was how weird it was to see people lining the street to watch us go by, many of whom obviously had no idea who was in the motorcade and why it was heading down this particular road. Some of them waved, even at us in the last car, because motorcade, right? It felt a lot like being the goldfish in the bowl, to be honest.

The meet & greet itself was pretty cool. The First Lady spoke for a little while before handling babies and shaking hands.

During her little talk, she talked about the long service of some staff, and then specifically named my friend, the mission's requisite spy, by name. I was standing close to this friend when Mrs. Bush singled her out like that, and the expression of shock and gratitude on her face was pretty special. She actually had her jaw hanging open a little bit.

Overall, I have to say I was impressed with the First Lady. She came across as smart and personable, and she handled both the bigger, more formal occasion and the smaller employee gathering with style.

Which is more than I can say for the visit of the Secretary of Health and Human Services, who came with two full busloads of his closest friends to see the early clinics where the US was making services available for people with HIV. Trying to organize the visitors into small groups and choreograph how they were going to move through the hospital was difficult enough, but herding them on the day was impossible—with the result that we spent about 90 minutes longer there than we should have. This is the kind of thing that rains on the organizers' parade in a big way.

My role at the ceremony site was to stand at the back with a yellow kerchief around my neck, thereby identifying me as a Toilet Monitor. Yup. My job was to help direct any visitors in need toward the facilities, and escort them if necessary. I kept that bandana for a long time, I'll have you know.

But the real reason I bring up this particular visit is because it so clearly shows the value of doing your homework. Kinyarwanda is one of those languages that makes a kind of flipped "r" sound for the letters *l* and *r*. So "Kigali" could just as accurately be written "Kigari", and in fact Kirundi (the sister version of the same language, used in Burundi) has done away with the letter *l* entirely.

Knowing that, you might now be able to judge just how

awkward it was for the Secretary of HHS to present a cow to the facility named "Elroy". Some time later, we visited the same facility as part of the SSH work, and learned that they had re-baptized the cow "Babette". Babette, sadly, was not very adapted to Rwandan conditions and didn't do very well.

13

IN WHICH WE MAYBE SLIGHTLY
MISAPPROPRIATE A WORK VEHICLE

Kosovo, 2008

One evening, my buddy Liz and I had been out for dinner and a drink or two. She was dropping me back at the team house on her way home, and we idled there for a little bit to finish up our chat. Out of the dark street emerged a Kosovar woman, frantically waving us down and motioning for us to roll down the window.

She kept repeating the phrase (more or less): "*Sie hat das Baby gehabt, sie hat das Baby gehabt.*" Now, Liz and I both knew enough German to understand "She's had the baby," but it took a little longer for the penny to drop. "Oh, you mean she's having the baby now?" I asked. Using a mixture of German, Albanian and gestures, she gave us to understand that she wanted us to take her daughter to the clinic.

Liz and I had a quick conference, weighing the pros and cons. Of course we wanted to help. And if we didn't, it would be pretty easy for the mother to spread the story of how two expatriate staff in their fat Land Rover refused to help a woman in active labor get to a doctor. So there was a real reputational risk if we didn't help.

There was no centralized taxi service in the city at that time, so people relied on having the number of a guy, or hoped to flag a taxi down in the street. The other catch about trying to call someone was that 1) plenty of people didn't have landlines, and mobile phones were still pretty scarce back in the day, and 2) the infrastructure was so underdeveloped that even if you had a landline, you could easily wait 20 or 30 minutes, if not longer, for a dial tone. Pick up the phone: dead air. You just waited, if you had time, and maybe at some point you'd get lucky.

On the other hand…. Transporting civilians for non-work purposes was not exactly kosher, and of course if any, er, fluids were to get on the upholstery, it would be a little difficult for us to explain away. But in the end, the feeling that we really ought to help outweighed our concern about getting in trouble, especially knowing that it could be tricky for Kosovars to travel around the city at night because of police checkpoints, so we said OK.

The other wrinkle was that they couldn't go to the regular hospital, because this was during the time of the "parallel system" in Kosovo. When Milošević ended Kosovo's autonomy within the state of Serbia in 1989, the Kosovars were forced out/left1 the official government structures such as schools, the university, hospitals, administration, etc. So the "clinic" we were taking the young woman and her mother to was the "Mother Theresa" clinic, named after the famous nun, an ethnic Albanian, born in Skopje (now Macedonia). Which was fine, except that we had no idea where this clinic was.

Now you have to picture Liz, who is short enough that she could barely see over the steering wheel of this honking great car, and me in the passenger seat, smiling encouragingly and sending mental messages to the baby to *stay put* for another few minutes.

The mother gave directions in simple German: "*Rechts! Rechts! Links!*" which Liz was able to follow easily enough. The daughter sat in the back seat, gripping the handle up next to the top of the window, saying "*Sot! Sot, bre!*" meaning "Today! Oh man, today!"

After some 15 minutes of this, the mother motioned for us to stop. She got out of the car, but the daughter stayed where she was, so we did the same. What was going on? No sign of the clinic.

Meanwhile the daughter is continuing her soft cries, "*Sot! Sot!*" She clearly did *not* understand German, so I was left trying to cobble what few words of Albanian I had into something that might sound encouraging. I think I managed what was supposed to be an "It's OK!" and something about breathing. I possibly even calculated that the baby would be a Scorpio, like me, and may have said something really embarrassing about us sharing a star sign... certainly not my most shining linguistic moment.

After what seemed like ages, the mother finally re-emerged with a young man at her side. Ah—the father-to-be. OK. Good thing we have nowhere to be, and it's not going to attract any attention at all that a big, white NGO vehicle is driving around and then sitting for 10 minutes in parts of Prishtina where foreigners probably never tread. But now the father is with us, so off we go.

Liz still had to follow the directions in minimalist German, but I figured at least the father's presence relieved me of my self-imposed obligation to try to put anyone at ease. After another good 10-15 minute drive, we suddenly pulled up alongside the Mother Theresa clinic. The hopeful family in the back piled out of the car, said a quick thank you, and made a beeline for the entrance.

Maybe Liz had thought about this beforehand, but it was only at this moment that I realized we'd been left somewhere in an area of the city we weren't at all familiar with, in the dark, and *no shimmer* of how to get home. This is, of course, never a great situation to be in, but if we were to happen upon a police checkpoint, it could theoretically get a little awkward explaining how we came to be in a part of town where we kind of had no business to be, at night, in an official NGO car.

We headed back the way we came, and by a series of lucky breaks and some *really* lucky guesses on my part, we managed to get home in one piece.

A few days later I saw the mother out in the street again, and asked after the baby. It was a girl. But you know the story wasn't written for TV, because they didn't name her after Liz or me. Shocking, I know.

14

HOW TO MAKE FRIENDS WITHOUT
STARTING WWIII

Russian Federation, summer 1994

S onja and I met through Russian class. We used to hang out
in the lounge of the Slavic Studies department at the
University of Bonn. This was kind of a cool place to meet people
who actually knew what they were doing, and had been to some
of the (to me, at least) exotic lands east of the Iron Curtain,
which hadn't been down all that long.

Our friendship was cemented during the second semester of
Russian, which comprised essentially nothing more than learning
reams and reams of verbs. Perfect, imperfect, conjugation pattern,
what case they took and whether prepositions were generally
required (and if yes, what cases they took, and how the meaning
potentially changed if different prepositions were used, or the
same preposition with a different case). Exhausted yet? Imagine
doing that for something like 200 verbs.

Sonja and I made up flashcards and quizzed each other for
hours (and hours, and hours), mostly sitting on the main quad if
the weather obliged. I'm sure it was good for my German, too,

since we probably had to learn some Russian verbs I didn't even know in German.

What made the whole thing tolerable was our need to make up mnemonics to help us keep all the verbs straight. I loved the German for that: Eselsbrücke, or "donkey bridge". Your brain as a donkey, being led over the bridge. Or something. The thing was that I always tried to make them really logical, whereas Sonja just kind of went on what the words sounded like, even if there was no association at all between the meaning of the donkey bridge and the word in question. But what she came up with was so random and sometimes really funny, that often hers were easier to memorize than mine.

After about a year and a half of Russian, we went to St. Petersburg for a 6-week language and culture program. It was good: we did some exercises, memorized Russian poetry (I still remember the one by Lomonovsky) and listened to our teacher's dreamy monologues about the wonders of her city.

Sonja decided it would be fun to get out of the city for a bit. She found a day-tour bus trip, from St. Petersburg to Novgorod and back, and cheap as chips because it was meant for Russians. It was really only when we got on the bus that we realized the theme of the tour, which was Orthodox churches.

Well, the upside of that was, we didn't care very much that we couldn't follow most of the tour guide's spiel. The churches themselves were beautiful, and it was great just to get out and see the countryside a bit.

Behind us sat a group of three or four young people, more or less our age. I couldn't figure out what language they were speaking. Around mid-day we took a longer break, and Sonja and I found ourselves gravitating towards the only other group of obvious foreigners. Feeling still pretty weak with the Russian, we tried English and even German on them, and I might have even tried Japanese: no dice. Truly the only language we had in common was something approximating Russian.

The great thing was, since everyone was crap at it, no one cared if we made mistakes or massacred the language in some way. We spent a very long time having a basic conversation, in which we learned that they were from Korea, also students, and also in Russia for a study program. In both teams, one more courageous individual emerged who did most of the speaking on behalf of his or her group. So the conversation went something like this:

"Where are you from?"

[much conversing in native tongue, agreeing on the answer judged most likely to be understood by the opposite party]

"Korea, and you?"

[same on our side, plus what should we ask next and do we know how]

"Germany. How long are you staying in Russia?"

And so on. This mode of communication proved very effective for filling the break time without having to enter into any dangerous territory, such as what they'd had for breakfast. And when we got back on the bus, our new besties shared their oranges with us.

15

LIFE AS THE ENEMY

Serbia, Kosovo

My first stay in Serbia was for a language course called *Medunarodni skup slavista*, or "International Slavists' Conference". Sounds grand, doesn't it? It's embarrassing, but I have essentially zero memories of the actual language instruction. On the other hand, the hours spent learning traditional songs and some dancing were not totally lost: I can still sing the better part of a couple of them, which doesn't mean I should.

I liked Belgrade (the "white city"), even if the hotel we stayed in was decidedly on the seedy side. My friend Sonja and I regularly went to the old fort where the Sava and Danube rivers meet, a confluence that pretty much explains the existence of the city.

We also visited Novi Sad, the capital of the Vojvodina, or the bit of what is now Serbia that used to be part of the Austro-Hungarian rather than Ottoman Empire. The difference in architecture and style is striking, so it's definitely worth seeing both.

But what mostly sticks with me about that visit was the hotel we stayed in, which was in the old castle that looks down over the city from the other side of the river. It's a beautiful, if slightly

Transylvania-esque building—until you get to the inside. The interior was pretty worn and very dated, an impression that was decidedly strengthened when someone found a bat in their room. Oh lord, it really *was* Dracula's castle! This is why I will always remember the Serbian word for bat, well, also because it's fun to say: *šišmiš* (sheesh-meesh).

We might have thought we were a bunch of random students, but apparently the Serbian press thought we were newsworthy. Considering this was back when Slobodan Milošević was in power and sanctions were in effect against the combined state of Serbia and Montenegro, I guess you could kind of see their point.

It's not like there were tons of Western tourists wandering around Belgrade, or any tourists, really. So at one point a couple of newspaper dudes showed up and took some photos (I believe some mandatory folk dancing was involved), and interviewed a couple of the students, including me. When the guy found out I was American, well. I'm pretty sure a close-up of me appeared in the article, along with a lot of Americanized stuff that I never said, but whatever.

Not long thereafter, when I went to live in Belgrade for a year, I was advised in the strongest terms to keep my head down, not to let on that I was American if possible, and never, *ever* speak English on the street. You can understand why, I mean, this was in 1997, so not that long after the wars in former Yugoslavia, and what most Serbs felt was very biased and unfair treatment of their side by the West, with Big Bad America at the fore. The funny thing was that, almost universally, people's reaction upon learning that I was American was uncontrolled laughter.

I got this once while traveling by bus from Belgrade to Sarajevo. The bus passed through the Serb part of Bosnia and Herzegovina, Republika Srpska. Thankfully I'd been warned to expect being singled out and forced to pay for a "visa", which was totally illegal according to international law, because the RS was not, in itself, a sovereign state. But when you're surrounded by dudes with guns at one in the morning, it's probably not the time to stand on principle.

It was a little nerve-wracking giving the guy my passport and watching him disappear into the little police hut, but after a few minutes he duly came out and returned it, with a very nondescript stamp of a car inside a rectangle, and the date. (They could at least have put something interesting on the stamp, a little "death to America" or "die, you imperialist pigs". Losers.)

Later that day, we stopped for lunch and a break. A young woman approached me and asked why they'd taken my passport off the bus, and only mine. When I told her I was an American from California, she pretty much doubled over with laughter. I wasn't sure what the joke was. Surely my Serbian wasn't *that* bad? When she finally caught her breath, she looked at me with this incredulous expression on her face, and said, "So let me get this straight: you *choose* to be *here*, in this pile of shit, when you could be over there in paradise? Awesome! Shall we trade passports?"

Funnily enough, I spoke more Serbian in Kosovo than in Serbia. So many of our Serbian contacts spoke good English, and relished the chance to practice, we wound up holding a lot of our meetings in English.

But Kosovars who came of age when Yugoslavia was still a thing had usually learned Serbian in school, and many had gone to university in Belgrade or Zagreb. Some had bits of German, but not many spoke good English. So I wound up using my Serbian quite often (which caused some consternation among the Kosovar communities we served, until the Kosovar staff started pre-emptively explaining that I was American and too dumb to speak Albanian).

The Serbian came in super handy at checkpoints. Much of the time I'd be the only foreigner in the car, with Kosovar staff.

My mere presence as a potential witness was already a handy feature, but when they opened my passport and saw that I was a US citizen, they usually made some little comment or other, which opened the door for me to respond in Serbian. "Oho! An American who speaks our language!" Free pass.

But my personal favorite had to be in the Zurich airport, in transit to somewhere or other. I bought something small and so was fishing around in my coins for Euros, and a Yugoslav dinar coin dropped out. I made a comment about the shop probably not wanting that one, to which the guy behind the counter responded, eyes wide: "Oh, you know Serbia? I am from there!"

"Oh yes, whereabouts then?" I responded in German.

"Niš."

And now I switched to Serbian: "Oh, but I know Niš!"

The poor guy nearly fell over. We chatted for a bit, and he just couldn't believe his luck to stumble on an American, of all people, who speaks Serbian. At this point another guy came in to re-stock the fridge. Counter Guy says, "Look, this is my friend! Marko, look, she is American, and she knows Niš! She speaks our language!" Marko was so excited, he insisted on giving me something for free from the shop, despite my protestations.

It was such a sweet gesture, I feel bad that I actually hated the drink I got, but at least I know not to try Red Bull ever again.

16

IN WHICH WE ARE SITTING DUCKS

Between Ohrid and Prishtina, September, 1998

The only checkpoint where I'd say I ever got really nervous was coming back from Ohrid, in Macedonia. Eddie and I had tried to get away for a weekend, just to de-stress from what was rapidly becoming a pretty difficult situation in Kosovo. The Kosovo Liberation Army (note to journalists: please always use the word "shadowy" when describing this group) was attacking Serbian police outposts with increasing frequency, and the numbers of Kosovars who'd left their homes and were sleeping in the hills was getting into the thousands.

This was actually the reason we were heading back at that moment: we'd been on the beach when Eddie's phone rang. It was his office, requesting him to come back to Prishtina and write a proposal to assist the displaced Kosovars. So we did some gymnastics with our tickets, and were able to get seats on a bus later that same day.

It was the season when the farmers were preparing their fields for planting, which consisted of setting small fires to burn off the stubble that remained from the previous year's harvest. As we drove along, we could see ribbons of fire stretching across the fields, pouring smoke into the sky and giving the sunset a spooky, menacing quality.

In the middle of all this, we reached a police checkpoint. Once again, Eddie and I attracted particular scrutiny because of our foreign passports. We were asked to get out of the bus, and identify our luggage so that it could be searched. Unfortunately I had a book in German that Eddie had given me in my bag; I don't remember the subject matter exactly, but there was a swastika on the front cover. Thankfully the guy didn't give it more than a cursory thumbing through, but I briefly had visions of us being held back and interrogated at length as foreign spies.

The really uncomfortable thing was that all the passport-examining and bag-searching wound up taking a good half an hour, and it was right around sunset, the Kosovo Liberation Army's (KLA's) favorite time to attack Serb police posts. You don't want to act nervous at a checkpoint, and you really don't want to give someone with a gun the impression that you're hooshing him along, but that was one of the longer 20 minutes of my life. Thankfully we finished up without incident, and were able to return to our fiery, apocalyptic drive back to Prishtina.

17

IN WHICH WE ACT LIKE IDIOTS AND GET AWAY WITH IT

Kosovo, ca. October 2018

Part of my job with the agency I worked for in Kosovo was to work with local youth groups, informal associations trying to do some good in their communities. The idea was to help them have good governance structures, and an intentional approach to identifying community needs and how they could be part of the solution. Or something.

When I first started, I was told about one active group, and another one in Lipjan (Lipljan to the Serbs). This second group had kind of lost momentum because Serb forces had taken control of the town, so it was considered unsafe to gather in any significant numbers. But after a few months, the Serb forces left the town, and it was judged safe for us to go back in.

A team of us went in to have a look. We concentrated on the school, since it had been a focal point of the village, and would normally have been an obvious gathering place. The problem was, this is where the Serb forces had set up their command station. However poorly or well they'd treated the building while they were based there, they'd pretty much trashed the place when they left. School benches overturned, furniture smashed up, other furniture piled into rooms to get it out of the way, and general debris everywhere.

Having had a mine-awareness training not long before, I have to say we did hesitate before going in, but curiosity won out. That said, we did keep an eye out for tripwires or other booby-traps, an abandoned building like this was the classic place to find them. At one point Mahmoud thought about going up the stairs to the second floor, but we decided it was probably not a great idea, so he didn't go. Another team member took a few steps up the stairs, but stopped.

Later, when I met Mahmoud again ten years after having left Kosovo, he told me that the second floor of the school had been heavily boobytrapped, after all.

18

MOM, THIS IS WHY I NEED MY OWN
PHONE

Kosovo, 1998

One evening, I was sitting around in the flat in Prishtina that I shared with my NGO colleagues, watching television. Three of us lived there, but T Roy (*po ose jo!*) was out with some friends, and Drew was upstairs with his girlfriend, who worked for a different agency. This was well into 1998, when the tension between Serbs and Kosovars was palpably mounting.

All of a sudden, I hear automatic gunfire. This, in and of itself, was not necessarily worrying, given the large number of gun owners among the general Serb population, and a tendency to shoot off a couple of rounds in celebration of, say, a wedding (dang it—we forgot to do that at ours).

My thing is, I hear shots, I listen for answering fire. Usually it's kind of a one-off, so you pause for a few seconds and then go back to what you were doing. (Much like how, many years later in Rwanda, if you heard an explosion on a Saturday, you knew it was just the army getting rid of leftover mines from the genocide, nothing to worry about.)

Only in this case, the gunfire was sustained, and it was all over the city. I had a pretty good view of the tracer fire going into the sky, considering that the front of our flat was solid windows. Suddenly that usually-pleasant feature didn't seem so handy.

Unfortunately, the back of our flat was also mostly windows, and behind the building on that side was an open field going up the hill, with a forest behind that was rumored to be a hiding place for KLA forces. So hiding behind the couch didn't seem like such a great idea, either.

There was no landline in the flat, and I was sharing a mobile phone with T Roy. And since he ranked higher than me, he usually got to keep the phone with him—with the result that there wasn't any obvious way for me to find out what was going on.

At one point Drew came downstairs in a bit of a panic, turned out all the lights and the TV, and then ran back upstairs again. Although I kind of took his point, it seemed a little para-noid to me, so I turned the TV back on... but definitely kept an ear out for what was happening in town. I figured if it really was the start of open conflict, someone would hear about it and come let me know.

Eventually, the gunfire died down and we passed a quiet night. The next day, I found out that all the brouhaha was because Serbia had won the semi-finals of the European basket-ball championship.

19

THE THINGS YOU'LL DO FOR PEACE

Kosovo, 1997

A lot of the work we did with the Balkan Peace Team was difficult to quantify, and oftentimes you're laying the groundwork for something that will become important years later. So it's not always easy to know whether or not you're actually making a difference.

One of the few times I really felt useful was when the Students' Union of the University of Belgrade asked us to help them get in touch with the Students' Union of the (parallel) University of Prishtina. Considering that the Serbian state did not recognize any of the Kosovars' parallel structures, the fact that they even asked the question was a pretty big deal.

And well, now that you mention it, we *did* happen to know several members of the Albanian Students' Union, including most of the leadership. The next time we were in Prishtina, we duly put out some feelers, which met with tentative openness.

Thus began a process that lasted a couple of months, with my partner Renate and I bouncing back and forth between Belgrade and Prishtina, carrying messages and helping both sides clarify how such a visit might go.

It dawned on me that this was shuttle diplomacy. There was an incredible number of things to be ironed out: how many people on each side, where the meeting would take place, whether or not there would be a joint declaration, how to treat the question of publicity, and on and on. And while both sides did genuinely want this first-ever meeting to go well, there was a lot of mistrust on both sides, and concern about how the visit might be perceived by their respective communities.

This is when I also came to more deeply appreciate the role of the diplomatic go-between, or broker. The Serbs didn't know the Albanians, and the Albanians didn't know the Serbs. But both sides knew Renate and me, and trusted us not to lead them into any nasty surprises. We were expending pretty much every ounce of political capital we had with both sides, praying that we were getting the nuances right, and doing our best not to misrepresent anyone. It was thoroughly exhausting—and a lot of fun.

One evening we met with a couple of guys from the Albanian side, in a building where we'd never been. They explained that the police, or people in their employ, were following them, and that other activists had already been jumped and beaten up, hence the attempt to fly under the radar. The meeting, which went on for a couple of hours, was lubricated by *rakija* (drinking was my contribution to the successful outcome of the meeting) and flirting (taking it and flirting back, just enough, was Renate's). The things you do in the name of peace.

The big day we'd been so looking forward to arrived, and in reward for all our hard work, Renate and I were invited to hang out in the Albanian Students' Union's offices, and they would tell us when it was over. Not quite the front-row seats we'd hoped for; then again, it was a positive sign that they felt able to hold the meeting without neutral arbitration.

Unfortunately, in the end, there was a misunderstanding (possibly deliberate) about the press, and so one side made the meeting more public than the other side was comfortable with. It didn't create any actual trouble for people as far as I know, but it eroded the trust we'd worked so hard to build, and so there were no follow-on meetings.

Still, it was a step forward to have made the contact possible, even if I count this as one of the many missed opportunities for things to have turned out more peacefully in Kosovo. And that is one of the things I feel most fortunate to have experienced in all my years abroad: to watch, close-up and in real time, how the little personal conflicts, misunderstandings, missed opportunities, people more interested in their egos than the outcome can snowball into a conflict that seems inevitable when one looks back, but which didn't feel that way at the time.

20

IN WHICH I DO THE KIND OF THING YOUR PARENTS HOPE YOU'LL NEVER DO: OR, DON'T TRY THIS AT HOME

Kosovo, 1997

Here is the story of how I think my life flashed before my eyes.

After 10-odd years of the Kosovo conflict being "frozen", with the Kosovars managing their own affairs through parallel structures and essentially ignoring the existence of the Serbian state, significant portions of the Kosovar population started to lose patience.

Young people in particular saw little future for themselves with degrees that were not recognized outside of Kosovo, in an economy crippled by years of sanctions against Serbia and Montenegro. This spurred the growth of a Kosovar opposition party that advocated a more active stance than Ibrahim Rugova's well-known passive resistance, as well as the emergency of the KLA, which engaged in acts of violence against the Serbian state.

As part of this trend, the Albanian Students' Union decided to stage a peaceful protest in Prishtina to demand the parallel university's access to the official/state-owned premises. No bonus points for guessing that this protest was not approved by any

Serbian authorities. I use the word "protest", but the students were clear that it was to be a peaceful march, designed to express an opinion rather than attack anyone or cause any damage.

The march was planned several weeks ahead of time. On the day, Renate and I showed up early at the Union office to check in with the leaders, whom we had come to know pretty well over the course of the past several months. As far as we knew, we were the only internationals present, though not in any official capacity, and we intended just to observe and make a report to our backers in the West.

I was impressed with the level of organization: there were a lot of people wearing armbands, which signified that they were in charge of crowd management and making sure no one did anything that would provoke an unwelcome reaction by the Serb authorities.

Renate and I then retreated to different spots on the hillside above the road where the march was to take place. We could see the crowd, all wearing white, gathered up the hill on the left... and as the hour approached, the Serb security forces massing on the right, in the bottom of the little valley.

The protesters started their march down the hill, with our buddies from the Students' Union at the head of the line. When they got to the bottom, they were forced to stop by a couple of rows of police in full riot gear, backed up by four or five Armored Personnel Carriers (APCs), and plenty of additional personnel.

The standoff continued for five minutes, then ten...then half an hour, an hour... No one up on the hill could tell whether negotiations were taking place. Either way, after a lot of standing around, I decided to maneuver myself closer to the point of confrontation, to see if I could learn anything more about what was going on.

Not long after I got down nearly to the front, roughly at the top of the hour, without any obvious sign of warning, the police starting beating the protesters in the front lines with their night-sticks, and we heard a series of dull thuds.

When I'd first seen the APCs, I'd wondered whether the authorities were planning to use something like water cannon, but now I realized that the thuds were the APCs shooting tear-gas canisters at the crowd. (Is it a good thing or a bad thing that I still remember the Serbian word for tear gas?)

Pretty quickly, people realized what was going on and started to run, me included. I turned around and did my best to hightail it up the hill, only I don't do so well on inclines, and by now I'd gotten a few good breaths of tear gas in me, which was not helping my mobility at all. I looked around and saw that most people had made it up over the ridge, and I was left with the stragglers—and some young men who had hung back in order to throw stones at the police.

Granted, they were probably too far away from the police to actually do any damage, but I figured that any act of intended violence toward the police could serve as an excuse for them to start using live rounds. And with my dark hair and leather jacket, it wasn't obvious from their vantage point that I was not a Kosovar myself.

As I did my best to run up the hill, I felt kind of an itching in my back, anticipating at any moment the feel of a bullet. "This is it," I thought to myself, "I'm going to die right here, 26 years old." A series of images came to my mind then: me as a kid, playing softball, dance class, all the studying I'd done in high school and college in anticipation of building a career one day, moments of tenderness with my parents, camping with my dad....

All this happened within a few seconds, a kind of re-evaluating of my life, mostly regretting how all that experience and investment was going to end on a hillside in a place most of my friends had never heard of, because I'd bought into this grand idea that a couple of foreigners could help tip the balance of events towards peace rather than war.

And then I was up and over the ridge, met by Kosovar house-wives with slices of raw onion and cups of water. I managed to ask someone what the onion was for. "The teargas," I was told. And it was true: just smelling it helped, but chewing on it was even better. The things you learn.

At some point I was kind of adopted by another one of the protesters who understood that I was American, and as we were running, a man signaled us to come into his house so we could hide until the police stopped searching for protesters. We sat there for a while, and they were terribly kind to me, although we really couldn't communicate because my Albanian was so poor.

Once the coast was clear, I made my way first to a café owned by a friend of ours that we'd designated as our rendezvous point, where I received a whisky on the house to help settle my nerves. Then back to the house where we stayed, where I was greeted by the landlady and her family, who let me sit with them for a while. I must have been in shock, because I remember shaking a bit and feeling terribly cold. They gave me a stiff drink and a blanket, and eventually it got better.

That night I tried calling my parents, since I thought the events could make the news, and I didn't want them to worry. It probably took the better part of an hour to get through, and I got my mother's answering machine. I left a really stupid message along the lines of, "if you see the news tonight, just know that I'm OK." But of course no press had been there, and the Serbs certainly weren't going to publicize it. To my knowledge the events of that day never made any international news media.

21

HOW HOT IS THE SAHEL, REALLY?

Burkina, 2014-2017

Part I: When we first moved to Burkina, a colleague advised me to stop wearing dangly earrings in the hot season, because the walk from the house to the car got them hot enough they would burn your skin.

Part II: Someone we knew had chickens. Not that uncommon, really, and as these things often are, they were left to pretty much run around the compound as they pleased. One day, one of the chickens laid an egg, in a shaded spot in the grass. Some weeks later, out popped a perfectly healthy chick. You noted the part where *the chicken never sat on the egg*, right? Burkina: the lazy chicken's ticket to a low-maintenance family.

Part III: One day, I was trying to get something out of one of the cabinets in the kitchen. What is it, anyway, with the super high cabinets in Burkinabè kitchens? You have to be like eight feet tall just to reach inside, let alone be able to see what you're groping around for.

Anyway, I'm tugging on this Tupperware box, trying to slide it out, and it's catching on a little bit of screw that's poking up from the bottom. So I'm sort of wiggling it around, trying to get it to obligingly jump over the screw and into my hand—and suddenly there's a hissing sound, and I feel something wet splash onto my hand.

No extra credit for guessing what worst fear popped into my head: spitting cobra, anyone? I screamed (so unlike me, but in this case I have to admit it) and jumped back, in a total panic. Eddie, who was sitting in the next room, kept asking, "What? What is it? What's wrong?" and for at least half a minute I couldn't get any words out of my mouth, mostly because my tongue was in suspension between the words "snake!" and "help!"

After a little bit, Eddie came in to see what was going on, and I was able to squeak out something about hissing and liquid and my imminent demise. Thus did my heroic husband take and look and find…. A can of Guinness, which he'd been keeping in the flour cupboard to use in making bread. In the heat, the can had popped a small leak, hence the hissing sound and small amounts of liquid spraying around. It's OK: who needs a pulse, anyway?

22

KAFKA WAS ON TO SOMETHING

Germany ca. 1994

If you've never seen the film *The Killing Fields*, you can stop reading now. Or read, but spoiler alert.

OK, you're still reading, so you've seen it. Remember the scene where the journalist is holed up in the French embassy with his Cambodian fixer, hoping to be evacuated? Crowds of desperate locals trying to get inside, end-of-all-time kind of atmosphere. The fixer, as a Cambodian national, has no hope of being evacuated, so the journalist forges him a French passport.

And then comes the devastating moment: one of the French embassy staff hands the journalist the doctored passport with the words, "*Je suis désolé, monsieur.*" He opens the front page, and you see the gray square when the photo is supposed to be: he'd not been able to get the chemical composition of the fixing agent quite right. And so he has to leave his friend the fixer behind, knowing full well that he's likely to be killed as a collaborator.

The night after seeing this film on TV, I had a dream so vivid that I still remember it in extraordinary detail. I was in a large building with many other people, and the message came through that everyone was going to be checked to make sure they had the right to be in Germany.

We were herded into a large white hall, and told to stand in one of the ten or so lines stretching down to the other end, where uniformed security forces were seated at simple wooden tables, checking papers. There was a great sense of urgency about the exercise, definitely a sense that a war or similar catastrophe was on its way, and being made to leave would be life-threatening.

When I got down to the front of the line, I presented my passport, which I was able to imagine with great accuracy since I carried it around with me at all times. The fact that it was a US passport caught his attention, and he started flipping through it. "I have a visa," I kept repeating, somewhat frantically.

Exasperated, he handed the passport back to me so that I could show him my visa. I could feel the thicker page where the visa had been stuck on, but no matter how I played with the pages, and amid a rising sense of panic, I couldn't get the right page open. Around this point, I woke up.

In fact it was a part of my stay in Germany that I dreaded, the yearly visit to the immigration office to renew my student visa for another year. I spoke German without an American accent, studied and lived there, and had adapted to many elements of German culture. In short, most of the time I felt that I belonged more or less as much as any German.

But then once per year I would have to go to this anonymous, uncomfortable office and beg (that's what it felt like) to be allowed to stay. It was a real lesson, experiencing how a whole life can depend on a little piece of paper that requires being able to negotiate an unfamiliar bureaucratic process in a foreign language. It scared me, and I was an educated, white person from a developed, "friendly" country. How much more terrifying must it be for people in a more complicated situation, or with darker skin, or a weaker grasp of the language, or with a family depending on them?

23

IN WHICH IRISH FOLK MUSIC CALMS
THE SOUL

Kosovo, Skopje, York, August 1998

I can't even remember exactly why the International Rescue Committee (IRC) and a couple of other NGOs decided we needed to remove international staff from Kosovo for a little while. I think the UN agencies got the order, so the NGOs felt they had to follow suit, even though it seemed an exaggerated response from our perspective. But since the INGOs couldn't get a license to put CODAN radios on our cars, we relied on UN escorts to maintain radio contact with Prishtina when in the field, so when the UN left, we felt we had to, as well.

After some logistical malarkey, we formed a joint convoy with a couple of other NGOs, and drove down to Skopje, where we settled into a hotel to wait things out. I'll never forget the horrible feeling I had as we drove out of the city. It was as though we were abandoning our colleagues, who were also our friends. Not that at that point we truly anticipated a major flare-up of anything, but there's just that feeling that if it's unsafe enough for us, it's too unsafe for them, too.

I spent the first day or two of our voluntary exile mostly

working on a project proposal we were revising for USAID, something focused on long-term development of the kind we were still doing in the eastern part of Kosovo, where things were quieter. We had to fill in a logframe ("logical framework"), which is basically a big table with objectives and sub-objectives and sub-sub-objectives, activities, indicators, and everyone's favorite: critical assumptions.

What needs to be in place for your project to work, which is outside your control, but would have a significant impact on the project if it doesn't happen the way you expect, and what will you do to guard against that contingency? I just loved the irony of writing the same critical assumption "the security situation does not substantially deteriorate" over and over while being "temporarily relocated" because of security.

After a couple of days, the bosses told us that we weren't likely to go back for another week at least, so if we had somewhere we'd rather be, we could take off for a bit (and presumably save the agency some money). Cool, thought I. Eddie had recently gone back to the UK to start his master's degree in York, so I thought it would be fun to go visit him.

I called to ask him what he thought of the idea, but got the British Telecom voicemail. Called again right before buying the ticket, same thing. And again the day before flying, and the day of flying…. Eloquent silence. But being stupid, I got on the plane anyway.

Now, as I learned very well during my time in Serbia and Kosovo, the key to lying is to know what you're going to say ahead of time, and rehearsing it a bit in your head so that you half believe it yourself. It's the getting flustered that gives you away.

Well, I didn't anticipate that the UK immigration agent would grill me quite as hard as he did—in fact, it was the most in-depth questioning I have ever experienced at an international border. Can't imagine why, either: I was only there with limited money and a weird story about having a job but being evacuated and going to visit my boyfriend. Why in the world might he think that I was planning to overstay and work illegally is beyond me. Point being, I got flustered when he didn't just wave me through, which just compounded the agent's suspicion.

Having finally convinced the guy I wasn't planning anything so dodgy as looking for gainful employment, I got through. I collected my bag and tried once again to call Eddie. No dice. Luckily, I had the phone number of Eddie's sister Helen, who lived in London, so in moderate desperation I called her—and got her partner, Nigel, who of course had never heard of me. And Helen was not in, because she'd gone to Brussels with her dad for a jazz festival, together with Dinah, Eddie's other sister and only other adult relative who lived in London.

Oh. Well, did Nigel perhaps have any suggestions for where I could stay, considering it was fast getting dark and I had no clue where to go or how to get there? [Trying, and failing miserably, not to sound desperate.] Gosh, said Nigel, wouldn't he love to help, but he'd been invited to some friends' for dinner, and obviously he couldn't just not go. Of course I understood [embarrassingly, fighting back tears; trying to sound grown-up and not like an American imbecile who's just come to London with no clue of what to do once she gets there].

Nigel: Sigh.

Me [with false cheeriness]: OK well thanks then.

Nigel: Sigh. Well, I guess they won't mind if you come along.

Me [oh thankyouthankyouthankyou and no, that's not *at all* what I was hoping you'd say]: Oh, how terribly kind, thank you so much.

So an hour or so later I rucked up at these people's house with my embarrassingly large and heavy suitcase, and I have to say was welcomed so graciously I nearly cried on the spot. And you have to wonder how Nigel explained me to them: "It's Helen's brother's maybe-girlfriend from, er, some place in the Balkans, and no, I haven't met her before, and neither has Helen, but she's clearly clueless and a bit lost, so…. whaddya say?"

Having been subsequently put up for the night and then helpfully directed to the right bus, I pitched up in York the following afternoon. And once again, I called Eddie's number— only this time, he answered!

He'd only been in London for the weekend, doing some debriefing stuff from his past job before coming back up to start his orientation. He'd been in London the whole time I'd been drifting around and imposing myself on the kindness of strangers! And he had come home to a series of increasingly desperate-sounding messages from yours truly. Give him 10 minutes, he said, and he'd be down.

That evening, Eddie suggested we go to a little pub down the road called the Blue Bell. It was a small room with plenty of history, and most of all it was cozy. We found seats by the fire, and Eddie organized us a couple of pints.

As we sat and chatted, we became aware of a group of about five people sitting around a table at one side, wearing cream-colored fisherman's sweaters and playing Irish folk music. They weren't professionals or hired entertainment; they were just a group of people who liked to get together and play, and they'd chosen this pub on this evening to do it in. I could feel the music reach in and blow away the stress and worry of the past few days, telling me I'd made it, and Eddie still wanted to see me, and Kosovo would (probably) still be there in a week's time, and that for now all was well.

24

PRISHTINË/PRIŠTINA

April, 1997 – January, 1999

O ne of the great privileges of my life has been to have a front-row seat to the start of a war. I know it sounds crazy, but the humanitarians usually only show up once the proverbial shit has started hitting the proverbial fan. So seeing the train crash happening in slow motion: the missed opportunities, the pride and personalities at play, the little coincidences that can have a big influence, was fascinating and miserable at the same time.

My time in Kosovo began at almost exactly the same time as political plates underwent a tectonic shift, from ten years of a strategy built solely around non-violent, some would say (too) passive resistance, to more direct confrontation. After 10 years of "frozen" conflict, in which a generation of ethnic Albanians grew up in a parallel system that offered them an education that would not be recognized outside of Kosovo and precious few job opportunities, a good portion of the population was ready for a thaw.

The less than two years in which I followed the Kosovo "situation" (a word I grew mightily tired of) saw the emergence of the

Kosovo Liberation Army, which attacked symbols of Serbia's authority, and a second Kosovar political party, which advocated a more assertive and confrontational stance than Ibrahim Rugova's LDK (Democratic League of Kosovo).

By the time I left, Serbian police actions had displaced thousands of ethnic-Albanian villagers, and the situation had grown dire enough to catch the attention of Western powers. I left Kosovo at the end of January 1999, and roughly six weeks later, NATO started bombing Belgrade.

One of the most iconic things in Prishtina, for me, was the enormous clouds of crows that came out every evening around sundown. As another day drew to a close, you'd begin to hear the call to prayer from the numerous mosques that punctuated the city, each built in a simple version of the Ottoman style, with a domed roof and one or four slender spires rising above the rooftops.

As the voices reverberated across the hillsides, the sound would be joined by the calls of hundreds, if not thousands, of crows flying in formation like schools of fish against the darkening orange sky. There was always something a little ominous in that sound to me, like a presentiment, or some kind of superstitious sign that something bad was on its way. Easy to say in hindsight, I know, but I remember standing outside the BPT flat on the balcony, watching those birds swarm through the sky, and feeling melancholy and a menace at the sound of their cries.

Indoors, the sound track to this period was *The English Patient*. Eddie had the CD, and we listened to it nearly every day, sometimes more than once. In a similar way, much of the music evoked a grand sense of things going awry, of something tragic.

In more upbeat moments, we also listened to a great deal of Goran Bregović, who is best known in Serbia for the soundtrack to the film *Underground*, but who also did the music for Johnny Depp's 1994 film *Arizona Dream*. We were also huge fans of the film *Before the Rain* (*Pre Kiše*), which also has a really wonderful and evocative soundtrack. The film's plot is a circle, cleverly and beautifully illustrating the cycle of violence between Slavs and ethnic Albanians in Macedonia.

One nice thing about working in Prishtina was that the social distance between expats and national staff wasn't that big, so it was relatively easy and common to socialize together. There also weren't that many international staff, at least at the beginning: eight international NGOs and maybe 15 expats.

Though maybe 10% or so of the ethnic Albanian population was Christian and the rest Muslim, no one had any problem knocking back a *birrë të Pejës/Pečko pivo* or three—the local beer that came in half-liter bottles. The story went that the person who got the rarer green bottle instead of the usual brown was the spy at the table. Actually people joked a lot that I was a spy, mostly because I spoke Serbian, I think. I made a point to keep cracking jokes about it so that no one would start to take the idea too seriously!

The thing about socializing with local folks, though, was that they usually felt obliged to give you the party line about how their side had suffered because of "the situation", no matter how many times you'd already heard it or whether you could sing it all to the tune of Dixie while standing on one leg.

We understood where it was coming from, but *man*, that shit could get tiring. (And interestingly, once I'd let people fulfill their national duty by giving me the mandatory walk through the last 600 years of local history, it was amazing how many people would quietly admit that maybe Serbs and Albanians would have to find a way to live together, or that independence for Kosovo was not going to happen any time soon—it would still take over ten years from the time period I'm talking about for that partic-ular dream to come true.)

It's pretty exhausting having people try to get you on their side all day, and we all got to the point where if we heard the word "situation" one more time, we couldn't be held responsible for our actions. So, in the privacy of our little expat existence, we did what any self-respecting aid worker does, and made fun of all parties concerned.

There was a great pet shop in Prishtina; don't ask me how they kept going. Eddie got an aquarium and two little turtles, wee little things just maybe two inches long. He named them Madeleine and Mira, for the US Secretary of State and Slobodan Milošević's wife, respectively. This might be what we call gallows humor.

Golly, they were cute. Plus, it was incredibly soothing to watch them swim around. The *English Patient* in the background, and swimming turtles. I'm pretty sure that at times each of us spent easily an hour or more in front of that fish tank, just watching the little archenemy turtles do their thing.

And then he got Carmen, a beautiful, bright red Japanese fighter fish. Carmen was elegant, and gorgeous. We loved Carmen, and so did Madeleine and Mira. The problem was, they liked to take bites out of her fins, which made Carmen less gorgeous and was probably not terribly comfortable or healthy for her, poor thing. We loved Carmen, and we worried a lot about Carmen.

And then came the time when we went away for a few days, and the heater in the aquarium broke and overheated everything, and pretty much boiled our ladies alive. Our first casualty of war.

25

IN WHICH I GO NATIVE

Ouagadougou, 2016

O ne of the things I did like about CRS was I felt they got the whole faith-based thing right. They're Catholic and there's a very strong Catholic identity within the organization, but you don't have to be Catholic (or even religious) to work for them, unlike <cough cough> some other agencies that shall remain nameless.

This meant that in some countries they have large or near-total percentages of Muslim staff, who are happy enough to sign on to the overarching values that the organization represents. My personal favorite at one time was the receptionist in the country office for Rwanda. You walk in, and there's a massive, hardwood, carved crucifix on the wall to your right, and to your left a Muslim woman in a headscarf.

One of the people I got closest to in Ouagadougou was the Head of Admin, Fatima. She's just one of those people who has a good head on her shoulders, lots of compassion, and a great sense of humor. If you saw her Monday through Thursday you'd never guess she was Muslim. Unlike some other women in the office, on normal days she not only didn't sport a headscarf, but wore things that were just this side of too racy for work. But every Friday, clad in an embroidered robe, she'd disappear for an hour or two while she went to a nearby mosque for prayers.

She was also one of those Muslims who'd send a text on Christian holidays wishing well for you and your family, and that you deepen your faith during this holy day. A bunch of times I suggested I could go to the mosque with her on a Friday, and she always welcomed me, but somehow I never got my act together.

Then, one day, I decided that enough was enough and I needed to go. I wore my jelabya from Khartoum to work, which is entirely shapeless but has beautiful embroidery on it. It's my one vaguely African garment, and it fulfills the basics in terms of modesty.

People in the office absolutely loved it. I'm always cautious about wearing African dress because it can feel a bit like going native and/or advertising how cool you are: so hip, wearing the local garb. So superior to all you Europeans who stubbornly stick with your Western attire. So in most countries I'd bring it out sparingly, but in Burkina there seemed to be no hint of "what are you doing in our clothes?", and I always received many compliments.

The hour arrived and Fatima picked me up to go to the mosque. We arrived, and I very inexpertly pulled out the one scarf I had that seemed vaguely up to the job of covering my hair. Thankfully Fatima helped me with it and helped make sure that all my hair was really covered. I was a little self-conscious about how it looked, but she seemed to think that as long as the hair-covering was taken care of, I could be wearing a fuzzy bear's head for all it mattered.

As we walked in, there was a voice speaking on some kind of amplified system. Fatima informed me that it was the sermon, that the imam came early and spoke at some length before the midday prayers would begin. There was an outside patio area filled with men, and Fatima indicated to me that we should go into a small building at the side. I engaged in some rather inelegant gymnastics as I tried to remove my shoes and get into the building without soiling my feet, and then we were inside.

Call me really daft, but it was really only at this moment that I realized all the prayers were going to be in Mooré, a language I can decipher about as well as Inca. And here I'd left my babel fish at home. So it was going to be one of *those* events, where I sit politely with no clue of what's going on and pick up on what I can through body language.

Of course, picking up on body language would be easier if everyone weren't doing the same prayers with the same movements all the time. But it was still interesting. The little building was really very crowded, though it did have windows and a fan, so was bearable in terms of heat—quite a feat in Ouagadougou. And people were very considerate about moving aside to make room for late-comers.

I think they were impossibly curious about me, especially since I didn't know any of the movements or how to pray. But they were all perfectly polite, and when Fatima introduced me to a number of her mother's friends and some other older women, they were all as kind as they could be without speaking French, and seemed to think it was very cool that I had come to pay their mosque a visit.

I'm pretty sure that in many other parts of the Muslim world, there are rules about non-Muslims entering mosques, especially during prayertime, but I have to say that no one batted an eye on that front.

Then again, perhaps we weren't technically in the mosque, since we were sort of outside. I really don't know, but the point is no one seemed to care. A lot of families are also mixed, with Muslims, Catholics and Protestants sometimes all found among direct siblings. So the lines between the different religions are perhaps a little more porous than what most Americans experience.

The funniest thing about this whole adventure was the reaction of people at work when they found out I'd been to the mosque. The news spread amazingly quickly. Some people seemed amused, while others were more surprised than anything. Clearly, I had accidentally busted some expectations.

26

BEWARE THE ICE BEAR

Germany, 1993-1997

Michael and I knew each other for at least four months before he figured out I wasn't German and I figured out he wasn't German. He was another one I met through hanging out in the students' lounge of the Slavic Studies building, and we were also in Russian class together. Michael, Sonja and I wound up forming a bit of our own little group, though because Michael was Slovak, he didn't need to pound the verbs quite as much as Sonja and I did, so he wasn't always around.

The thing about getting together with Michael and Sonja was that we didn't have to *do* anything in particular. Through my friendship with him, I began to understand a key difference between West-European/American culture and that of the Eastern bloc.

Since I'd never learned that much about Europe before starting German my junior year of college, and then being there practically on the heels of the Wall coming down, I was fascinated by the differences in culture, as well as the idea of countries having to redefine their governance systems essentially from scratch. Of course, since then I've learned that you never start from scratch—there is no point zero—but that was a later lesson.

What I started to understand through my first trip to Russia, and then more in-depth with Michael, was that people in Western Europe and the US generally felt they need to *do* something if they get together with friends or family, whereas in the former socialist countries to the east, the mere fact of being together was worth a celebration. Of course this doesn't hold 100%, but think about how often you hear (or have had) conversations along the lines of:

Want to get together one time soon?

Sure, when?

Next Tuesday?

Great! What do you want to do?

[much debate ensues about what activity would be pleasing to both]

I don't want to overstate things here, but at the time the best word I could come up with for it was "transactional", by which I don't mean that people see friendships as a zero-sum game or a buying and selling relationship, but in contrast to the "socialist way", I felt that doing things with friends could often have an undertone of "OK, saw that friend, did a fun thing and had a good time, *tick*!"

Whereas in Russia or with Michael, I always had the feeling that there didn't have to be a point to getting together; getting together *was* the point. I think the time it really hit home for me was when Michael invited Sonja and me to his flat for brunch. He made a huge stack of *palačinky* (like crêpes or British pancakes), and I know he'd made a bunch of other stuff, but it was the pancakes that impressed me because they are so fiddly to make and he'd made so many.

So much work, just for a casual brunch apropos of nothing in particular. And the point wasn't to show off his culinary skills or give us a taste of something exotic: it was enough work to be an act of affection, but also common enough that the company would stay in the foreground rather than the food.

Another thing I learned was not to let Michael pour the drinks. He introduced us to the "ice bear", which I think means Polar Bear, but "ice bear" is just so appropriate somehow. It's a glass of champagne/sparkling wine with a shot of vodka. The problem is that you don't taste the vodka at all, so it's easy to think you've just had a glass of champagne, and if you're dumb like me, you think well that wasn't so bad, and so you take another one.

Oh, such a mistake, that.

Not embarrassing at all.

Michael also introduced Sonja and me to the wonderful Hana Hegerova, Czechoslovakia's answer to Edith Piaf, only she sings in Czech, Slovak, German, French, and Yiddish. Believe it or not, she's on Spotify.

27

IN WHICH I NEARLY RUIN THE REPUTATION OF A LARGE AND IMPORTANT ORGANIZATION

Kosovo late 1998

One day, I'm beavering away at the IRC office, and the phone rings. It's Vlora, the secretary, telling me that a journalist is calling, and since all the other expats are out of the office, could I take the call?

So, like an idiot, I say "Sure." What could go wrong? Can you tell I'd never had any media training?

After the introductions, the journalist gets around to the main point: Did I have any comment on the Serbs who had allegedly been abducted by Albanians in a couple of places in Kosovo?

Now, in fact, I had heard about this. Maybe a week before, we'd been visiting a representative of the Serbian authorities (I can't remember what exactly: local Red Cross chapter, maybe?), and he had complained to us about Serbs disappearing, having been nabbed by vindictive Kosovars.

He told us about a particular case where a Serb man was returned unharmed after a ransom was paid, but there were other stories where the men never came back. Nevertheless, it was a few isolated cases, and since the Kosovars protected each other, there wasn't a whole lot the Serbian police could do.

So, I replied to the journalist something along the lines that we had heard unconfirmed stories, but that it really wasn't in the remit of our organization, so we weren't doing anything specific about it.

"It's not in your remit?" the journalist asked, his voice registering something between disbelief and horror. "No, we're a humanitarian organization; we don't deal in kidnappings," I repeated.

This back and forth went on for quite a few minutes before the penny dropped.

"Oh—, do you think you're talking to the ICRC (International Committee of the Red Cross)?" I asked.

"Well, yes. Isn't that who you are?"

"No," I said, "this is IRC, as in the International Rescue Committee, not the ICRC."

Well, that cleared *that* up. Thankfully, the guy had a sense of humor, so we were able to have a conspiratorial little chuckle over the near-miss. Which would have been pretty bad, considering the ICRC's global profile and well-known mandate to visit prisons and report on the conditions of detention.

And now you know why NGO workers all need media training.

28

IN WHICH I GET MY FIRST TASTE OF
SAVING THE WORLD

Claremont and Los Angeles, 1991 and 1992

It's funny being back in the greater LA area as I write this. Strange echoes of the last time I was here, 25 years ago.

My last summer at Pomona College, I got an internship at the local chapter of the American Red Cross. It was a job I was extremely unsuited for: matching young people to volunteer opportunities in the community, and supporting them through the summer. It should have been great, but those young'uns were so unreliable, and their parents occasionally so rude, I was a bit out of my depth. Teaching a babysitting class really wasn't any better.

The compensation for all that was getting some exposure to the work that people more commonly associate with the ARC: emergency-response stuff. I helped organize a yearly conference that was held at Harvey Mudd (another college in the same complex as Pomona), and there got to take the Emergency 101 class that qualifies you for fieldwork. This got me on the roster of the Claremont chapter.

The first event I was called out for happened during the summer of my internship. A chemical spill in a local factory had produced some potentially dangerous gasses, so the police had cordoned off an area of about a mile around the building in question, and evacuated the residents inside that zone while firefighters (complete with dramatic-looking hazmat suits) went in to assess the danger level and contain the spill.

One of the interesting things I learned about the Red Cross during my time with them was that they have the mandate to provide food and water for emergency-response personnel while they are on a call, and receive no money from the government for this service.

Now you may be imagining some big tables with vats of chili or something, but in this case, since we were only going to feed about 20 people, we took orders and then went down to a nearby fast-food burger place. And then we drove around the perimeter, handing out burgers to the cops. It was fun, for sure, though I was honestly a little nervous about the clouds of poisonous gasses ostensibly lurking not that far away. There was a little gallows humor, but I couldn't tell how seriously to take it.

Almost a year later, following the Rodney King riots of April and May 1992, I got another call from the Red Cross. FEMA was setting up points where people affected by the riots could come and apply for federal assistance. The ARC was helping out at these registration points, handing out water and snacks in anticipation of long waits in the sun, helping to direct people to the right spot, etc. Would I be available to go for a day or two? Of course I leapt at the opportunity.....

...and was sent to Watts, a name associated with race riots in 1965. I knew things had changed a bit since then, but since I didn't know what they'd been like in 1965, that didn't mean a whole lot to me. I just knew that my little white, middle-class self was going to spend the day in a place I probably wouldn't dare set my pinkie toe in on my own. So in that sense, I felt I was lucky to be able to go and see first-hand what this neighborhood was like.

Mostly I was surprised by how normal it looked. Single-family homes, most very tidy, the only obvious difference from some neighborhoods I knew being a bit of waist-high chain-link fence around most of the properties. Obviously there's plenty you can't see from the street like that, but it certainly didn't match my TV-created image of large apartment blocks and people hanging around on the front step with nothing better to do.

The best part of the experience was that I was there to be of service to the local residents who'd suffered some kind of damage or loss during the riots. It was an interesting role reversal from the stereotype, and I got the opportunity to chat with some of the clients, which was great. I was also uncomfortably outed as not knowing any Spanish, thankfully by one of the FEMA guys (who was just giving me a hard time) and not any of the residents.

What killed me, though, was seeing the burned-out buildings right among those tidy homes. The one I remember most was a Foot Locker. But there were also grocery stores and little shops, in short, most of the places where people could meet their basic needs nearby. Now they were going to have to travel an hour just to buy groceries.

It seemed like a terrible own goal, causing more suffering to the local population than any of the big, impersonal corporations whose outlets were hit. Of course I understood the motivation for the damage that had been done; it was just kind of incredible to see it.

The second day we were taking supplies to a couple of shelters. After a couple of hours loading the vans, we hit the road—and also traffic. It took us all day to make the run to two shelters.

And thus I learned the most important lesson from all of my emergency work with the Red Cross: when the apocalypse comes, we're screwed. Forget emergency services, or anyone coming to put out a fire or restore a phone line or even pass information. They'll all be sitting in traffic.

29

IN WHICH I LEARN THAT CARS AND MUD
ARE A BAD COMBO, PART I

Kosovo, 1997

The first time I ever went to the field with IRC, they assigned the receptionist to go with me. A young woman who'd recently returned to Kosovo after studying in Australia, Vlora spoke very good English and so could double as a guide and a translator.

The guide bit was handy because of course there weren't really any maps, and road signs were pretty minimal as well. The directions to the village were basically "take the main road west out of town, and when you see that village we went to that one time, turn right and carry on another 20 minutes or so." Sounded dodgy to me, but Vlora knew the road, so OK.

I drove, which was great for my self-esteem because I had to stop for a cow in the road, which I'd never done before, suburban girl that I am. Learning new driving styles: one of the great perks of working in a bunch of different countries.

After a while we got to the village and made the required right turn. Once through the village, though, the road started to narrow and get bumpier, basically transitioning from unpaved road to a track just wide enough for a car to pass through. And it was muddy. Muddy, and getting muddier.

Well, we were in a pickup truck, and what's the point of being in a big NGO car if you can't use the 4-wheel drive, right? The only problem was, neither of us knew how to do it. It turns out this was one of those cars where you have to get out and manually turn a thing on the hubcap 90°. Who knew?

Also, Vlora has now had to openly admit that this suspect bit of road was not, in fact, the way to our village.

"Vlora, didn't you say you'd recognize the village where we were supposed to turn?"

"Hey, don't blame me. It was the same houses, the same chickens!" she said, sounding just the teeniest bit defensive. Because chickens are famous for changing how they look from village to village.

OK. So we're in the wrong place, and we can't figure out the 4WD, and there's no way I'm trying to back up all the way to where the road gets wide enough to turn around. The only thing for it is to do a three-point turn where we are. The problem is, there's a ditch on the left, and someone's fields on the right.

"Vlora," I say, "we can't drive over these people's food."

It's not just that I'm obviously a foreigner, but there's a big IRC logo stuck on both sides of the truck, so it's not like we can do this incognito. But not seeing any other option, I turn right and smash about 10 feet of someone's cabbages.

And now that we're in the open, in the distance I see a house, surrounded by a mud wall as Kosovar homes usually are..... and about five heads looking at us over said wall. OK, it's bad enough to drive over someone's food, but being seen by the owners of said food (within the first two weeks of starting work for a new employer) is really, really uncool.

"Vlora," I say a bit urgently, "you have to get out of the car and apologize to these people for driving over their food."

"No, it's OK," she says, because I guess pick-up trucks just appear in the middle of people's fields every day.

"Um, no, " I insist, "please—you have to get out and apologize for us."

And, because I outrank her simply by virtue of being a naïve and inexperienced foreigner, Vlora duly gets out of the car and yells an apology to the heads behind the wall. They made some obviously conciliatory motions, and so we finished the other two points of our turn (OK, it was probably more like a seven-point turn, but I was seriously afraid of that ditch) and headed home. Because, having made our little side trip, we now had *absolutely no idea* of how to get to the project site.

I do know how to use 4WD now, just sayin'.

30

IN WHICH I LEARN THAT CARS AND MUD
ARE A BAD COMBO, PART II

Kosovo, 1998

One day in early spring, Eddie and I were invited to a brunch in Prishtina. The house was up some stairs on a bit of a hill, so we parked down below, facing forward toward a restraining wall about five feet high.

When we got back to the car, some of the ice on the ground had melted, and we found that the car was now parked in the kind of place where you'll find fossils a few million years later. In short: mudsville. We got into the car, and Eddie tried backing out, which resulted in nothing more than one of the back wheels spinning rather violently and going absolutely nowhere.

Eddie got out to inspect the situation, which he assessed as well and truly stuck. Tow-trucks being not so much a thing at this point, we were a bit flummoxed as to how to get out. We couldn't go forwards because of the wall, and backwards was just killing the tires.

At this point a young Albanian man approached us and motioned for us to stop what we were doing. He ran off and found a piece of board lying around, which he proceeded to shove under the offending tire.

In broken German, he then instructed Eddie to drive rapidly a little bit forward and then backward, trying to rock the car onto the board and so out of the mud puddle. It took us a while to get what he was after, though, so the first few times consisted of him saying "forward!" and then "back!" and me translating from German to English for Eddie until he got the hang of it.

Eventually we did catch the edge of the board, and were able to back out of the spot onto the road. Before then, however, there was a lot of rocking back and forth, with plenty of wheel-spinning and flying mud. That would be flying mud that........ generously splattered our Good Samaritan's formerly spotlessly white jeans.

Of course we were mortified, and apologized profusely. I think I offered to pay to get them cleaned. He adamantly refused, and made it clear that it was an honor to sacrifice his jeans to the greater cause of helping the foreigners who were going to help Kosovo get its independence from Serbia one day. Well, he might have overestimated our influence just a tiny bit, but he really wouldn't take anything from us except for a thank-you, so that's what we left him with.

31

IN WHICH I LEARN THAT CARS AND MUD
ARE A BAD COMBO, PART III

Rwanda, 2005

S hould it be embarrassing that this little tale comes in three parts? You'd think I'd know by now that mud and cars don't mix, right? What can I say; when the rainy season hits, you get kind of used to feeling like a drowned rat half the time, which I guess can mess with your judgment.

At one point it had been quite a while since Eddie and I had been on a date night, out of the house, just the two of us. So we decided to treat ourselves to dinner at Sole Luna, which was known for being one of the better pizza restaurants in Kigali. One of the reasons for its popularity (besides the good pizza) was that, by virtue of being at the top of a kind of ridge, it had a great view over part of the city.

This meant that, to get to the parking area, one had to drive one block down a pretty steep road to the right, and then drive parallel to the main road over to the restaurant. That block going down was paved, though, so although it felt a bit like some of the more vertiginous moments in San Francisco, we made it fine.

The trouble started when we tried to leave. The road from

the paved bit to the restaurant had been pretty bad, and we'd had a good shower while sitting in the restaurant, so I decided to continue on to the next block up to the main road, in the hope that it would be better. No prizes for guessing that the road up the hill to the main street was not only steep, but not paved and so muddy and pretty darned uneven. But I had my handy 4WD car (no hubcap adjustments required), so decided to give it a go.

And thus did I learn one of the most important driving lessons of my life: Watchers of American television will have the impression that a biggish 4WD car can handle just about any terrain. Not so. The 4WD helps, but it is decidedly *not* a guarantee that your car will win the battle of car vs. road. Especially when the road has mud in its arsenal.

We started up the hill, and I pretty quickly figured out I wasn't going to make it. So I decided to back down and go back up the way we had come. The problem was that the road was so uneven, it was nearly impossible to actually steer as the wheels kept getting caught in the ruts and valleys.

I want to emphasize for the record that I saw the drainage ditch at the side of the road. I knew it was there. I tried to avoid it. I was not successful in avoiding it. This was not my fault, but the road's fault. That's a legal opinion, which I will defend until the day I die.

I got out to check out how bad things were. They were pretty bad. Both left-hand wheels were hanging in the ditch; the passenger (LH) side was smashed up against the hillside, and the car was resting on its axle. 4WD notwithstanding, I had at most two wheels to work with, unfortunately both on the same side of the car.

To further wound my pride, people who actually knew what they were doing were making it up the road in regular little town cars (though to be fair, not everyone was successful). One of them stopped and the driver told me he would call a tow truck for us.

Yeah, sure. This in a city that couldn't even manage a taxi service with a centralized dispatch. But lo, about 20 minutes later, what should appear but what might well have been the only tow truck in Kigali? Good news, indeed. They guys took a look at how the car was lying, and then gave us a price, which we managed to negotiate down to something we felt was reasonable.

Only, we'd spent all our cash at the restaurant. Cue a phone call at about 11:00 pm to our friend and Eddie's colleague John, and a somewhat shamefaced request to come by with money, and while he was at it, why not a bottle of whiskey as well?

Eddie and I found a place to sit on the side of the road, and waited for the tow-truck people to do their thing. After about 20 minutes, they told us they had to go get gas. (And I hate to say this but) because, Africa. You didn't know 20 minutes ago that you didn't have gas?

While waiting for them to come back, Eddie and I made the classic mistake of saying, "Well, at least the power hasn't gone out." No joke, it didn't last a minute after that. This was one of those moments that drove Eddie and me to develop the phrase: "I chuckle at you, O Life! Bwah—ha ha ha haaaaa!" (Think of the Count in Sesame Street, and you'll get the rough idea.)

John did in fact show up at some point, and once the tow truck was back, we watched them try to pull the car out, using our car's headlights to see by. No joy. It's really quite something to watch a tow truck not getting any purchase.

So they hammered a stake into the ground about five meters away from the car, attached a chain to the front of the car, looped it over the stake, and then drove the tow truck down the hill to pull the car up in the opposite direction. Just one of those miracles of ingenuity that are an everyday result of poor infrastructure and lack of resources. You gotta admire it.

Since it was about 1:30 am when we finally got home, we didn't assess the damage until the next morning. Under a rather extensive layer of dried-on mud, the dents ran the full length of the car. I'd like to tell you that I didn't get them repaired because I liked the effect—I always think a car that's obviously been in some kind of accident and yet is still on the road sends the message, "I don't give a shit if my car gets dinged, so you better not mess with me!" Truth is, I just never bothered.

IN WHICH I BECOME A PINCUSHION

August, 2009

M oving back to Zambia was a bit of a nail-biter in the sense that, as much as we loved living in Sarajevo, we'd noticed that we had a tendency to look back on our time in Africa with rosy tones. Good heavens—had we become Africa bores? Those tiring people who go all misty-eyed when they speak of *Africa* (it always gets a *tone*), and how everything there is just so much more "real, you know?" Had we idealized it with the benefit of being away from all the downsides, plentiful as they are? Would the warm fuzzies survive first contact with reality?

The short answer is, yes: we'd spent so much of our life as a family of four in Africa, that's what we know how to do. Move with the family to Washington, DC, or Harare? No contest. The African option is our comfort zone.

Anyway, as part of easing the transition to a new country and back to the continent, I kept back a few vacation days so that we could take a long weekend as a family and just kind of take the measure of things again. Not knowing the country at all, I did a little searching around and landed somewhat arbitrarily on a place called Chaplin's Barbet—and no, that's not a typo; it's a Zambian bird, I promise. It was a small guest house situated on an essential-oil farm, which sounded cool, and not too far from Lusaka.

In the end I did find the place a little disappointing, as there wasn't a lot to do. No pool, which is pretty much the solid stand-by option when kids are involved (ours were seven and nine at the time), and we'd arrived in Lusaka toward the end of the winter dry season, so shall we say the countryside was not showing itself at its best. Actually, having spent the past seven years in Rwanda and Bosnia-Herzegovina, both of which are spectacularly beautiful, arriving in bare, dusty and windy Lusaka had been a bit of a shock.

So we weren't exactly being blown away by the scenery or the facilities, but our family is pretty good at making the best of things, so we put on our cheerful smiles and did our best to settle in. Our first real break came when we met the house dog, which was enormous and fierce-looking but was missing a leg. He turned out to be terribly affectionate, and proceeded to lie at our feet, drooling profusely.

After nightfall, I left our room to go over to the loo, which was in a separate building. On the way, I looked up at the sky, and nearly fell onto my behind. It wasn't just the usual plethora of stars that you can see when spared the usual urban light pollution: for the first time in my life, I understood what the Milky Way is, and why it's called "milky". So many stars, you can't really differentiate the individual spots of light, just a brushstroke of white running clear across the sky.

So much of our lives is disappointment. You hear about how wonderful something is supposed to be, or you grow up all excited by the idea of Santa Claus, and as you get older and reality sets in, you discover that it's all not quite up to how it was billed.

And then, very occasionally, you get really lucky and experience the opposite: you discover that something you've been hearing about your whole life is even more wonderful than you'd ever understood. Not only is it really a thing, but there's a *reason* it's renowned. I actually ran back to the room and got Eddie to come out and see it, as if it was going to somehow disappear in the next five minutes, because I couldn't stand the idea of his not getting to see this completely unexpected miracle.

The next day, we decided to take a walk through the fields where they grow the plants for the essential oils. It wasn't particularly beautiful per se, but it was fun to see the great fields of geranium, lemongrass, and lavender. At one point we stopped to breathe in the scent of the geranium plants, and just enjoy the panorama laid out before us.

Until, that is, Marion let out a yelp of pain. We looked her over and found that a large ant had buried its pincers in her. I tried to pull the ant off her, and was finally able to, after a big yank—only I'd only got the back bits. The head was still doing the ant equivalent of the Martian Death Grip on poor Marion's leg. It did finally come with a second good pull, but by this time a few more had started to crawl over her shoes.

At this point we belatedly realized that we were standing over what must have been some kind of ant city. There was no mound or hill to see, but given the aggressive nature of their defense, it could only have been a big settlement. (She says, as if she has a clue.) And boy, were they defending. Both kids had probably ten big ants on their shoes, with a few heading up their pants, so we began to desperately try to brush or pluck them off.

And then I started to feel the little spots of burning pain, not only through my socks, but up my legs. I looked down and felt I'd just been dropped into a B horror movie. Ants were all over my shoes and my jeans, and several had clearly crawled up my legs under the jeans, and were picking their points of attack wherever they fancied.

The obvious thing to do was to pull down my jeans and whack the suckers off me. The problem with this plan was the group of about 15 people working in the fields just across the main path, about 30 meters away.

Now, I don't know what your ideas are about acceptable dress in Africa, but Eastern and Southern Africa (Angola excepted, maybe Mozambique but I've never been there—it's the Brazilian influence) tend toward the conservative. Spaghetti straps and skirts above the knee (or shorts on a male over about 12 years old) can be tolerated if worn by foreign types, but wouldn't really be considered appropriate for your average Joe or Joanne. In some countries (and I'm not sure how widespread this is, but my sense is that it's fairly ubiquitous), it's thighs rather than breasts that carry a sexual or erotic connotation.

Thighs. That part of my body that is going to show (never mind my butt!) if I pull down my jeans to get at the ants. I'm frantically smacking on the outside of my jeans where I feel the sting of a bite, but it's clearly not working well enough. So, in the end, there was nothing for it. Eddie and the kids stood between me and the workers, to try to block their view of my nether regions as much as possible, and I yanked 'em down. I then committed ant massacre.

Thankfully, none of the workers gave any indication that they'd seen my little display, and we were able to carry on our merry way. From then on, though, every time we wanted to stop and admire a plant or bit of scenery, we were careful to examine the ground and make sure it was safe. Unfortunately, the lawn back at the lodge was also pretty badly infested, which made our games of frisbee a little too active for my taste. Good thing the dog didn't bite.

33

IN WHICH WE SEE THE WORLD AND MAKE NEW FRIENDS

Hamamet, Tunisia, May 2016

It's not that we set out to have a vacation in a spot where Western tourists are afraid to go and so get a really good deal, but the opportunity just sort of jumped into our lap, so what can I say? We heard about this place from some friends, and since we always spent summer running around seeing family and such, we were well in need of some relaxing family time.

So without knowing much about it ahead of time, we bought our tickets to Tunis and got the number of a friend's brother's uncle's cousin who would give us a ride from the airport to the resort in Hamamet.

It was pretty dreamy. A lot of the stuff wasn't open because it was so far off-season, but they had an external group of "animators" in, whose job was to run the few activities that were going on. There was a little hut in the middle of the main grounds between the hotel wings, where you could get ping pong balls or sign up for archery. This was also the booth from whence poured the resort's theme song 12 hours per day.

We made friends with the animators because our kids were

practically the only people doing the activities, and of course because our children were particularly charming and intelligent and well-behaved. So every morning, as we were having breakfast (Marion: "I only start counting the chocolate croissants [she'd eaten] at six"), the theme song would start up, and we'd look down at the booth, catch the eye of the animator, and do the little mime of waving your hand with a pretend lighter back and forth in the air.

Apparently one of the reasons they had the animation team in was because it was a busier weekend than some. It was Easter week but also some bank holiday in Libya, and since the attitude to drinking and clothing was more relaxed in Tunisia, a lot of Libyans apparently liked to come over to spend the holiday.

Such it was that I got into a conversation with a young couple from Libya; it must have been over their kid doing something particularly cute. The man spoke better French than the wife, so I mostly talked to him. Again, far from throwing a disapproving eye over my Western holiday clothes, the husband mostly just wanted to friend me on Facebook and persuade us to come visit one day.

I was glad for this conversation in part because I'd never spoken to anyone from Libya before, and it was nice to have one of those conversations where governments do what they do, and we regular people just get along. I just wished I could have spoken with the wife as well. What an interesting conversation that could have been.

We had plenty of friends and family back home and in Ouagadougou who questioned the wisdom of going to Tunisia "so soon" after the terror attack where several tourists were killed. One thing I can say for certain is that our safety was a prime concern for the hotel. There were guards at the front gate with German shepherds, and another guy out back by the beach with another German shepherd. (We met the woman who raises the dogs at the hotel and she let us come to the back and see the German shepherd puppies. Kiddie heaven.)

Also, the beach—I mean, you couldn't really ask for it to be safer. There just weren't any tourists out there, maybe the occasional guy with a camel wanting to be paid for photos with the animal. As far as you could see to the left, and as far as you could see to the right, was just pure beach. So the idea of someone sneaking up on us was more a factor of entertainment rather than fear.

Generally speaking we didn't see much of anything cultural during our visit, which I know should be a capital crime in Tunisia. But even just our presence as Westerners/Europeans in the off season was enough to put a smile on people's faces. I once asked the man who seemed to be in charge of guest services whether he enjoyed his job, when we got talking a little bit about the poor state of the economy and all the other hotels that had closed for want of European visitors. "I love my country," he said with a shrug.

34

WHEN THOSE SIMPLE THINGS GO
HORRIBLY WRONG

Kigali, 2002

A lthough this story didn't happen to me or my family, it did involve some close friends of ours. I want to tell it because it's emblematic of the kind of thing that always lurks in the back of your head as an expat, especially since we do tend to live in the swankier parts of town and drive the better cars and such. I'm murky on some of the details, so with apologies to those who actually lived through it:

School runs were always a drag (proof that not everything in Africa is wildly different or exotic—or even exciting), so our friends Christine and Sophie managed to come up with an arrangement whereby a driver from Sophie's husband's work would pick up the four kids and drop them off every day after school. The kids were all in preschool together at the Belgian school, so they had the same pick-up time.

One day, the minivan pulled into Sophie's drive, and the driver got out to walk Sophie's two boys into the house. While he was gone, a pickup pulled up behind the van and two guys got out, one with a gun. They threatened the driver as he came back out, took the keys, and drove off—with Mike and Suzanne still in the van.

The driver immediately ran back inside to tell Madame about what had just happened, which left Sophie with the incredibly unpleasant task of calling Christine and telling her that her children had just been abducted at her house. Both women are pretty level-headed, so there wasn't quite panic, but obviously everyone feared the worst.

Eventually, Mike and Suzanne showed up at Sophie's front door, a little shaken but otherwise on good form. Apparently the guy who thought it was OK to take the minivan either knew it really wasn't OK to take a couple of kids, or just didn't want to deal with them. Either way, he'd driven for a while and then let the kids out. It must not have been too far away from Sophie's house, because Mike recognized where they were and managed to lead them back.

In the meantime, Sophie had called the police, who actually made an appearance (a rare occurrence in the absence of bribes or "gas money"). They were there when Mike and Suzanne arrived at the house, and spent some time taking statements from them. Then one of them pulled out a gun and started waving it around in front of Mike. When Sophie asked him what in tarnation he was thinking of, he replied, "I just want to see if he was traumatized by the gun he saw!"

35

THE SPIRITUAL SHOWER

Kigali, 2006-2007

One day my friend Amalja and I were chatting, and one of us bemoaned the lack of variety in terms of faith communities in Kigali at that time. Amalja is the daughter of a Protestant pastor in the Netherlands, who at the time was still very attracted by some aspects of the Christian faith, but put off by others. And I was at a point in my life when I had recently decided that I believed in God, and felt most affinity for the Jewish faith, but was many years away from the decision to formally convert.

So we identified a few friends who were also interested, and we launched a little religion group that met around once per month. By happy circumstance, each participant represented a different faith tradition.

Over the two or so years the group met, we had one person each from the Catholic, Protestant, Jewish, and Baha'i traditions. It was unfortunate that we couldn't identify an interested Muslim or Buddhist, but even just with the four it was a rich experience. Before each meeting, we'd identify a topic or theme of common interest, such as prayer, discipline, or sin, and each person would prepare a little bit so that she could represent "her faith's perspective".

This in and of itself would probably have been interesting, but we'd also bring in our own personal experience, challenges, things we'd tried to do, what we wanted to do more of, and how it seemed impossible to cultivate a full professional, spiritual and family life all at the same time. In addition, a number of us had spouses or partners who did not share our faith, so negotiating that was always a ready topic of conversation.

Our discussion always managed to crystallize the points of agreement between the different religions, and also to throw the differences into relief, but not in a confrontational way. Much the opposite: in learning the thinking and tradition behind other philosophies and practices, it became much easier to appreciate them.

At the end of the evening, it was fascinating how each of us always left feeling cleansed somehow, as if we'd had a "spiritual shower". And for as much as we'd learned a lot about other faiths, the fascinating thing was that we all left each evening feeling strengthened in our own faith.

Later on, Amalja owned up to the fact that she'd had to study quite a lot of Biblical Hebrew as part of her (Christian) theology degree. Language geek that I am, and thinking it would be cool to read the Torah in Hebrew, I asked if she would teach me.

So for the last six months or so of our time in Rwanda, Friday afternoons meant lemon tea and a stack of dictionaries (including her father's German one, which was so old it still used the pre-War *faktur* script), photocopied verb tables, and Bibles in English and Dutch.

We had a great time, and I even sort of learned a little bit, despite the fact that the method (start at "B'reishit" aka "In the beginning" and explain/look up as you go) was not really my usual. Without wanting to offend anyone, I have to say that I sure learned how much of the original text seems garbled or as though there might have been small copy errors here and there.

Which isn't surprising... but now if anyone talks about taking the Bible literally (or spends too much time interpreting something based on a translation, without verifying the Hebrew), I smile my wry little smile and leave them to it.

36

THE BLOCKADE THAT WASN'T

Kosovo 1998

This story is about the import ban that Serbia put on Kosovo in 1998, effectively cutting the province off from all sources of foreign goods.

Now, chances are you fall into one of two categories. If your reaction to that first sentence is "what blockade, and what or where is Kosovo again?" you belong in the first category. If your reaction was, however, more along the lines of "I remember the Kosovo conflict and read a fair amount about it, but don't remember anything about a blockade of Kosovo," then you are in the second category. There is a third group of people who were actually there and will remember it, a vanishingly small minority.

This is because, at the time, a glassy-eyed world was being Obi-Wan-ed by Serbia, repeating "there's nothing to see here" every time a piece of actual news threatened to break free and dangle itself like a shiny prize in front of the collective consciousness. Please note I'm not blaming the journalists here. They were doing their best to get the stories out, but as a journalist friend of mine noted, there are only so many times you can write "it's going to blow".

So here you have it: the blockade that officially doesn't exist —or, for those too close to the action to pretend nothing was happening, that thing we don't talk about:

"Honey, where's the milk for the baby?"

"Darling, you know that our friends the Serbs have decided that we should buy locally. Perhaps our wee pumpkin would like to eat toilet paper tonight? There's plenty of that!"

Now we international types were largely spared the effects of the "informal" blockade, for several reasons. First of all, some of us traveled regularly enough to Belgrade to stock up, and second, at least with IRC, we'd been encouraged to lay in a stock of non-perishables in case demonstrations or conflict left us confined to quarters for any length of time. So we had long-life milk, pasta, and sugar, for example, all of which were essentially impossible to find in the shops.

I'm talking about Soviet shelves that look full, but when you look closely you realize it really is all toilet paper, packets of cookies and other things that are hardly core household items. The milk shortage was no joke. A colleague of mine paid a farmer to bring his milk in from the village every morning. You'd be having a meeting, and suddenly he'd jump up and leave the room with apologies that the milk guy had come. He'd keep it in the fridge in the office, and then take it home so his wife could boil it for pasteurization and then give it to their baby.

For the third reason we internationals did better than most, let's talk about what I'll call the Dominique factor: that special way we all cultivate of blinking our eyes innocently, and adopting a slightly infantile tone of voice that says, "But I only need to do [insert harmless-sounding thing here]. Why should that be a problem?" (This technique is called "Counter Obi-Wan-ning" and is only known to a select few. You can thank me later.)

At this point, it is especially clever to invoke an actual child if possible, failing that a sick relative, or any other predicament you can conjure up to win the sympathy of the DWG (Dude With Gun).

Dominique had the added advantage of having, in addition to an American passport, one of the strongest French accents I've ever heard ("But Eddie, I em more Amereeken zen I am Fronsh." Uh huh.). So she could bat her baby blues at the DWGs and explain to them, in all innocence, that the 12 kilos of sugar in the back of the car were not (<there's nothing to see here...>), in fact, to share with anyone or even (gasp!) sell, but because "you know, I need it for making jam!"

The best thing about this story is that she was telling the truth: some fruit or other was in season, and she wanted to make jam, and even if she had to go to Skopje (Macedonia) to get sugar, well OK then. Never mind there wasn't a pound to be had anywhere in the city.

Skopje was close enough to Prishtina for a day trip, and although we'd lose about half an hour at the border (new visa, *every time*, but hey), the drive in and of itself wasn't bad. And it was seriously nice to be able to get out of the increasingly oppressive atmosphere of Kosovo for a few hours.

At one point during the blockade, a bunch of us went down to Skopje for the day. About half an hour in, Eddie and I passed a small supermarket. Nothing special, your usual little spot where you can dash in and grab something while you're out and about. But remember that at this point we've been staring at empty shelves for several weeks.

So my heart skipped a beat when I saw an entire shelf, as in like five rows ten feet long, of *just cooking oil*. No joke, I got tears in my eyes. I didn't think I was making a scene, but the way Eddie dragged me out of the store while I protested "but look! Look at all the oil!" might be a hint that I was looking just a tad hysterical. No security personnel were called, so I figure it can't have been all that bad and that Eddie is exaggerating.

37

THE MAGICAL WEEKEND

Kosovo, 1997-1998

So, in the story of how Eddie and I met, I last left you with me sticking my business card into Eddie's pocket while he danced away wearing the strawberry-flavored exfoliating shower gel.

We met up a few times over the next six months. I'd give him a call if I was coming down to Prishtina from Belgrade, and we'd try to get together. As circumstance would have it, most of the time he already had plans, so he'd invite me to join the group.

Which, honestly, was OK with me because I wasn't looking at him in a romantic way yet, and once I even had a crush on an Albanian colleague of his who was with us.

Then came New Year's Eve, 1997. My colleague, Renate, and I were both down in Prishtina over that long weekend, and were both invited to the same party. Now, Renate is a perfectly nice person, who has provided a lot of emotional support to peace activities and veterans in former Yugoslavia over the years.

And, I'd been sharing the same flat and working with her pretty much non-stop since the previous April, so let's just say I

needed a break. So I decided to skip the party, and called Eddie
to see if he wanted to hang out at all. He was amenable but had
also been invited to said party and intended to go, so we were just
going to do something quick and then he'd head off.

We tried to find a place to get a quick drink or a coffee in the
early evening, but most of the cafés were closed for decorating in
anticipation of the festivities later on. We were able to convince
one to give us a quick espresso, but no chance of finding
anything to eat. So Eddie invited me back to his house for pasta
pesto. OK, he wasn't exactly showing off his (actually consider-
able) cooking skills, but a jar of pesto was a pretty exotic treat, so
it was still a nice invitation.

So we went back to his place, which he shared with his
colleagues Dominique and David, who were not home yet. He
made the mistake of letting me put the pesto sauce in—hey, it's a
little jar, so I thought the whole thing was supposed to go in. Not
my fault! But otherwise it was a perfectly nice meal.

In the meantime, Dominique and David had arrived home,
so introductions were made, etc. Apparently they thought we
were already a pair when they walked in, but honestly that really
wasn't on my mind yet. I was just glad to have a nice place to be
instead of hanging out on my own in the *very* spare BPT apartment. So when it came time for Eddie to go to that party where
Renate was going to be, we agreed that I would stay at the house,
and he would go to the party for a while but not stay too long.

This is how I wound up seeing in 1998 with two people I'd
met all of maybe three hours previously. Did I mention that
people like to shoot their guns in the air when there's something
to celebrate?

So while I believe there were a few fireworks, it's fair to say
they were overshadowed by the multiple volleys of automatic
gunfire sounding all around the house. The three of us did this
little dance, then, trying to get close enough to the windows at

the front of the house to see fireworks, but wanting to stay back enough not to get caught by a stray bullet. And yes, it was kind of scary.

Eddie did eventually return, and we all chatted for a bit, and then it was time for bed. Given the action going on outside, and my total lack of desire to go back to the BPT flat, we agreed that I'd stay the night. And we slept, and that's all we did, and I know what you're all thinking, you people with a dirty mind.

That happened later.

And the day after that, a bunch of folks decided to head down to Skopje for the day (scene of the infamous cooking-oil incident). Aside from Eddie and his housemates, there were a couple of folks from Oxfam and IRC, so there were six or seven of us in total.

We went shopping, had genuinely exotic things like salad for lunch, and generally wandered around the historic center of town. It was a thoroughly delightful day: easy company, a break for me from the usual scenery, and for all of us from the mounting tension in Kosovo, a bit of *cou cou*! between Eddie and me, well, you get the idea.

Upon arriving home, we had a small challenge: It was day three of a long weekend, so the markets had been closed, and anyway there wasn't a lot available even when they were open, considering the famous blockade and general boringness of European fruit & veg in January. When I think now how terribly futuristically trendy we were without realizing it, eating locally produced stuff, and only in-season, please.

(Aside: by contrast, you really can't properly appreciate the joy of cherry season when it's not restricted to two weeks per year. Walking down the street with a kilo of cherries that cost maybe a dollar, just popping the little suckers into your mouth as you go, feeling the sun on your face… Magic.)

So basically we had our own version of one of those cooking

competition shows, as in "Please create a meal for four using only the following ingredients: cabbage, potatoes, white onion, bananas, pasta, canned kidney beans, dried soy chunks, and whatever condiments and spices you can find in the cabinets."

I have to say, both David and Dominique did some serious magic. David channeled his Nepal days and did something amazingly curry-ish with the soy chunks and beans, and then Dominique produced *bananes effing flambées*. I mean, wuh? Not that I was complaining, mind you.

Even if I'd wanted to, I would have struggled to put a coherent thought together given the mental dissonance of eating *bananes flambées* while overlooking a shopping center that's been repurposed into a collective center for refugees, in the middle of winter, in Kosovo.

In this way I managed to give myself a break of three full days from my regular life, and start what I thought was going to be a nice little affair, given that I was based in Belgrade and he in Prishtina (a good 6-hour drive if you take advantage of the 120 km/h speed limit), and I was leaving in April, anyway. Of course things didn't quite work out that way, but that's another tale entirely.

38

A TALE OF TWO CAPITALS

Belgrade and Zagreb, April, 2007—April, 2008

When I was working for the Balkan Peace Team, I was based with my co-worker in Belgrade. We had our own little flat (actually, not that little), very centrally located. The only problem I had with the flat was that my co-worker and I had a room each to sleep in and the living room was basically our office, so even on your "day off" it could be really hard to get away from work. That plus living with the same person for that long…. Well.

But Belgrade itself I loved. It was comfy—now, I don't suspect most people would expect me to use that word, since the country was still under sanctions and Milošević was still in power. In fact, as I mentioned before, I was cautioned not to speak English on the street. Clearly the people who thought up these suggestions had never seen the McDonald's in Belgrade. Always, always full. Mostly with adolescents who would nurse a shake or some other beverage, and maybe a small serving of fries—date night! And the place to be seen, clearly.

The point is, as I traveled around the region, I developed a distinct preference for Belgrade over Zagreb. I confess that I didn't spend loads of time in the latter city, so it's not a fair comparison, but just on kind of the aesthetics of the place and how people are dressed and such, I felt that Zagreb was a hard and shiny place, where women's hair is perfectly coiffed and they all wear high-heeled shoes and everything looks great but they'd never give you the time of day. (Sorry, Zagrebians.)

In contrast, Belgrade was like that old pair of shoes that you probably should have thrown away a long time ago, and certainly they've seen better days, but they fit your feet so well and they're so comfy, they're still your go-to. Everything had a run-down feel, but in a "nu? What can you do?" sort of way.

39

MOVIES THAT WRITE THEMSELVES

Berlin, Autumn of 1992

E ver have that moment when you feel like you've been dropped into the perfect scene for a movie? OK, well this story and the next both had that quality, and I'm noting for the record that anyone who wants to make an actual movie based on this stuff (which would be great) will owe me for the story rights.

My last year at Pomona, there was a German exchange student called Maja and a German regular student called Mieke. The three of us and a few other German types hung out a fair amount, and so the following year when we were all in Germany, we decided to meet up for Oktoberfest in Munich. Some of us also went to Berlin.

It was Mieke's birthday, and she invited three friends from her old middle school in East Berlin to get together to celebrate. Maja and I were also invited, but the focus of the evening was clearly on these four women, who had not all been in one spot since sometime around 1982, well before the Wall came down. As the evening drew longer, the ashtrays filled up, and the sky grew darker outside, each woman told the story of what she had experienced in the previous ten years, at times falteringly, at times highly emotionally.

Mieke

Mieke's father was a Protestant pastor, and her mother was a professor of Egyptian Studies. Because they were intellectuals, in the Communist system there was no way Mieke was going to be allowed to pursue an academic track. Her parents got around this somewhat by putting her in a church school, but this also brought its own problems since the state frowned upon religion and didn't like any kind of parallel thing they couldn't control.

At some point Mieke's mother went to an academic conference in the West, where she met an American professor. She fell in love and took off with him to the US. After some time, she asked Mieke to join her there. And although it was a wrenching disruption to her life, Mieke understood that the opportunities she would have in the US far outweighed what she would miss by leaving home, and after long negotiations with the state, she was finally allowed to leave.

She'd finished high school and gone to college in the US, but now wanted to complete a German degree as well, following in her mother's Egyptian footsteps (and if you start singing "Walk Like an Egyptian" right now, I'll kill you). She chose Munich for the strength of their Egyptian Studies department, and had moved there some months previously.

So now remember that while she was at college, the Wall had come down and Germany had reunified. It had been three years since East Germany ceased to exist, which isn't that long, but if you're living it day to day, it is a decent interval to make your accommodations with the new system and way of life.

Unless, of course, you were Mieke—"fresh off the boat", as it were, and totally new to all things West German (now just "German"). So there were a million new things to learn, not only regarding starting at university, but how to rent a flat, get a phone line, all that. Much of which any German would be expected to know, but which Mieke had to learn by asking.

Asking, in her very strong East Berlin accent. No way you can fake this one. Mieke's accent is strong, and it marks her without doubt as someone from East (not West) Berlin. So now she's asking about really basic stuff ("how do I get a phone line?") in an accent that marks her as a native German. Had she lived under a rock for the past 5 years?

This was actually something I could relate to, since even when I arrived in Germany I had a good enough accent that most people thought I was German. But of course I'd only had two years of the language, and there were plenty of things I didn't know, especially vocabulary. Once I walked into a department store and had to ask for "that thing that you, uh, it's in the kitchen, and, uh, you use it to [cue hand motion]…"

"Oh!" exclaimed the shop assistant. "You mean a *Pfannenheber*?" Uh……. Well, *Pfanne* is a pan, and *heben* is to lift, so it seemed like a good enough candidate for a spatula.

"Yes, that's it!" I say with the sweetest smile I can muster, trying to ignore the sideways glances I was getting for appearing to be a fully developed adult and yet not knowing a perfectly normal household word. Mieke and I definitely bonded over this one.

Frauke

In the new, unified Germany, both form and function demanded that some politicians from the former East Germany be able to rise to positions of importance in the Western parties and political offices.

Frauke was to all appearances an average 20-something woman in East Germany. Blond, dressed like a university student…. Only she lived with her father, and only her father, because her mother was one of those up-and-coming former East German politicians who was making her name even in the West.

Oh—and no one could know that she had a child, since Frauke was born out of wedlock and had never been openly recognized.

So she went through life, doing the things that German students do, still living in East Berlin because that's where home was, seeing her mother more often on the nightly news than in person. And watching her rise in political stature, even as her visits to Frauke—never frequent—became all the more rare.

Julia

Julia was the same age as the others: around 25, but in many ways she seemed more mature. This was at least in part due to the fact that she had a child—which was why she had a flat big enough to seat all six of us. Julia was the one who wanted to go clubbing after dinner.

Clubbing? I was more wondering when we can go to bed?

But there was a reason for her enthusiasm, and it was a simple one. She'd gotten pregnant around age 19 and quickly married the child's father—and so had never had the opportunity to do all those fun and crazy things that pass for entertainment with young adults, like going to bars and clubs. Instead, she studied and got a degree in business while her husband studied engineering. They were set up for a pretty good life in East Berlin.

And then, the Wall fell. At which point Dear Hubby split for the West, taking their combined savings, and leaving Julia holding the baby and with substantial bills to pay.

The best part was that her Business degree, being as it was, based on Marxist theory (or probably capitalist theory with some Marx quotations thrown in), was not recognized in the new, unified Germany. Surprise! That degree you just spent five years of your life to earn: worthless. You're a businessperson; sell the paper your degree is printed on, and see if you can make a profit.

Requalifying for the same degree was out of the question. No way could she handle full-time studies and taking care of the baby. So, she did what every self-respecting woman would do, and got a cosmetology degree. It had worked out pretty well for her. She was working, saving money to go back to university and earn a more useful degree, and doting on her little girl.

Julia's story really stuck with me. Imagine losing all your savings, your husband, and your job prospects all at the same time, and all because of some bigger-picture political thing that you've had nothing to do with.

The husband ditching was hard, but what got me most of all was the non-recognition of her degree. Surely if she's really that incompetent, she'll just not be able to find a job? Later I came to understand the protectionist role of the guilds in Germany, and the way the educational and professional system seems set up to protect certain types of people and thwart the ambitions of everyone else. It just seems wrong to me that you're considered qualified and then you aren't, just because your country went away.

Sabine

There's an expression in German for a porous border where bushes and trees provide some cover for would-be illegal crossers like Sabine and Jonas. One such "grüne Grenze" lies between Hungary and what was Czechoslovakia at the time.

Sabine and Jonas met when Sabine was on a trip with her school. Americans may be surprised to learn that it's not that uncommon in Europe for older students to go on class trips abroad as part of their education. A bit of language, a bit of culture, a bit of teenage fun.......

Anyway, Sabine from East Germany and Jonas from Czecho-slovakia, newly in love, went for a stroll one day in the woods, and discovered the border with Hungary when they accidentally strayed a bit too far and found themselves confronted by a patrol of Hungarian border police (our friends the DWGs). Oops.

Thankfully they were innocent enough and close enough to the actual border that they incurred, rather than the wrath of the

Hungarian state, more a finger-wagging and a free! (if uncomfortable) trip back to the other side. A simple enough tale, only that it gave them an idea.

Once Sabine had returned to East Germany, she and Jonas continued to correspond, deepening their relationship and eventually deciding that they wanted to spend their lives together. Now they had to decide where to get married, and where to live. At this point in time neither one of them could imagine trying to build a life in their respective home country, or anywhere in the Eastern Bloc. Pressure was building on the Communist systems in these countries, and more and more people were making a run for it, so after much reflection, they decided to do the same.

Once again, Sabine went down to Czechoslovakia and met up with Jonas, where this time they fled over the *grüne Grenze* into Hungary. From there, they gradually passed into Austria and then West Germany, where in an ironic twist of fate, they wound up settling in West Berlin.

Ironic because, while the young couple had over many months been gradually making their clandestine way to the West, the Wall had come down and Germany was unified. There was nothing preventing them from going back to live in East Berlin, where things were more familiar and rents a whole lot cheaper—except Sabine's inability to stomach moving back to the place she'd started from, after all the risk and effort she'd taken on to get out.

40

IN WHICH I REALIZE THAT I WILL NEVER, EVER BECOME A POLITICIAN. EVER

Germany, 1993-1997

Something very cool about German universities, at least when I was there, is that they have a whole student government that functions like a scaled-down version of "real" provincial or national governments. They even have university versions of the national political parties. In my day, the main ones were the Democratic Socialists, the Christian Democrats, the Free Democrats, and the Greens.

(Aside: I should stipulate that the Christian Democrats [CDU] are in fact not entirely nationwide; the Christian Socialists, who use the word "socialist" to mean "community-minded" and are most emphatically not "red", exist only in Bavaria and are in a formal alliance with the CDU, which exists everywhere in Germany *except* Bavaria.)

When I first heard this, I was completely convinced that my leg was being pulled from here to China. Can you imagine having an alternative Republican party that exists only in Texas? Well, probably. But that's the way it is, go figure.

These university parties run annual elections with the entire student body, which determine the composition of the student parliament. There are also the equivalents of ministries, called a *Referat*, which are supposed to represent and assist certain groups of students or causes. So there was, for instance, an ecology *Referat* dedicated to promoting things like recycling and energy conservation in the university, an LGBTQ *Referat*, and a Foreigners' *Referat*, dedicated to the interests of international students.

It was through this last that I came to student politics during my time in Bonn, pretty much (OK, entirely) by accident. I'd found the whole process of applying to and registering at the university intimidating, and I even spoke passable German, which not all new international students did. And so when I learned that there was an office dedicated to representing the interests of foreign students and helping them work through the bureaucracy of enrolling and getting set up at the university, I decided to volunteer there.

I made some great friends through the *Ausländer-Referat*. I most clearly remember Ahmed, a Palestinian student of medicine, and a man with the most wonderful name of Ali Al-Nasani. Just say that out loud and savor it. Ali's ethnic background was Iraqi, but he'd grown up largely among native Germans, and as such had a very strong local accent.

Also, dude, that man talked fast. I really liked Ali, but sometimes it was kind of hard because between the *Bönnsch* (local accent) and the speed, I really struggled to understand him half the time. We used to joke that your average German walking down the street would assume that I was the German and he was the foreigner, and of course they couldn't be more wrong.

Ali was also super handy, because he was the only one of us who spoke French, and we got a fair number of students from francophone Africa looking for information. One time, when I'd been volunteering in the office for a couple of years, Ahmed and I got two guys from Cameroon who spoke neither English nor German. And, well, not Arabic, either. So off I went to see if Ali was in the building (he often worked in the ecology office as well), and when I found him he promised to come but needed 10 or 15 minutes to wrap up something else.

Arriving back in the office, we managed to get our clients to understand that they should wait a little bit. Ahmed, who by this time had learned of my affinity for languages, said, "You don't speak French? You speak everything else!"

I laughingly demurred, and then, probably because I'd been on a study trip to Russia not that long before and just kind of had the language in my head, I said "*nichevo*", or "nothing" in Russian. Immediately one of the Cameroonian guys sits up and says, "*Ty govorish po-russki?*" "You speak Russian?" Uh, well, kind of. But what the heck? Why does this Cameroonian guy speak Russian?

This was before I learned how many Africans were invited to study in the Soviet Union or other Soviet-bloc countries as part of their bid to increase sympathy for the Communist system. Proxy politics and all that. In fact, many years later in Rwanda, one of our son's best friends was a Rwandan boy named Igor. When I finally had the chance to ask the father about it, he told me he'd studied in Bulgaria and kept very fond memories of the place. So Igor was Igor, and his brothers were Boris and Marko.

And so I found myself explaining how to take the German test and potentially additional studies before beginning university, and how to apply for financial aid, in very halting Russian, to a couple of guys from Africa. Because of course, right? Fortunately, Ali showed up soon thereafter and saved me from further embarrassment.

Another time early in my tenure it was the German language

that tripped me up. The students were going to strike over plans the (national) government intended to introduce, which would inflict penalties and even expel students if they took too long to complete their degrees. (At that time, the average actual time to complete an ostensibly 5-year program was more like 7-10 years. Plenty of reasons for that.)

As part of the process, the student government had to call a series of meetings designed to reach as much of the student body as possible, in which they were to make their case for why the new policy would be unacceptable, and so that the students would vote for the strike.

One of the groups they wanted to have speak was the international students, who stood to be put under a lot more pressure if they needed more time due to gaps in prerequisite knowledge or German, or if they had to work on the side because they most likely had to finance their studies themselves. For some reason it was decided that I should both write the speech and deliver it on behalf of the international students. I suppose it was because I was credibly a foreign-born student (unlike Ali, who was clearly a local boy the minute he opened his mouth) with strong enough German to be well understood even with the inevitable slippages that come when you're nervous.

And boy, was I nervous. I mean, hello. Big auditorium filled with native German speakers, and I'm supposed to get up and make a speech on an issue I only sort of understand? And then I realized that the other speakers had pretty much written out their speeches, while I had only made bullet points and intended to speak more or less contemporaneously. Oh my, oh my.

Also, in all the TV shows and movies I'd seen with speeches of this kind (because really, when had I ever seen anything like this live?), they were always rousing and inspirational—but the people speaking before me didn't seem to be rousing much of anything.

When it came to my turn to speak, I was shaking so much that it was just as well I hadn't relied on a written-out speech, because it would have been impossible to read. But the real fun was about to come. "Expel" is such a friendly little word. Sadly for me and my tongue, the German version of this is "*Zwangsexmatrikulation*", which is obviously neither little nor particularly easy to pronounce, especially when you are not a native speaker and you are trying not to embarrass yourself in front of a couple hundred people. Yeah, as in "don't think of an elephant".

But something happened as I continued to speak that I hadn't expected. The more I had to say *Zwangsexmaktulation*, and the more I stumbled over it, the more the public got on my side. I made some passing reference to how anti-foreigner the word was, obviously in more than one sense, and got enough sympathetic laughter to keep me from retiring from the podium in disgrace. And when I got to the last bit and went ahead with my prepared slogans despite not having heard any from the others, I actually got cheers and the biggest applause of anyone who spoke that day.

A bunch of my friends were becoming more active in the Green students' party, and since I was already sort of in student government by virtue of my participation in the foreigners thing, I started going to the party meetings as well. Next thing I knew, I was running for "office", i.e. a seat in the student parliament.

Now, the Germans usually use a list-based system, meaning there are no districts. People vote for the party of their choice, and depending on how many seats this equates to in the relevant parliament, that many people are selected, in order, according to a list agreed within the party before the election. So no one was voting for or against me personally (thank heavens); it was purely a question of whether the Green students' group would win enough votes for me to get in.

And, scarily, it did. Suddenly, after having spent less than two years in the country, I was an MP—even if the parliament in question was just for the university and of limited influence. And not only that, the Greens were the biggest group in the parliament, and therefore tasked with putting together a coalition with enough votes to form a majority.

Awkwardly, the only group that really had the votes we needed was the equivalent to the CDU, i.e. fiscal and social conservatives. Not that there was any fiscal policy to set per se, but there was a budget to be allocated every year, and decisions to make about which *Referate* to approve, or special requests to be approved and denied. So it wasn't just a talk shop, either.

Only we did a lot of talking. Oh my Lord, yes. The coalition negotiations were lengthy, convoluted, and frankly infuriating. This was the first and most important lesson I learned about politics: there's no such thing as sticking to your principles. If you try to be honest and straight-up, some other unscrupulous soul or souls will figure out how to use that to force you into a weaker position (aka screw you over). The compromises are inevitable, messy, and yes, potentially hard to explain to people who haven't been in the thick of it like you.

There was a lot of wrangling about the central governing body, vaguely equivalent to the cabinet. I can't even reconstruct what that last issue was about, but it had to do with what that body was going to be called, and to what extent power was collectively going to be shared—with the Greens, of course, pushing a more communal model, and the Christian Democrats wanting something more clear-cut (which would, in their eyes, presumably assure them a certain amount of power—something they might not be able to quite manage in a fuzzier system).

And thus came perhaps my most lasting contribution to German politics ever, when I said "The substance of what we're saying is pretty much the same thing. We could call it a boccia ball for all that it matters." As so, for the remainder of the negotiations, the governing body was the boccia ball.

Let me beg your indulgence for a momentary digression: When we were finally ready to sign, the wonderful Sabriye Tenberken was to become President of the student body. When she signed the agreement on behalf of the Greens, someone saw her signature and made a joke about how clumsy it was. "What, is her arm broken?" Which was awkward, because she is, in fact, blind.

For her Tibetan studies, Sabriye needed a way to write the Tibetan language in Braille. None existed, so she just did the obvious thing and created one. As you do. The alphabet was later examined by scholars of Tibetan and deemed to be very well adapted to the Tibetan language.

After her studies, Sabriye used this alphabet when she founded the first school for the blind in Tibet. She has since gone on to create some projects in India, as well, and is the founder of the NGO Blind Without Borders. She's well worth a google.

What I remember most about Sabriye is her absolute lack of attitude about being blind. She'd been raised in an environment that brought out her independence, and so she was capable of an awful lot on her own. Perhaps for this reason she was then comfortably unabashed about asking for help if she wanted it. I recorded myself reading a couple of books in English that she needed for her studies, since they did not exist in Braille edition, and in this way learned an awful lot about the Karakorum pass.

My favorite, though, was when she told me that she uses colors to help her remember numbers—and not just straightforward colors like blue or red, either. One was kind of a pale, translucent blue; another, a bright yellow like sunshine. When I shared with her my confusion about her ability to name such subtle colors, she explained that she'd been able to see enough as a child that she remembers generally how the world looks. And because the blindness is caused by a restriction in the blood vessels to the retina, when she drinks, she can see better. Well cheers, then.

Politics at the university in Bonn were also marked by the fact that the national seat of government was still in the city, even though the capital had already moved to Berlin. This meant a lot of law and politics students (of whom the women in the latter group were almost universally identifiable by their pearl necklaces), who were looking for chances to intern with the "real" political parties and thus gain useful connections. Some leftie types were of course also trying to get into politics, but it seemed less direct somehow.

Anyway, I can't compare with other universities, but in Bonn at least we all took ourselves terribly seriously, with lots of grand speeches and posturing. As the representative of the section for foreign students, I occasionally had to give a report to the full parliament, which was a thoroughly terrifying experience. My German was quite good by this time, but certainly not very tried in situations of emotional distress, and this certainly counted as one! It frustrated me that I never seemed to be able to get my point across with any real clarity, and then of course the ripostes would come from the other side, some of them genuinely racist or walking the border, and I didn't have the linguistic sophistication yet to give 'em a what for.

After a year of this, I was done. I'd sat through innumerable meetings that were at least three times longer than they needed to be because everyone had to have their say, been forced into several compromises I wasn't keen on, had the stress of trying to keep track of what was going on enough to be able to report on it, and generally invested a lot of time and energy in things that didn't seem to really bother anybody outside of the political crowd.

I stayed with the foreign students' desk for a while, but that was about it. Still, although it was really only sticking my toe in the water of politics, I think I learned quite a lot about what it's like, and knew it was definitely not for me. But today, it does give me a little more sympathy for the people who really are trying (or came in trying) to make a difference, and just get bogged down in the machinery of it all.

41

IN WHICH I MAKE A SMALL FORAY INTO
THE WILD AND WONDERFUL WORLD OF
SMALL JEWISH COMMUNITIES

One of the great pleasures in my later years abroad was finding ways to be a part of a Jewish community, whether an indigenous one existed or not. As a result, I have had the privilege of worshipping with some of the smaller Jewish communities out there, each with its own history and particular characteristics.

The first synagogue I went to outside the US was in Bonn. To be honest, I went once and never again. The armed guards outside the building took me aback at first, although it was clear enough to me why one of the few working synagogues in the country at that time should be seen as a target.

It's also pretty obvious that the congregation is probably relatively stable, which is, I assume, the reason for the hesitancy in welcoming me for services. I didn't get the feeling they were used to having visitors. It was the first time I'd been in a synagogue where the women sat separately from men, upstairs in a balcony. It kept them pretty far from the action, but then many of them didn't even seem to be particularly following the service.

I was reminded of a reason someone once gave me for the separated seating; since only the men are required to pray, it makes sense to keep the women separate where they can tend to the children without bothering the men. Still a thoroughly sexist explanation, but at least one that doesn't mean to imply flat out that women are inferior to men, if you can kind of squeeze yourself into that reasoning.

Some years later, when for fun I took a Yiddish course in Bonn, I learned that the city had once housed one of the most flourishing Jewish communities in Germany. Who knew? In that class, I met an African-American woman, Shana, who was getting her degree in Yiddish. I'll leave to your imagination how welcome her fellow scholars made her feel.

Living in Bonn was no picnic, either. Since the embassies had not yet moved to Berlin, a large proportion of any dark-skinned people you'd generally see around town were diplomats. So people kept addressing Shana in French, which was not only insulting but also inconvenient, since she didn't speak that language. (As opposed to Amsterdam, where everyone spoke naturally to her in Dutch, which made her much happier even though she didn't speak that, either.)

Rwanda took a while to get going, because there was no community to speak of when we arrived. The first thing we did together was a Passover Seder. It was really made possible by an Israeli guy called Yoav, his girlfriend, a friend of ours from the US embassy, and me. When we arrived on the day, we were astonished to meet our Indian friend Rajan, with his nominally Catholic French wife. Wait, you—But, also you—?

Rajan ran a travel agency that did all the standard airline stuff, but, as I noticed after I knew he was Jewish, also organized trips to Israel. He sounds Indian and is one of the most amazing cooks of Indian cuisine I have ever known, but if I understood correctly, his family belonged to a group of Jews who'd migrated to India from Iraq back in the day. He'd moved to Israel in time to do his military service, and spoke fluent

Hebrew. Perhaps for this reason, Rajan was always responsible for the hummus.

We discovered other Jews to invite, and it became a nice little community of seven or eight Jews and their families, who were not necessarily Jewish. We celebrated the holidays with a mish-mash of everyone's customs: a bit of Hebrew, a bit of English (OK, mostly English), and lots of good food and laughter.

In Sarajevo, you famously find the Catholic cathedral, the Orthodox cathedral, the main mosque and the old central syna-gogue within the same square kilometer. The "sound of Sarajevo" is the church bells ringing on Sunday morning, say, and the call to prayer picking up from all the tiny mosques that dot the hill-sides, colliding into each other as they bounce around the moun-tains, ultimately becoming a great, companionable cacophony of religions nestling up against each other.

And yes that's not the whole story, but it is a significant part of the story. Sarajevo is also famous for the Sarajevo Haggadah, a book that contains the order of service for the Passover Seder. The pre-war population of Sarajevo rightly valued their Jewish community as a gem of history and a model of peaceful co-existence.

During the war, when the city of Sarajevo was broken up into different factions and besieged from the outside, the Jewish community leveraged the fact that they didn't belong to any of the three main ethnic groups (ethnicity and religious affiliation being synonymous in that part of the world) and so were consid-ered neutral, to run an ambulance service that served the entire city. They were not hindered by having to stay in any particular enclave. For this reason, they are still widely appreciated by the post-war population.

Which, sadly, has not prevented the younger Jews from emigrating in massive numbers. When I was attending services, there was a hard core of maybe 15 folks who came every week, and counting only the Bosnians, the median age was probably around 70. Having lived for so many years under Tito's regime, when religion was not exactly encouraged, the community found themselves re-establishing practices and customs based on what they could remember from childhood.

This led to some interesting customs, which I found occasionally surprising, such as blowing out the Shabbat candles rather than letting them burn (I believe this was largely a measure to conserve the candles). They're also very big on brined hard-boiled eggs, which are apparently one of the things Sarajevans most associate with the Jewish community.

But my entry was not so easy. On my first try, I had missed Friday evening, and so decided to just walk down to the synagogue on Saturday morning and see what was going on. As I arrived, a man was just getting out of his car and heading for the door. Our exchange went something like this:

Him (in a challenging tone): What do you want?

Me: I'd like to go to services.

Him: Why?

Me: Uh… because it's Saturday morning.

Him: Yes, but why?

Me (increasingly confused at this circular conversation, hoping to land on the magic words that would get me past this gentleman): Um, because it's Shabbat morning and I would like to go to services?

Him: Are you Jewish?

Me: Well, technically no, but….

Him: It's Saturday. The synagogue is closed.

Me (Huh???): Um, OK, could you tell me when the services are on Friday, so that I can come back?

Which he eventually did, while making it clear they wouldn't be waiting outside with open arms if I did decide to come. I should add that despite my replying in the local language to begin with, he insisted on using English, to the point that I gave up and did the same. I've always hated that, though. It always seems to be to be a vaguely passive-aggressive way of saying you don't speak the language very well.

I did keep coming back, though, reasoning that if I just kept showing up, eventually someone would be friendly to me. And, very gradually, it worked.

The rabbi was a local young man now settled in Israel, who came only for the High Holy Days and Passover. In his absence, one of the congregants habitually acted as *Hazan* and led the prayers—from what had to be one of the most jumbled, cobbled-together, illogical prayer books to see the light of day, at least in modern times. A Xeroxed copy of copies of copies of at least three different source texts, it jumped around in such a way that one was constantly flipping back and forth in order to follow the service.

It didn't help that the gentlemen prayed at something just short of light speed. It was months before I was even able to follow the service, let alone speak along. It didn't help that all the transliteration was done with Serbian/Croatian/Bosnian phonetics in mind, meaning I had to read everything silently to myself about three times before I could get what was intended. Plus, all the songs were wrong. I didn't recognize a single melody. And for someone who gets much of the joy of a service out of the singing, I found it pretty disappointing, until I got used to the "new" songs.

The community was the object of a fair amount of interest from scholars, Israelis and tourists, which meant that you never quite knew whether you'd arrive to find a quiet gathering of 15 people, a group of 30 visiting students, or an Israeli film crew. During one such visit, I was treated to a service upstairs in the "real" synagogue, with hardwood pews and floor and stained-glass windows.

Normally services were held downstairs in the community center, because the upstairs was too expensive to heat. One day, a group of Croatian students of Spanish, who'd been touring Sarajevo, came by to visit during Friday-night services. The group was big enough that it made sense to go upstairs, which was already exciting. And then the Hazan says, "And this evening, in honor of our guests who are learning Spanish, we will do the service in Ladino." And boom—just like that, the regular congregants shifted gears and off they went.

Blanka was probably the person I got to know best of the regular congregants. She made me feel welcome and didn't seem to hold it against me that I hadn't lived in Sarajevo for 50 years. From her I also learned how close Ladino is to Spanish, much in the way that Yiddish leans heavily on German. She told me the story of having visited Spain some time back (possibly in the '60s). She had never learned Spanish, but she and her husband just spoke Ladino the whole time, and while they got some funny looks from people, they were able to get by just fine.

If you think about it, it's logical that a population like the Jews would learn to navigate the palimpsest of cultures and languages wherever they found themselves, and under what regime. True to a certain extent of the entire population of the Balkans, what with Ottomans and Austro-Hungarians swooshing back and forth, and borders shifting like the tides, this seems to be especially true of the Jews, who add another layer of their own making by trying to maintain an identity as a people, as well as the language(s) and customs that go with it.

This was illustrated to me best when the Bosnian-Israeli rabbi was in town for Passover, and offered a talk on sayings and their cultural roots. As he gave his lecture, he ping-ponged between Bosnian, Turkish, Ladino and Hebrew, and probably others that I couldn't make out. I was lost most of the time, having mediocre Bosnian and none of the other languages at my disposal, so I people-watched instead. Was anyone else having trouble following along? Certainly none of the Sarajevans. What I loved best was when he cited one of the Ladino sayings and was quickly corrected by several of the older generation in the room.

Zambia was a sadder story. Where once a Jewish community thrived, the one I found in Lusaka was pretty close to being on its last legs. Why Jews in Zambia? Turns out the South Africans had a quota for Jews around WWII, so many refugees who made it there from Europe were told to keep on trekkin'.

Many wound up in Zimbabwe, and some even carried on farther north to Zambia. Solomon, whom I first contacted about coming to services, was an importer and investor in real estate. The task of dealing with the authorities and bits of bureaucracy was made slightly easier in his case by the fact that his father, one such refugee from Europe, had gone on to play a significant role in Zambia's fight for independence.

By the time I lived in Lusaka, though, the community was down to a few "locals" born in Zambia, Botswana or Zimbabwe; another group of resident Israelis; and other temporary sojourn-ers, such as a couple from the US embassy and yours truly.

There were some tensions among these groups, not least because the Israelis were able and wanted to do most of the service in Hebrew, which was not necessarily that easy for the native English speakers. On top of that, the official head of the Jewish community in Zambia (something of a magnate in chicken farming by day) was not very welcoming to non-Jews, and I got the impression that he was rather too attached to the notion of being in control.

The synagogue building itself, an unassuming, one-story thing in downtown Lusaka, was half occupied by a school, since the community was not vibrant enough to make use of the whole thing (or to afford the bills for its upkeep).

But it wasn't all doom and gloom. One year, in preparation

for Passover, one of the members donated enough money to repaint the community hall, which had been unused since I'd been going there (and, I got the feeling, a lot longer). A couple of guys volunteered to go in and straighten the place up, getting rid of old furniture, repainting everything, and fixing what needed fixing.

The new room's inauguration was a grand Seder, with kosher food and wine courtesy of Chabad, an (Orthodox) organization that seeks to support Jewry worldwide (and makes sure everyone is doing it right, by their definition). Tickets were sold, and a good 50 people probably came out for the event. The room looked spanking new, and it seemed that perhaps some new life was coming back into the community. Everything was great.

The only problem was that the Chabad guys were allowed to run the show (the price we paid for the matzah and kosher wine they'd donated), and they did the Seder for *real*. I think we were there for like two hours before we got to eat more than a bit of matzah and some lettuce. Remember that the average congregant was on the older side, so you can imagine all these poor folks near to expiring for hunger while the Hebrew went on and on. There was a lot of surreptitious matzah-snacking going on, I'll tell you.

That year we had a Purim celebration, High Holy Days services, and a matzah-making session for the kids. Things seemed to be looking up. And then somehow it all kind of fell apart. The Zambian government took the railway concession away from the company of the day, and suddenly all the Israelis had like a week to leave the country. And with the passing of Dr. Mike Bush, one of the anchors of the community, there just didn't seem to be enough energy to keep any kind of regular services going.

The community had never exactly had a lot of money, and the historic center of Judaism in the region (outside of South Africa) was really Harare, as the former capital of Rhodesia, with a secondary presence in Livingstone, the erstwhile capital of Northern Rhodesia (later Zambia).

So things were pretty tenuous there for a while, and then, somewhat out of the blue, the news popped up on the Jewish listserv that the head of the community had sold the synagogue to the school that was already occupying part of the site. Since then it seems that things have pretty much wound down for good. I've received a few more e-mails, some of which suggesting that there were rather a lot of politics going on in the background, and then a few notices of people passing, but that's been it.

My Jewish experience in Burkina is easy to relate: there wasn't any, at least for quite some time. My first contact with another Jew was in our second year there: I made contact with her through a Facebook group, and invited her to our Seder.

She was a Sephardic Jew from France, so it was interesting to compare customs and songs. She also didn't speak great English, but gamely struggled her way through her bits of the Haggadah, and afterwards she gave me a bit of a history lesson on the Jews in France, which was a lot more complex than I'd realized.

The following year I met Noah, the head of Canadian Cooperation, and his (nominally Muslim, but who's counting) wife Khadidja. And then there was the guy from the Danish embassy. The next Passover, I received the following text from Noah: "The other 33% of the Jewish community in Ouagadougou has kosher wine, so why don't you come to our place for a Seder." I'd never been 33% of a community before.

42

IN WHICH MARION DISCOVERS A
DOWNSIDE OF GLOBETROTTING

Beccles, England, 2013 or 2014

The closest we lived to the equator was Rwanda, which was about two degrees south (the equator itself runs through Uganda, just to the north). As a result, the sun rose and set at essentially the same time every day, pretty much at 6 and 6.

For our kids this was great, as they always knew that we would have dinner around the time it was getting dark, and then they'd maybe play for a little while, and soon we'd be getting into our bedtime routine. And they could wake up more or less with the sun.

That might have worked fine in Rwanda, but in the US or UK during the summer, sleeping and waking with the sun was not an option. At my mother's apartment, the kids used to sleep in the office, and she'd tape black garbage bags to the windows in an attempt to at least delay the early-morning prowling.

One summer, when Marion was two or three, we were in Beccles, England, where the long days are even more extreme than in the US. The kids were young enough that we were trying to keep them on a routine of a nap after lunch and then getting to bed at around 8 pm. This of course meant putting them to bed when it was light, but we maintained our bedtime routine as much as possible to help them get settled.

To compound things, Eddie's family has the habit of saying "dinner" for the mid-day meal, and "tea" for the evening meal. (Much hot air has been expelled over the historical reasons for this, and the relationship to the custom slightly more familiar in the US of saying "dinner" at mid-day and "supper" in the evening. It's the "tea" in the evening that confuses me. But I digress.)

So now imagine our poor wee thing of a daughter, with Grandma putting her mid-day plate of food in front of her, saying "Eat your dinner, darling."

At which point Marion, turning to me in alarm, says, "Is it nighttime, Mommy? Are we going to bed soon, Mommy?" To which I had to explain that this was lunch, and then we'd have a little sleep, then play some more, then dinner, then bed. Phew.

Which is why, ever since, the family loves to make a big deal about having the "the mid-day meal" (nudge, wink) when our family is visiting.

43

BABIES, BRIBERY AND BUREAUCRACY
EVERYWHERE AND ALWAYS, AMEN

The move from York to Nairobi was our first one with the whole shipment thing, so we were still terribly naïve and actually believed them when they said we'd have our stuff in six weeks. Looking back, this promise is so laughable that it kind of still makes me chuckle.

We'd long since found our flat and been using borrowed stuff for the bare basics when our shipment finally arrived fourteen weeks later. Hurray! So in a few days we'll have our things, right? Ha. Customs delays, and I don't even know what all else they cited as an excuse for why our things were being held hostage. At some point we got frustrated enough to go down to the offices of the clearing company ourselves to find out what was wrong.

We got the usual promises and foot-shuffling response, until in a moment of frustration I held Eirwyn, just a year old, up in the air and said, "This is the baby who has no bed!" Much oohing and aahing ensued, and he was passed around to be admired from close up by several of the staff.

And funny thing, our stuff came within a day or two. "The baby must have his bed!"

(Aside: When we were unloading our things into the apartment, our housekeeper, Patricia, was so excited and overwhelmed by all the hustling and bustling that she ran up and down the stairs the whole time, pointing to me and saying "This is my madam!")

Thus started my career of shamelessly exploiting my kids to all sorts of nefarious ends. Got into a potential bribery situation? Play the kid card! Need to needle your way toward the front of the line? No problem!

Now really, I didn't exploit it so much for queue jumping as to win the hearts of bureaucrats. I'm convinced that much of the obstructionism in African bureaucracy is not necessarily a bid for a bribe (though I'm sure that would be happily received in many cases) as an attempt to show people who's in charge. So in my dealings with officials, I always made an attempt to not only be polite, but to show a reasonable amount of deference, and in subtle ways give them to understand that I know they have the power in the situation.

Playing (or being) dumb always helps, too. I once got pulled over for being a little too optimistic where an amber light was concerned. The policeman told me what I'd done, and I started with my usual apologetic spiel (works about 80% of the time), and then he said, "Normally, I'd have to give you a ticket." I could pay on the spot, or go to the police station the following day.

OK I said, I'd go to the police station, if he could only tell me where it is? Because no way was I giving this guy money on the street. Fuggedaboudit. Well, "normally," he'd have to give me a ticket—or I could pay him now. No, I repeated, that's OK, just tell me where the police station is so I can go there tomorrow. Honestly I was so slow that it took me until after he'd given up and let me drive away that I realized he'd been looking for a little top-up.

The other thing is that I learned the very common custom of

the long greeting, and making a point of greeting everyone in the room individually. The long greeting was first introduced to me in Rwanda.

When greeting someone you know, you don't just give them a peck on the check or a hug: first comes the double-hug thing where you go in as if for an air kiss, but head in a bit farther, but not so far as to be a full-body hug—on both sides. Then you stand there and keep holding hands as if for a handshake, and inquire as to the health of the person, their family, work, their cows.... Oh, yes: gotta know if the cows are healthy. (Not being sarcastic here: cows being the traditional store of wealth, their condition is of grave economic and status-driven significance.)

It's funny how you don't realize you've learned things until you encounter someone who hasn't learned that lesson yet. I can't tell you how many Europeans I've seen get really huffy with people, becoming visibly angry, playing up how important they are or why they can't be asked to do this or that.

Far from acknowledging their opposite's power over them, they are doing the exact opposite: making themselves important or their task incredibly urgent, presumably as a way of intimidating people into doing what they want. I'm here to tell you, this strategy will pretty much always backfire. Emphasis on "always".

One time when my mother was visiting, the two of us drove up to Uganda for a week's holiday. This meant crossing from Rwanda by land, one of very few times I ever used a land border in Africa. (To be fair, the whole thing was pretty smooth, a sign that some of the investment in border infrastructure was paying off.)

When we arrived on the Ugandan side, it wasn't obvious where we were supposed to go, so I found an official-looking person to ask what the deal was. I began with the full greeting, and then asked my question, to which he replied that we first needed to go over there and buy insurance, and then come back over here for the visas. A simple enough interaction, but my mother commented on the formal greeting I'd given him, and it was only then that I realized how much it had become second nature.

At the visa counter, the immigration official asked how long we were staying. When we replied that we were coming for a week, he looked pained (in a joking—but not 100% joking—kind of way) and asked, "Only one week?" And here I reached for another automatic reaction, the famous kid card. I told him I had two wee ones at home, who obviously couldn't be expected to be without their mother for more than a week. He proceeded to heartily agree, and was thoroughly cheery with us for the rest of our interaction.

The kid card was so good that I even started playing it outside of Africa. We'd once ordered some ultraviolet-protection swimsuits from Australia to be delivered to friends in Germany, where the plan was to pick them up during our visit and bring them back to Lusaka.

The problem was that the German authorities wanted me to pay duty, but I was going to re-export them almost immediately. It was one of those situations where in the spirit of the law I shouldn't have had to pay, but for some bureaucratic reason he was required to collect the duty. At some point you could see that he wasn't unsympathetic, but in the open-plan office, it was kind of tricky for him to let us take the packages without paying.

We went around and around in circles for a while, and I invoked the poor children who needed the suits in Africa. Finally, the official looked down at my son and gave in, saying something about doing it for the kids. The only thing was, my "son" was in fact my friend's! He was at that age when he'd easily blurt out something like "but *that's* not my mummy, *that* one is!" But thankfully he kept quiet, and we were able to take our packages and go. And they say German officials have no heart.

Another good one is to make a point of going through the same bureaucratic hurdles as everybody else. Once I was trying to get my annual car registration paid, which included paying the fee at a bank branch located within the motor-vehicle area. There were about 15 people in the line ahead of me when I arrived, and only about half an hour until the bank closed, so it was looking unlikely that we'd all make it in before closing.

About three times, people offered to let me go ahead of them or told me I should go to the front of the line, but I always responded with, "If you wait, then so do I." After a while I heard a couple of people talking behind me in the queue. My Kinyarwanda wasn't great, but I did understand "She's a good muzungu," and the murmur of assent. It was really nice to feel like I'd done something to earn their respect.

I have to say, I also got a good taste of the opposite, watching one VIP after another get ushered past the line and straight into the bank, thereby decreasing the chances of our making it inside before closure. In the end, I did make it in—and I was the last one, I'm ashamed to say. While I was very glad not to have to come back another day, I felt really bad for the ten people or so who'd come after me and also waited a good 20-30 minutes, to no avail.

There is one story I heard toward the end of my time in Rwanda, which sticks in my head because it was recounted as an example of indecipherable African behavior, and yet I think I understood it. The story was as follows: Jasmin had just arrived in Rwanda, with her infant son in tow. Her husband Srđan (say Srjan), an engineer and killer tennis player, had been there for a year or so, and things were finally looking settled enough that it was worth bringing the family. Much like Eddie at the beginning, Jasmin arrived pretty much expecting to be chopped to pieces by people with machetes within five minutes of getting off the plane, and she hadn't lived abroad before, so let's just say she was on the nervous side at the beginning.

After about a week in-country, she took Srđan's car to drive around Kigali a bit, do a little shopping, whatever. On the way she was stopped by a couple of police officers as part of a routine control. They then showed her that the insurance was out of date, and said they couldn't let her go unless she got more. Jasmin tried to say that it wasn't hers but her husband's work car, that she was new in the country, that she couldn't sit there with her son in the car, but no dice. She was so nervous, sitting there with her son in the back, trying to negotiate with police in a language she didn't know well, she started to cry as she was pleading with them.

Finally she called her husband and explained the situation. When he arrived, he took over negotiations with the police, saying it wasn't her fault, she was new and didn't know, etc. He was trying to convince them to let her go long enough to buy some additional insurance. Finally they agreed, but on one condition: Jasmin had to apologize to them for crying.

What was that about? Wasn't she the wronged party here?

What I think was going on is that she lost control of her emotions. You'll hear about how it's not cool to lose your temper in Africa, and it's true. Make a joke of it, get them on your side by humanizing your story, whatever you need to do—but don't lose your cool. So when Jasmin started to cry, it was embarrassing to the police officers in the same way it is when someone makes a racist comment at the dinner table, or if someone exposes themselves. The whole situation is uncomfortable for all concerned.

44

THE POWER OF POWER (AND ITS ABSENCE)

I think Belgrade was the first place I lived where the power went out for any length of time, and even then, it was usually only for a few hours. What I remember from our flat in Belgrade was being shown by an American volunteer how to repair a fuse. She'd learned it from a friend who'd learned how to do it during the war.

In Kosovo, things were a good sight dodgier. For reasons we could never quite grasp (except perhaps for length of piping), the hot-water heaters were usually hung immediately above the bathtub. Which was fine, except when we got the advice to unplug them before taking a shower. Which is a sign of what, exactly?

Kosovo is also where I first experienced brownouts and low power. The first hint was that our oven never got properly hot, so it apparently took several hours to cook our dinner (according to Julieta, our lovely housekeeper). Also, the TV had a tendency to start flipping, which was annoying enough that we got current stabilizers for our flat (IRC) and the floor above (Concern). The IRC one was fine if you didn't need anything else in the flat to have power. We discovered this the first time we plugged it in and the fuses on everything else blew. The one in the Concern flat didn't short everything else out, but it wasn't grounded, so you had to turn it off with something wooden or it would give you a shock.

When we first arrived in Nairobi, there was a load-shedding program in place such that we had power 12 hours on, 12 hours off, with formula so that you switched off, days or nights, every couple of days. We were staying in the Concern Country Director's flat, which was spacious enough but really dark.

We were too far from everything to walk, and even going up and down the street felt like too much sun, so I mostly stayed in and went slowly insane trying to keep our 9-month-old son entertained. I remember seeing an ad for some promotional thing where one of the prizes was a washing machine, and bursting into laughter. Who had power and water *at the same time*?

Now, Rwanda. Initially it wasn't that bad. There were outages, but they didn't usually last more than a couple of hours. We acquired quite the collection of candleholders, and always knew where the matches were. It's actually crazy how much light a bunch of candles will generate, though of course it's not necessarily your first choice if you have little kids running around.

But as time went on, the outages got longer and more frequent. A load-shedding program was put in place but not adhered to. By 2016 they were saying that the water levels in the lake where the power plant sourced its water had gotten so low that they had to drastically reduce production, or the levels would go down so low that they'd not be able to generate any power at all.

Of course, the load-shedding didn't work, because every time they shut the power off, they'd get phone calls from this or that minister: the power in his house was out; they're having a "very important" workshop in this or that location, etc. As a result, certain parts of the city always had power, and others (like ours) had it less and less frequently. By the last year we were in

Rwanda, we were counting the hours we did have power rather than those we didn't. Four to six hours per day was pretty standard, on the days when there was anything at all.

We did get a generator in our first year, but it had been used to power a sub-office, so it was huge, and it was *loud*. Plus, it kind of threw fumes into the living room. But it was really the noise that just got to you after a while. So we used it only when the fridge needed topping up, or if we really wanted light in the evening.

We'd originally had a 100% gas stovetop and oven, but I gotta tell you, the gas oven was just not the way to go. Everything came out burned on the bottom before it was properly cooked on top. I don't recall having this issue so much in the UK, but all the gas ovens we had in Africa were a royal pain in the butt. So we changed that stove out for one that had an electric oven, two electric burners and two gas. This was great because we still had the two gas burners when the power was out, and the decent oven when we did have power. Which wasn't Thanksgiving. I once cooked the turkey for the whole four hours on the generator.

The gas thing was its own pain, though. There was no piped gas; you had to buy bottles and exchange them yourself. This was a pain if your brand was having a shortage, or if the gas ran out in the middle of making an omelet. Once I thought the gas was out so I unplugged the hose from the bottle, only to discover that there *was* still gas. It started leaking out with a horrible high-pitched scream. In a panic, I rolled the canister outside into the back yard, where at least we wouldn't be asphyxiated. But I didn't have any way to stop the gas from coming out, so had to just stand there while the screaming announced to the whole neighborhood how stupid I was.

When we first started having cats, we had Katchoo and Kiwi. I say "having cats" like they would come in the house, but mostly we just fed them and they hung around a bit. Until Kiwi was killed by some dogs one night. We got the guard to bury him out at the back of the house, next to the retaining wall, and promised the kids we'd have a little ceremony for him after school. So there we were, standing solemnly over his little grave, trying to belt out comforting words over the din of the generator not six feet away, engulfing us in fumes.

Our 10th wedding anniversary was a bit like that, too. We'd splurged on a nice bottle of wine and planned to split it over a pleasant evening, which we did. It was just a little less romantic than expected, accompanied as it was by the interference patterns from the four or five gennies running in the immediate vicinity.

As the Rwanda power crisis worsened, we stopped buying meat and cheese, and kept everything else out of the fridge that could be. You'd really be surprised how well many things do unrefrigerated for a while. The problem was, both fridge and freezer can actually keep things decently cold for 12 hours or so, but only if you don't open them. So you really want to minimize how many times you need to go in and out.

Of course the freezer is a problem, because things could thaw but then refreeze, and you'd never know, right? Hot tip: Fill a plastic cup halfway with water, freeze it, and then keep it in the freezer turned on its side. If things start to melt, the water will start to drip, and you'll see that even if everything has refrozen in the meantime.

Our kids got so used to things not being cold that they started to prefer it. I'd always thought it was weird when Rwandans ask if you want your drink warm or cold, but even I got to the point where I could do a warm Fanta. I draw the line at beer, though.

When we went to the UK on vacation, where everything is cold by default, the kids were constantly complaining that the drinks were too cold and giving them a stomachache. (To this day I dislike the American custom of putting ice in everything.) When we got back late to our little holiday cottage one evening in Beccles, two-year-old Marion said, "It's getting darker, Daddy, time to get the candles!" We showed her the magic thing called a light switch!

In Burkina the problem with no power was no fans. It's hot enough on a good day, but when the air's not moving, it's just a killer. Plus, of course, the ambient temperature is so high that the fridge struggles more to keep things cold. (The amount of heat it used to throw off during the hot season could fry an egg.) And then when there was power, turning on a light brought imminent risk of the light bulb exploding, because falling shards of glass is what every parent wants in their living room. We spent a fortune in light bulbs before we finally found an electrician (our third or fourth try) who actually saw what was wrong and fixed it properly.

45

IN WHICH I PLAY "MISCELLANEOUS" ON TV

Rwanda, 2002—2005

When I worked at the US Embassy in Rwanda, I had a yellow badge, placing me between the red badges (national staff) and the blues (possessing a US security clearance). Sure, they did a kind of security check on me since I was going to be managing USG funds, but I didn't need access to classified information, so I didn't bother going through the full security-clearance process.

The only time it really mattered was when I needed to go upstairs to where the big dudes worked: the Ambassador, Deputy Chief of Mission, security officers and the political section. Our weekly econ meetings were held here, which coordinated the political and economic sections with USAID, CDC and the little hodgepodge of funding streams I was in charge of. If I came a little early for that meeting, I'd have to hang out in the lobby, where the receptionist could watch me, until someone else was ready to go in.

Of course, I could have been planting a bug, but nothing so

cloak-and-dagger was really part of my embassy experience—except, of course, for being friends with the resident spook.

My American embassy colleagues used to ask me all the time why I didn't apply for a security clearance. Perhaps they didn't realize what life was like for the lowest-ranking person with a blue badge at post, but I knew, because this person happened to be my office neighbor.

She was an embassy spouse and I don't even remember what her job was, only that she had an encyclopedic knowledge of the FAR, which is basically all the rules for US Government procurement. She also got to do things like sit in the upstairs section for an entire weekend, watching some dudes haul up carpet and strip floors, or on the roof, in the rain, watching someone repair an antenna. In short, she was Babysitter In Chief. Yeah, no thanks.

But in one area I *was* bottom of the pile. It was logical, really. Since I managed all the little miscellaneous funds at the embassy, it only made sense that I would deal with random correspondence that came in, which didn't clearly fall into anyone else's area of responsibility. Kind of like that desk drawer that holds scissors, a tape measure, your coffee cup, four marbles, an expired parking pass, and a couple of really old tea bags. Oh, and a random piece of string, because.

And so it was that I had the honor of receiving gifts addressed to POTUS. Yes, sometimes random citizens of foreign countries feel moved to present gifts to the US President. Who knew. You'll be reassured, I'm sure, to learn that all gifts, no matter how small, must be officially received and catalogued by the Prez's protocol office. Whether they're then thrown away or put into storage à la *Raiders of the Lost Ark*, I don't know.

And so it was that I had to find a box for a rather poorly executed wooden statue thingy and pack it in nice and tight, along with an Ode to President George Bush. I wish I had made a copy of this masterpiece. It was truly special, praising Bush's warrior qualities because of the war in Iraq: you get the picture. I then also had to learn the ins and outs of writing a cable for the protocol office to let them know that this package was coming, and roughly what was in it. Honestly, I spent more time on this whole gift than I would have on easily 10 project proposals for one of the funds I actually managed.

But actually, most of the random messages came from Americans. One was a guy who was trying to collect bottlecaps from all the factories when Coke is bottled. Was there such a factory in Rwanda, and if so, could we provide contact information? Well, why yes, there was one such factory (better known for beer, but who's counting), and here was the address.

Then there was the woman who wanted information about the Girl Scouts in Rwanda. This one came down with a note from the Ambassador saying that she had been a girl scout, and so we might as well see what we could find out for them. So *this* former Girl Scout got on the case, and learned that although there was an organization that called itself part of the Girl Scout movement, it was more like a local NGO devoted to peace and international understanding. So I sent a little paragraph, noting the connections with the Ambassador and myself, and the person wrote back thanking us for the prompt and interesting response. Wow, warm fuzzies all round.

Oh, and there was a man who wrote to President Bush asking for a bicycle, as one man in Christ to another. For this one I got the all clear to send the President's regrets without passing through Washington. I didn't pretend to be him or anything, I just found a nice French phrase saying the president was unable to respond favorably. Three weeks or so later, I got another letter from the same man: "Dear Brother in Christ President George Bush," [I sent you this letter, you replied thus, etc.] "and now I would like to know, *was it really you yourself* who said no?" Dang, he got me.

My favorite, though, was an artist from Colorado who asked the US Embassy's help: 1) to acquire a machete of the type used in the Genocide, because there were so many machetes on the internet that she didn't know which was the right one, 2) to find a real a Rwandan flag, because she could find photos on the internet but she wasn't sure how true the colors were, and 3) to know whether or not it was safe to travel to Rwanda now (this being a good 10 years after the Genocide). All of this was because she was having an artistic phase based on the Genocide, and she wanted to be sure it was authentic.

So I pulled out my best diplomatic plume. As for the machete, I'm not sure I even responded to that part. There was just no way to answer that didn't seem in poor taste. For the flag, we suggested she contact the *Rwandan* Embassy in the US, given that the *US* Embassy's job is to promote *American* interests, hence our possession of many US flags but not so many Rwandan ones. As for safe travel, we indicated the presence of several tour companies in the country that could arrange visits, including to the world-famous mountain gorillas. Trying so, so hard to keep it together and stay polite.

The crazy thing was that I met her a few months later. A friend or relative of a friend of my mother was traveling to Rwanda, and would I stop by just to say hello and make sure she has my number and all that good stuff? Sure. We met on the steps of a church-run guest house in downtown, and chatted for a little bit.

She told me how inspired she'd been by a story she'd read about a little girl who gets a goat, and how with the income she has from the goat she's eventually able to finish her schooling and get a good job, happily ever after. (Wow, I guess we development types have been missing an obvious fix here: give every girl a goat and we'll have 100% education! Wouldn't it be great if things were so simple.) Anyway, then she got onto her art, and it slowly dawned on me... Wait a minute, did you write to the US Embassy a while back? As someone I know would say, *fake laugh hiding real pain*.

Oh, and did I mention I really was on Rwandan TV? The ceremony awarding the small grants was covered in print and moving pictures, which makes it sound way more exciting than it actually was. You pay the journalists for their "gas money", and they come. I'd like to say it wasn't prime time TV, but then I couldn't tell you about the time I was out with friends and saw myself on the restaurant's TV set. Thankfully, it drew the correct amount of interest (none), so I was spared the fawning mobs that might otherwise have annoyed my friends.

46

AH, THE ROMANCE OF TRAIN TRAVEL

Nairobi to Mombasa, 2001 and Zagreb to Lyons, 1997

My second-favorite train experience of all time was a first-class, overnight trip from Nairobi to Mombasa. Eirwyn was about one-and-a-half years old, and I was around four months pregnant with Marion. Air travel was prohibitively expensive, and we'd been wanting our own Out of Africa kind of train ride, so this was the time to do it.

Now, in case you have illusions about the whole first-class thing, let me clarify a few bits. On the positive side, it meant we had actual horizontal beds to sleep in, and most important, a cabin to ourselves. Thankfully, Eirwyn was small enough that we could plonk him on the floor and he didn't really care.

This left the two bunks available for Eddie and me. The top one folded up during the day, and the bottom one made a seat. There was a little washbasin, but we still needed to go down the hall to the communal bathroom. So it was a good cut above the other classes, but you'd be hard pressed to describe it as "luxurious". But even first-class tickets were distinctly cheaper than the plane, and the train was our little adventure, so we were happy enough.

The train itself looked run down, but we were fairly confident it wouldn't actually break down just as we happened to be inside. So, full of adventure and optimism, we got on. A porter immediately helped take our bags to the room (this *was* first class, after all) and made sure we were all comfy. We were left alone to settle in, until he walked down the corridor ringing the bell for dinner. So we followed like good little baby chicks after their mama, into the restaurant car, and found a table. The décor was definitely reminiscent of the 1930s, lots of wood and brass.

Then the waiter served the first course, which was soup. Really? Soup. On a train. Maybe on the Shinkansen, but on a bumpy old thing going only 25 miles per hour? Of course the soup was also served in a very flat bowl, with great round spoons that demanded maximum protocol and delivered minimum soup.

I don't actually remember what the rest of the meal was, but we definitely had a mains and a dessert. What I most remember is that the waiter was dressed impeccably in black, with brass buttons and a sparkling white shirt under the jacket. It was only on closer inspection that you'd notice how frayed the jacket was around the edges, and the fact that none of the spoons matched. You really had to hand it to these guys: they were pulling out all the stops to deliver a first-class train experience with practically no resources.

One of the reasons I don't remember the food very much is probably that I was too busy staring out the window. The train cuts through Nairobi National Park on the way out of the capital, so we had an unimpeded view of the bush and the colors of the setting sun. We saw some zebra and antelope, nothing exciting, but that didn't matter. We were clicking and clacking our way through the bush, breathing the fresh air through the open window, and watching the day fade away.

The night would have been OK except that we were afraid of being burgled and so didn't really dare sleep, and because of the stops along the way. As long as the train was moving, we got some air through the open window, and it was just about cool enough to sleep. But at every stop we'd lose the air movement, it would get stiflingly hot, and the local mosquitoes would come to check out the passengers.

We were more worried about mosquitoes than usual, because we were descending from the plateau that largely protects Nairobi from malaria. As it got warmer, the more full of mozzies the train got, and the more malarial the mozzies got. And, you know, there was that tiny detail that getting malaria while pregnant is bad news for both mother and baby. And when fatigue had just about sent us back to sleep despite the heat, the train would start up again—preceded by a horn blast from the engine. With only the restaurant car separating us from the engine, I think it's safe to say that horn would have woken Sleeping Beauty.

The following morning we emerged sweaty, dusty and sleep-deprived for a continental breakfast. I loved the marmalade. It was so much less sweet than a lot of the stuff we'd buy, so I asked what kind it was. Joke's on me: it was the cheapest kind I knew of, which even came in a can rather than a jar. I suppose it was cheap because sugar is more expensive than fruit. Guess what I started buying when we got home again. The fancy stuff was supposed to be by royal appointment to the Queen, but honestly, I liked this local stuff more. It gave me a good chuckle to think that I was eating better than the Queen of England...

My favorite train experience of all time was when a couple of us BPT volunteers made the trip from Zagreb to Lyons. Adam, my colleague in Belgrade, and I met up with Jude (from Split, in Croatia) after traveling to Zagreb from Belgrade by bus. We were headed to a monastery or something near Lyons, where we were going to have our semi-annual meeting with the BPT coordinating committee.

Armed with our stash of nibbles and the famous Croatian Kraš chocolate, we boarded the train around 3 pm, and quickly found a promising cabin. There was a sole occupant when we got on, whom we were able to "nudge" out by being three twentysomethings speaking foreign and generally being a bit loud. We didn't do any of that on purpose, I promise... Certainly once we had the space to ourselves, we made a point of smoking enough that people would look in the fogged-in window and leave us alone.

The really great thing was that this was a proper old Yugoslav train, complete with plush red-velvet seats on both sides and sliding glass doors into each compartment. The sound of the train running over the tracks was no modern whoosh, but a solid bah-BUM bah-BUM, a steady heartbeat carrying us through fields where you might still see a haycart piled high, and little towns with their spired churches and detailed tile-work. We curved around lake Bled in Slovenia, through Ljubljana, and into Italy. I'll never forget skimming along by the harbor in Trieste, leaning out of the open window, watching the sun set over the distant water.

And we certainly weren't bored: it was the first time we were going to present on our work and the situation in our respective geographic areas, and we were seriously nervous. Many cigarettes were harmed in the making of this presentation. We did have some bread and cheese or something, but I swear we mostly lived off of adrenaline and nicotine for that whole train ride.

However, we did want to get some sleep. This was the best part about this old train: its red plush seats slid down and met in the middle, thus forming three pretty decent beds crossways. We even had that wonderful train sound to lull us to sleep. The only problem was that we were terrified of sleeping so soundly that someone could steal our passports. American, British and Austrian, they were pretty good pickings for someone from the Balkans trying to make their way to the West. So we put our papers under our heads and tried to sleep…. Only to be rudely awakened by border guards as we left Italy and entered Austria, and then again as we left Austria and entered Switzerland.

The next morning we arrived in Geneva, where we had a criminally expensive coffee at a café across from the train station, and then boarded our connecting train for Lyons. It makes me sad that the old trains are being "modernized", and that no one will experience that same atmosphere anymore. Though I suppose you'd have to make do without the clouds of cigarette smoke for that extra atmospheric element nowadays. And they call it progress.

47

PEOPLE

It should be obvious by now that only people with a certain unusual bent will generally gravitate toward the overseas life. And our lives have been shaped and enriched by our friends and colleagues. A few deserve special mention.

T Roy — The first thing to know about T Roy is that his name is not actually T Roy. The T comes from Chad the country, formerly spelled Tchad in English because that's how it's spelled in French (otherwise it would be "shad"). We got in the habit of talking about T Chad, at which point all sorts of things and people started getting a T in front of their name, and for T Roy it just stuck.

T Roy was my first boss in the aid business. When IRC hired me on as an intern, I got assigned to the project he was leading. Eventually I got hired onto that project for real, but we didn't work much together as he'd been moved to the team providing emergency response for the injured and displaced as the conflict between ethnic Albanians and Serbs got tenser and more violent.

T Roy was a flies 'n' shit man, as in his specialty was water and sanitation. Sanitation sounds vaguely OK but really it pretty much always means latrines. I'll never forget T Roy talking about his schooling and saying that his studies gave him a whole new appreciation of the phrase "Eat shit and die".

What I really loved about T Roy, though, was his down-home quality. From West Virginia, he'd not exactly followed the usual trajectory of his peers. I'll never forget the day he pulled up his shirt and showed us his various scars, which included both knife and bullet wounds. He was completely unpretentious. He'd done a number of jobs over the years, and so was full of interesting tidbits like the proper way to cure concrete. "I used to think it was ridiculous when office people said they were tired," he said after a few months of managing the emergency team. "I always thought real work was what you did with your hands, and that was the only honest way to earn a living. But *man*, I'm exhausted!"

Unfortunately, the way to greet people when driving in West Virginia was apparently to just kind of flick two fingers up from the steering wheel, a kind of "wassup" with the fingers. Not a problem, except that in response to the traditional three-fingered Serb nationalist salute, the Albanians had adopted the two-fingered "peace" sign. So every time T Roy thought he was saying "hey" to a passing motorist, his fingers were saying something like "long live an independent and Albanian-run Kosovo!"

Steve — Steve pitched up in Kosovo around the time when things were getting kind of hot with the KLA. I can't remember what his official role was, something political, but it didn't take long to figure out that a bit more was going on.

Steve was, namely, a charming guy—played guitar, told funny stories, was interested in what the NGO crowd was up to.

Very interested.

The thing was, he wasn't even that bothered about disguising what was going on. "Where did you go today, what did you do, what did you see?" was his stock phrase, repeated often enough that it became its own little jingle, like an inside joke. People had their own takes on whether or not it was OK to play Steve's game and tell him what they had in fact been up to that day.

Some felt that it crossed the line by effectively making NGO workers into spies for the US Government. Then again, I figured there wasn't much we were going to tell them that anyone influential couldn't find out by other means. If a KLA cell made contact with an NGO convoy, don't you think someone in Prishtina would have heard about it?

Speaking of convoys, at this point there was no such thing as traveling incognito, not that there really ever is for a white Land Cruiser, but there's exposure and there's exposure. For those like me who were heading east most of the time it was no big deal; we could pretty much go about our business of trying to promote long-term development in a country that was going to be at war in about six months.

But for those going west, any NGO cars and trucks had to be escorted by the UNHCR, because the Serbian government refused registration for the INGOs, so they were not allowed to operate radios in the cars. So you get my point that a run-in between the "shadowy/existence not yet officially confirmed" KLA and a fat aid convoy of several NGO cars and two UNHCR vehicles might attract just a little attention.

Which didn't stop Steve from asking his questions and soaking up whatever little tidbits he could get about KLA and IDP movements and such. To be fair, he paid the piper in kind, with entertaining tales that often made us feel we were getting a little glimpse behind the curtain of the US government. This is how I learned that you can't open the window in an armored vehicle, for example to talk to the leader of the little KLA band that's just stopped you, so that you actually have to *open the door*.

Marko — And then sometimes you meet real, bona fide heroes. They say times maketh the man. Well, crazy Kosovo times produced some pretty incredible people.

One such was Marko L. One day a letter came to our office in Belgrade advertising an opening ceremony for the Human Rights Defense Committee of Leskovac. My colleague Renate and I were intrigued to say the least, because Leskovac is exactly the sort of mid-sized, southern, industrial town on the downswing that formed Slobodan Milošević's fan base. When the Serbian state needed really nasty police from outside Kosovo (and thus lacking any personal connects that might complicate their motives), Leskovac was the first place they'd go. So we decided to go check this guy out.

And it really was just a guy. His outfit was pretty much a one-man show, but he'd managed to put some flyers around and write about the human-rights situation in Serbia. We met him in his living room over cups of Turkish coffee. He explained how he'd come up with the idea to form his NGO.

He said after reading the papers and reading the papers, he starting thinking "I must be in Hawaii!" As in, what they presented was so disconnected from what he saw around him every day, he might as well be on a tropical island. One day he'd simply had enough, so he sold his seed shop and used the money to start the organization.

I couldn't believe the way he made it sound so obvious, like wouldn't everyone just cash in their livelihood (he *sold his seed store*), put their daughters' education at risk (not for lack of money to pay the fees, but think political retaliation in the admissions process), accept being watched and followed, have their electricity cut off and generally deal with a lot of bureaucratic caramel, just because of something they read in the papers?

Sure.

In fact, I left this encounter profoundly humbled to have met the real deal, someone who is prepared to risk everything for those principles we like to say it's our moral destiny to defend. He wasn't famous. He could get thrown in jail for months and who outside his immediate circle would know? He had no protection. And yet when we mentioned the first student protest planned by the Albanian students' union in a couple of weeks' time, without hesitation he said, "I'll be there."

And that was his refrain. Any time there was a protest or something going on: just give him 24 hours' notice and he'd be there. Once he slept in his car on the street in Prishtina the night before a protest. This caused some consternation in the neighborhood because of the "out of town" plates on the car.

We managed to do Marko one small favor, which was to introduce him to the Women in Black in Belgrade, a well-known women's human-rights group. On his own in Leskovac, Marko had no easy way to network with other human-rights organizations or make himself known to potential donors. So through the women in Belgrade, he was able to start to make connections on the national scene and get some funding.

This is how he was taken up as a person of concern by Amnesty International during the Kosovo crisis. After his release, he continued his work and is now known among peace-activist groups across Europe. (I know this because now I can follow him on Facebook, which is insane when I think that he hardly had a telephone back in the day.)

Nadja — If you know that I'm a language geek and you know that I was studying East European history and languages, then maybe you won't be too surprised to learn that I once had a go at learning Romanian. Yes, I did this just for fun. The problem was, the class was (logically enough) located in the department for Romance languages. Of course no one takes Romanian as their first Romance language, so a good 80%-90% of the class already had some background in French or Spanish to help them. Which I did not.

The other small percentage were people like me who had more of a background in the Slavic languages and were studying

Romanian more out of geographic than linguistic curiosity. One of these was Nadja, who turned out to be one of those "ethnic Germans" who were allowed to migrate from the former Soviet states to Germany. She was from Tashkent, the capital of Uzbekistan. We found each other because we were equally lost when the teacher would say "well this obviously means *this*," because of some word in French or Spanish that everyone was expected to know.

We got revenge, though, with the roughly 30% of Romanian words that are of Slavic origin. If I can geek out on you for a sec, this is what I think is really cool about the Romanian language. You have a bunch of Latin-based words that have been tweaked over the years because of Romania's geographic proximity to the Slavic realm, and then you have all these actual Slavic words grafted onto a Latin grammatical base. (I could geek out even more here, but I'm restraining myself for you, so be thankful.)

Many of these words have to do with religion or philosophy, since the main religious influences are Orthodox, but they also include newer words that presumably just came to Romanian through Russian. So, for example, Nadja and I first really bonded over the word for "car", *maşină*. "Машина!" we both exclaimed with no small measure of joy, finally recognizing something in this strange sea of Latin-ness.

Given our common sense of what was hard and what easy, it only made sense that we would study together, and so we got to know each other. I was of course intrigued by her background from Uzbekistan and the transition to Germany. And having lived for a few years in Germany already and being subjected to yearly visa renewals, I had mixed feelings about a population of "ethnic Germans", most of whom didn't speak any German and who had been living in Russia/the Soviet Union for some two hundred years, getting automatic citizenship.

I became more sympathetic when she described life back in

Tashkent, e.g., being pulled over by the police for imaginary traffic offenses and treated rudely because of her blond hair and blue eyes. Never mind that I might not consider her very German, she was German enough to attract uncomfortable attention from ethnic Uzbeks, so maybe it wasn't such a bad thing that she and hers could get out of Dodge when they did.

What killed me, though, was that she'd already graduated university in the Soviet Union and was an art-history teacher. But Germany didn't recognize her degree, so she couldn't translate her title into German. So it was OK for her to advertise herself as a преподавательница истории искусства, but not as a *Lehrerin der Kunstgeschichte*. Seriously? So she was starting over, and studying art history all over again, just to get the same degree she already had but to be allowed to say so in the language of the country. You have to hand it to the Germans, they sure know how to make sure that the ins stay in and the outs stay out.

48

OUAGADOUGOU

August, 2014 – May/October, 2017

The first thing about Ouagadougou is the dust. It's not unique to Ouaga; there are plenty of other Sahelian (and Middle Eastern, I'm sure) countries that also get a lot of sand and dust. But it's just one of those things that you notice right away, the way it covers everything and if you clean it up it's there again 24 hours later. The worst is in the winter, a word that evokes thoughts of cold, so let me just catch you right here and say the lows got down to maybe 16°C/61°F. Burkinabès and long-term foreign residents will experience this as real cold, but a lot of people reading this in North America or Europe wouldn't even put on a light sweater.

Anyway, the dust is what blots out the sunlight so you can get the cool. Think Oklahoma dust bowl. Setting the table with plates upside down so they won't get covered, washing out a clean glass because it's got a film of sand on it, and generally feeling like you are slowly drowning in an endless stream of the stuff.

The second thing, in my book, is the concrete. Whorls and great swoops and screw-shapes, they are apparently painted in the only shades the color police allow: tan/brown with accents of green and red. OK, so those are the colors of the flag. No one favors a little hint of purple or yellow? I say accents but if you are the roundabout called *Cinéastes,* apparently you have permission to use the accent colors as the main show. You have to love *Cinéastes,* with its vaguely drum-inspired shapes that rise up, succulent-like, in the middle of a traffic circle. But many of the ministry buildings are examples of this craze for concrete, and it's really incredible what people will think up with such a delicate building material.

The main ministries and presidential palace are in a part of town called Ouaga 2000, which was built for a conference and then converted into regular homes and businesses. The houses here are much bigger than in our part of town: upper stories are common, and I'm not quite sure but I think our Ouaga house would fit into the sitting + dining rooms of a friend of ours. People like to live there because it's where the big houses are, and it's convenient for USG employees, since the embassy and USAID are close by.

But I never really liked Ouaga 2000 for living in: the streets were too broad and there wasn't a sense of being able to walk to anything. You were in your home, office or car. By contrast, where we lived in the Zone du Bois, one of the oldest parts of the city, we had plenty of little markets and restaurants within walking distance. Not to mention the school, which was so close our kids could actually walk there unsupervised. Remember that they were ferried around in a car to school and other kids' houses in the other places where we'd lived, so having that autonomy was a big deal. As its name suggests, there are a lot more trees in that area as well (though it takes its name more from the forest to the north), so it was a little bit cooler around where we were, or so I've been told.

49

IN WHICH WE GET A CRASH COURSE IN BURKINA FASO'S POLITICS

Ouagadougou, October and November, 2014

I t's not every twelve-year-old who can tell you the difference between a revolution, a popular uprising and a coup d'état. Our kids will tell you that this is the popular-uprising bit.

The kids and I had arrived in Burkina in August of 2014. I'd gone ahead and found a house, which we moved into right around the time Eddie arrived with our dog, Seamus, from Lusaka. Our shipment hadn't arrived yet, so our furniture consisted of a dining table and chairs (made locally, and not super comfortable), a small desk and chair borrowed from the office, locally made beds for all of us, and a mattress out in the screened-in porch area off the living room that was vaguely suitable for sitting on.

And I guess if you want to be less human-centric, you could count the dog carrier that Seamus had traveled in and was still using as a bed.

Even before we arrived, a few people had made allusions to the fact that this normally peaceful country was going to have some interesting days ahead, because the current president, Blaise

Compaoré, was aiming to change the constitution so he could run for a third term—because apparently the 27 years he'd already been in office hadn't quite done it for him.

There was supposed to be a referendum on the question of modifying the constitution, which would then lead to the actual modification being approved by the legislature. What wrong-footed us all was that on Friday the cabinet met in special session and decided the referendum was unnecessary—and the parliament would convene the following Thursday to vote on the modification.

As you can imagine, this did not sit well with the population, at least in the cities, who were tired of the corruption, misrule and downright creepiness of the regime (Blaise's brother François in particular was rumored to engage in all sorts of dark arts, including the abduction and sacrifice of schoolchildren). The Friday of the announcement, the ride home was a bit dicey, as I had to drive directly by the university on a main thoroughfare. The signs were that the students had been out protesting earlier in the day.

After all that we decided to stay mostly at home that weekend, so as not to get caught up in any protests, especially if there were going to be confrontations with the police. International staff were also requested to stay at home through the following Thursday as a precaution.

Thursday arrived, and I woke up ready for an interesting day, but honestly I wasn't prepared for the interesting-ness to start pretty much from the time I emerged from the bedroom. It turned out the students were out in force again, and this time the police were prepared—with tear gas.

We were close enough to the university that whiffs of tear gas came into the house—slat windows are rubbish that way. We closed everything up as well as we could, but the kids could still smell it, and it was irritating our throats. So I chopped up a small onion and gave the kids pieces to chew, which helped.

Later I looked up *tear gas* in French, since I already knew it in German and Serbian; you can laugh, but it's one of those words that when you want it, you really want it. It was some hours before either of the kids had the presence of mind to ask why I knew about the onion trick, but since it was based in a rather frightening incident from Kosovo, I said I'd tell them later. Which I'm not sure I ever did, to be honest. Well, you've read it here.

After a while, the tear gas petered out, which allowed us to open doors and windows again. And with that, we could hear crowds in the distance. Not being comfortable leaving the house, and having no Internet access, Eddie had to rely on the guard to transmit what was going on. In fact, crowds had converged on the houses of known senior politicians in the CDP, Blaise's party. They would give anyone inside a few minutes to gather important items and vacate the house, and then loot it and set it on fire. Eddie saw a man running down our street with an air conditioner slung over his shoulder.

The scary thing was that we could see the smoke from these fires in two directions, which made us feel a bit boxed in. Expats were not the target of people's anger, so in that sense we were safe, but both Eddie and I were acutely aware of how fast the mood of a mob can flip, and then reason gets you nowhere fast.

It was a stupidly long time before we came to our senses and got the kids to pack runaway bags. We hated to scare them, but we needed them to be ready, and it was less scary to be ready than it would have been to have to run and be totally unprepared. Our road was not great—it was narrow and very rough—and although my Burkinabè boss had offered to drive down and bring us out, we weren't prepared to let him risk himself in that way.

About mid-morning I got a phone call from the Consul at

the US Embassy. Poor woman, I can't even imagine how many people she had to call that day. Apparently the embassy's Internet push system wasn't working, so they weren't able to post updates or situation reports (sitreps) to keep the American community informed about what was going on. She'd tried to reach the official warden of our little CRS warden group, but hadn't been able to get through, so she was calling me as vice-warden to see how everyone was getting on. If the mobile networks had gone down, I'd conceivably have been asked to walk to each person's house on our list to pass on important information to our group.

Internally within CRS, my informal role was to pass updates to the other expats and make sure everyone was OK. So when the Consul called, I was able to reassure her that everybody was home and safe. We actually knew each other casually from the school (baby mafia—wins every time), so I chatted with her briefly. I mentioned that we were a little concerned about the fires within a couple of blocks either side of us, and the fact that we weren't really sure whether we were safer trying to get out or just staying put.

A couple of weeks later, when the whole thing was over, the US Embassy hosted a "Town Hall Meeting", where all US citizens can go to hear the Ambassador give an update on the situation and ask questions of embassy officials. I got chatting with the Consul's husband, and he told me that during that day of October 30th they'd had a list of people they were watching out for, and our family had been coded orange. Sure glad we didn't find out what red means.

Our family was pretty isolated during this time. We'd only been in the country for about two months, so we didn't know many people and no one well. Our house was not technically in Zone du Bois, an older, relatively upscale part of town where a lot of expats lived, so we weren't in easy walking distance from anybody, even if we'd known people to go to. For internet we only had a dongle running off airtime, and the connection was pretty bad, so for hours on end we were cut off from the greater world. As a result, we had to depend on our guard (whose ear was glued to the radio) for news of what was going on.

It fact, large numbers of citizens, mostly youth, had stormed the Parliament building and torched it, as well as the Azalaï hotel next door, where most of the MPs were staying in anticipation of the vote that day (which, obviously, did not take place). A few days earlier, women had gone out on the street en masse with their wooden spoons, a traditional symbol of dissatisfaction and protest. This day, it was the population as a whole.

And, miraculously, it worked. Blaise stepped down with minimal casualties, where hundreds could have died if the police or military had opened fire on the crowds. By October 31st, protesters were again out in force, but Blaise was officially on the way out (with, allegedly, some 30 Land Cruisers stuffed with money—but who's counting?), along with the hated brother and their mother. François' house was soon ransacked and burned, and there were some additional casualties in clashes between police and protesters.

The funny thing was that October 31st was my birthday, so about half of my correspondence was worried colleagues sending IMs all day to find out how we were doing, and the other half were Facebook messages and e-mails wishing me the most wonderful of days! And hoping that Eddie and the kids were spoiling me! Ha. Obviously your average American wasn't glued to the radio over some incident in—where was that place again? But I couldn't resist writing back in some cases along the lines of "hm, so-so, you might want to check the news about Burkina today and get back to me."

But overall, by the second day, the general mood in Ouagadougou, at least, was pride and elation. They'd done it! Twenty-seven years brought to an end, with minimal loss of life.

And yes, some buildings had been destroyed, but there was no massacre. Which is why it felt very strange to open up the BBC website and read about violent clashes, burning and looting.

Yes, those things had happened, but they weren't the majority, and *weren't the point*. Now I realized how many people must feel when they see their country described in the Western press, with dramatic and negative headlines, and never anything else to round out the picture a bit. Even we Westerners went around kind of scratching our heads: were we seeing the same thing as the journalists?

Where were the cameras showing those same youths who'd been torching the Parliament building two days before, now organized into clean-up crews, going around town sweeping up broken glass and clearing the roads? Where were the interviews with young men and women who would be considered uneducated by most Western standards, who were literally putting their lives on the line, simply for the lofty right to take part in choosing their next president?

The next week or so continued to be dicey, with competing claims to the posts of president and prime minister. Should the head of state be a military man, or not? If the president *is* a military man, does that make the whole thing a coup d'état? Now we aid types start getting nervous, because coups mean aid restrictions, and aid restrictions mean less money for us, including the potential cutting-short of existing projects.

Of course there's a self-serving element in that concern, but there is also the genuine consideration that we've planned projects over a particular life span because we think that much time is needed to really have an impact, and if you cut things short, in some ways you might as well have thrown out the money you've spent so far. Not to mention our personal fondness for our Burkinabè friends and colleagues, who stood to lose their jobs.

As we learned later, this question of was it or wasn't it a coup kept lots of legal minds busy in Washington, D.C. In the end, the military man was made prime minister, answering to a civilian head of state, who was nominated in a vaguely participatory process over the following weeks. This and the fact that the parliament was allowed to execute its proper functions were apparently enough to avoid the "coup" designation.

So as we employed folks endured our mandatory "working from home" status while not getting much done, the kids whiled away their days doing not much. This situation was soon rectified by the school, which helped teachers to post work and assignments on "moodle", one of those online sharing platform thingamajigs. The kids loved it.

And if you believe that, there's a bridge I'd like to sell you. We were on a dongle for Internet, basically a flash drive that ran with a SIM card you could load up with airtime. The connection was, frankly, shite, and the school was pretty inconsistent in what was posted or not posted. For all of these reasons, the teachers couldn't exactly punish the kids for not getting assignments in on time, so the whole thing was more of a dry run than actual distance education. I guess it helped the school figure out how to do it better, but suffice it to say (and nothing against the platform itself, which for all I know is the best thing since Swiss cheese) "moodle" was a dirty word in our house for a while.

One of the "fun" things about situations like this is all the crazy coincidences that take on extra meaning because the overall situation is such a mess. On day two or so of the non-coup, when things were still running pretty hot in town, one of the senior staff members needed to go to the office for a satellite phone that someone had forgotten to take home with them on day zero. The guards, bless 'em, were still bravely at the office and doing an awfully good job of holding down the fort.

So the senior staff guy got the guard to open one of the doors to the main office building…only to find the room full of smoke. A cable had been left plugged into the wall and had started a small fire. Thankfully the guard had the presence of mind to grab the fire extinguisher and put out the fire, which impresses me a lot because even if I kind of know how to use one, actually doing so when needed requires a level of cool that I'm not sure I would have had.

The area immediately around the fire sustained some damage, as well as the whole cubicle in general, but other than that the office was unscathed, a small miracle considering that the whole thing was uncomfortably close to all our admin and finance records. The incredible thing is that the guard had been on the far side of the compound, and so had they not opened the door at that moment, it's likely that the office would have been largely toast inside before anyone noticed that something was wrong. Phew.

And speaking of forces of nature, here's a handy little tidbit: shooting into the air is really, really stupid. Forget that it's loud and a waste of ammo, besides terrifying people who don't know where the shooting is coming from. The thing is, remember that whole thing about "what goes up must come down"? And now add to that the fact that it comes down *as fast as it went up*, give or take some friction.

Which means that a bunch of bullets then come raining down at lethal speed, unfortunately not straight down from whence they came, which would only skewer the idiot who did the firing in the first place, but into unsuspecting things like the belly of a pregnant woman, going straight through the placenta and nicking the fetus' heel on the way through. Baby was born the same day, and he and mama are fine.

Now during all of this, once things had quieted down a bit, we were still "sheltering in place" but our family got a serious case of cabin fever. It still wasn't clear who was going to run the country, but surely while they were all negotiating we could sneak out for a quick bite to eat? I know it sounds crazy when you read it like that, but normal life was starting to pick up a bit, and we'd been stuck in the same four walls for days with no friends nearby, following the news but not daring to leave the house. So we hopped in the car and drove to a little guest house we knew with a restaurant and a pool, about a mile from our house towards town, but not anywhere dodgy (we thought).

In fact, we'd just ordered our pizzas when suddenly shooting broke out not too far from where we were, in multiple places—so there was a real possibility it was fire and answering fire rather than just someone blowing off steam. The owner ran and closed the main gate, and we all just sat there, waiting.

After a while, I was possessed by something that may have been professional instincts, and called the Country Rep to tell him what we were hearing. He told us to go home right away, but the hell I was going to potentially drive *into* a firefight when we were relatively safe where we were. Besides, we hadn't gotten our pizzas yet.

So we tried to wait for lunch and then eat calmly while waiting for things to cool off nearby, which was made more difficult by my CR calling every five minutes to find out whether we were home yet, despite my having made clear what a dumb idea it would be to head onto the street right then. By the time we'd finished our pizzas, the scene seemed to be clear, so we hightailed it home, where we found out that the shooting had been two rival self-declared prime ministers having it out over control of the national radio station.

The one big injury suffered in my wider circle during this time was the looting of the CRS warehouse, where we lost about $1m worth of commodities (aka food) intended for pregnant women and mothers of young babies as part of one of our largest programs. The guards tried to fend off the looters, but after a while they broke down the metal-and-concrete door, and something like a hundred people were able to make off with bags of food.

The CR and Head of Operations went to the site to see what they could do. At first they tried to explain to people that the food was intended for vulnerable people, but at some point they must have reasoned that the looters were also in need, in addition to being in overwhelming numbers, and they stood aside. The police came as well, but since the only response available at the moment was basically to start shooting people, they decided to stand by and let things take their course.

But lest you think that this is a sorry commentary on human nature, consider this: once the overall situation had calmed down some, and the CR went on national television and explained who the food had been intended for, people started returning what they'd stolen. The final amounts returned might not have made up for what was stolen, but it was still a decent chunk. And who, you ask, did us the favor of stockpiling the returned commodities in the communities before we could pick it up? The local mosques, that's who—and never mind that we were a Catholic organization.

Coming back to work was quite the experience. Everyone was bubbling over with excitement and pride. I doubt much work got done that first day! It felt like such a privilege to have been there during the whole thing, and to have kind of witnessed it firsthand, if only from our house. The other interesting thing was how I only realized once it was over how much stress I'd been under the whole time. The process of coming down from it all took at least a week, as I gradually learned to trust again that things weren't going to go berserk at any moment.

50

THE EMPIRE STRIKES BACK

Burkina, September and October, 2015

After the popular insurrection that deposed Blaise, a committee of elders selected a certain General Zida as transitional president. His job was to keep the country ticking over while organizing a democratic election process within one year. I'll leave it to the professionals to comment on the pros and cons of this period, but overall we can at least say that it was relatively peaceful and largely achieved its grand-plan objectives.

Relatively peaceful.

One afternoon I was sitting in my office, drowning under the usual pile of things that needed my attention, when I got a phone call from my husband. "Listen," he said, "I've just had a chat with the school director and he's telling me something about the President being arrested. I'm not sure what's going on, but you might want to check it out."

So I zoomed next door to the CR's office. Remember that iconic photograph of the people in the White House watching the operation to kill Osama bin Laden? The sight that greeted me when I opened the door reminded me a lot of that. The CR was sitting in front of his computer, composing a message to his boss, the Regional Director, with about six people looking intently over his shoulder. I walked in with my mouth already open to ask what was going on, but instead one of them just nodded at me and waved me over.

At that point, there wasn't much to write to the RD. The arrest of the President seemed to be confirmed, as well as the Prime Minister and all of the cabinet, though it was hard to know what was true. The main thing was, it seemed likely that whatever was going on was being orchestrated by forces from or friends of the former regime, which prompted the first talk of an attempted coup d'état.

Not knowing what else might be coming, the senior managers convened a quick meeting at which it was decided to give people 20 minutes to gather their things and leave the office. This time, I made sure to unplug everything!

At this point we'd been in Burkina only just over a year, but at least I knew the city a bit better, and so was able to take an alternate route home, rather than driving through the center of town and right by the Prime Minister's office. This route took me through the main shopping district, which looked to be pretty much business as usual, I assumed because word hadn't yet spread of what was going on. But it was crowded and traffic was slow, and I was certainly on edge the whole drive home.

Now there is probably a wide range of things you'd hope not to see on the first day of a major political and security incident, but let me tell you that coming home to find the gate to your compound hanging wonky and obviously broken would be near the top of my personal list. The hinges had been a problem for a while, but really? The gate had to choose this moment to go definitively kaput.

There were two main issues with this: 1) I couldn't get the car inside the gate, and so was going to have to leave it on the street overnight, which was a security issue, and 2) despite propping the gate up as well as we could, it was pretty obviously just kind of leaning in position, rather effectively advertising to all who might pass by that our compound was insecure. And let's just say that the moment when everyone is scurrying under cover is not exactly when you want to be looking for a welder who will travel across town.

Thankfully the whole thing had started toward the end of the workday, so the kids were already home from school. Little did we know that being home would be our every day for the better part of the next two weeks.

And then the phone calls started. Pretty quickly the senior management team established a division of labor, to cope with all the tasks that needed to happen on a regular basis. You'd think that we'd just be sitting around watching the news, but there is actually an enormous amount of work just keeping people in-country, in the regional office and at HQ informed of what's going on; answering inquiries from embassies and donors; and passing security information up and down the chain.

My job was to "manage" the expats, meaning I was the main liaison for keeping them updated and dealing with their concerns, passing on security information and things like the status of evacuation plans, and coordinating responses to the US Embassy.

Because let me tell you, we got a whole lot of requests from a whole lot of people. From HQ/the region: lists of all expats and their dependents currently in-country, with passport numbers and contact person outside of the country. From the embassy: list of all US citizens and dependents, with passport numbers. Also from the embassy: a list of all staff who work on US-funded projects, with their current whereabouts. Um. They do realize that our office is closed and we're not exactly going to send our HR manager to go look that one up? Providing input on sitreps, sometimes several per day. Answering concerned e-mails and Skype messages from friends and colleagues all over the world (not an unpleasant task, but time-consuming).

Then there's Twitter and Ouagamamas, a closed Facebook group mainly for Anglophone expats in Ouagadougou, as well as embassy updates, all of which provide information about the latest evolution of events, to be shared with the CR. For his part, he gathered security information from staff in different locations and with various connections in the police and army, from the local Catholic church and Caritas offices, and his own friends and contacts, which he would pass on to me for dissemination to the other expats. So that first evening we were already informed that it was definitely an attempted coup.

The first full day was the scariest, as the coup guys covered the capital with suppressing fire. That means every so often a DWG (Dude With Gun) goes out onto the street, sprays some bullets in the air, and then goes back to playing checkers or drinking beer or whatever it is coup guys do when no one's looking. The upshot was that we heard splotches of gunfire from different positions at fairly random points throughout the day, which was very effective for keeping us inside. Thankfully it never sounded like volley and answering fire, which would have been terrifying.

As we found out later, this strategy of suppressing fire was carried out across the entire capital, which, along with the rapid seizure of the radio and television stations, demonstrated that these guys had learned their lesson from the popular uprising the year before.

This was, in fact, one of the biggest challenges to the opposition—and opposition there was. It was clear that the coup enjoyed very little support from the general population, and many youth tried to play a cat-and-mouse game with the security forces, dodging around on their motos to avoid roadblocks and checkpoints.

But eventually the youth would be thwarted in every direction, and since petrol stations were closed, there was a real calculus about how much fuel people were willing to blow in a seemingly vain attempt to form nodes of resistance. Plus, after a few days, they were simply grounded due to lack of fuel.

What they could do was block the roads, which people did with anything handy: a felled tree, tires, a truck, anything that would make it difficult or time-consuming for a larger truck or armed personnel carrier to pass. The idea was to prevent the Republican Presidential Guard (RSP) from being able to move around and patrol the city. They couldn't kick the RSP1 out, but they could gum up the works a bit.

After the first day, though, things in Zone du Bois were pretty quiet. It's so eerie when you know major events are going down not that far away, but the only difference you can see on the street is that things are unnaturally quiet. Not that we went out much that first week or so, certainly not at all for about three days.

But then, you know, the kids needed to do homework, and books and things were still in the lockers at school… you can see where this is going. It should have been about day 3 when we decided with another family to conduct a lightning "ninja raid" on the school to retrieve the necessary items. Eddie and another parent made the raid on foot with a couple of kids in tow to vet what was brought home. My heart was in my throat the whole time they were gone, but the trip was uneventful—and allowed us to hunker down for real.

By about day five though, the crazies start to set in. You're running out of fresh fruit and veg, and although we always had plenty of canned food, you start to want an egg or an apple. One afternoon we were surprised to receive our friend Solveig with a couple of her daughters, looking to do a DVD swap since they'd run out of stuff to watch. They brought us some Nordic noir (always welcome) and raided our DVD shelf. We stood and chatted a bit, and exchanged information, but they didn't dare stay out too long so pretty soon they headed back home.

A few days later, to our great surprise and no less delight, Oumou the vegetable lady showed up at the gate with actual fresh produce for sale. The prices were probably double the usual, but given the hazards she'd likely had to endure to get to us, we were hardly in a position to complain. I expressed my surprise that she was working. She looked at me with a mixture of a lack-adaisical "that's life" and something like disdain for my privileged innocence: "One has to eat," she said. Indeed.

The contribution of this dynamic to the ultimate demise of the coup d'état would be difficult to underestimate. In an economy that's not doing very well anyway, a lot of people are living what we so casually call "hand to mouth". What this actually means is that what you earn today is what you and your kids eat tonight. The coup put a near-total stop to street trading, a rather obvious corollary of the fact that no one was on the streets. The middle classes had some food stored at home, but even they often relied on a daily shop to procure the fresh ingredients for the evening, so they would have run out of all but starches pretty quickly.

The fact was that once the coup lasted into a week or so, people couldn't work, they couldn't earn money, they weren't getting paid, they couldn't put gas in their car or moto, and they couldn't get out of the city. The increasing frustration and desperation that the general population in Ouaga felt during this time put a significant amount of pressure on the coup regime as things moved into the second week, and helped deepen the coup's lack of popularity.

Four days or so into the coup, we also ran out of wine, so I decided to risk a quick trip to my local wine shop. Please—I had my priorities. I saw about three vehicles on the little stretch of road to get there, where on a normal day it would have been thirty, and what I saw belonged to the Red Cross or other international NGOs.

To my relief, I found that the shop was open, which wasn't entirely surprising, considering that they were normally open until about 9 pm every day, including Sundays and holidays. The proprietor, who was certainly in her sixties if not older, was the matriarch of a clan numbering around 15, as far as I could tell, and at least three generations. The compound where the house sat was attached to the shop through a side door, so it was always possible to get a sense of the family's activity—and to know what they were watching on TV.

The little shop was a family business in the truest sense: the grandkids as young as nine or so would sometimes be on till duty, dutifully getting the bottles of wine from behind the counter, calculating the price on a little hand calculator, giving change and recording the purchases in a ledger kept above the cash drawer.

On a number of occasions I'd tried to give these kids a crash course in calculating the prices in their heads, especially when they'd tried to tell me I owed $600 for my few bottles because they'd made an error with the calculator, but it was more a game on my part because of course they weren't really into it, so I knew I wasn't making a dent. Anyway the kids mostly spoke Mooré and didn't even really know what I was on about half the time. OK, more than half.

Anyway, my wine lady, as I affectionately called her, would inevitably shuffle out to say hello, in slippers and a day dress that hung on her loosely enough to show, well, more than I would have thought she'd be comfortable with. She never seemed self-conscious, though, and she was obviously Catholic, which meant that she was less subject to strict ideas about covering up. Anyway her French was fine, so we'd often chat about the weather, or politics, or whatever. In this way, I discovered that she was a good barometer of public opinion.

When I arrived that day during the coup, she was in full catastrophe mode. Practically in tears, she told me what a disaster it was for the country, and, without swearing, used some choice phrases to describe the coup plotters and RSP. It's bizarre, I suppose, but my contact with her felt like my first real talk about was going on with your "man in the street", so I suppose it seemed more real to me afterwards. I bought my wine and scurried back home.

As the coup wore on, we became increasingly bold about making small forays out of the house, as long as we could make it back quickly if anything scary happened. Zone du Bois remained quiet, and as long as you didn't try to get past certain borders, you might never see a soldier or DWG. Neighbors came by for tea. Our neighbor and friend Andreas called one day to say he found fresh eggs for sale (*quelle miracle!*) and did we want any? Of course we did. Eddie started taking the kids to a friend's house to swim in their pool every day, just for half an hour or so.

In this way, although I would not want to say that I exactly *enjoyed* the coup, it was so much more human than during the popular uprising, when we'd been so isolated and didn't know people. Now we were part of a community, and people were sticking together. This time around we weren't alone.

So this was the paradox. During the popular uprising, we'd felt more insecure personally, but by day two already had the sense that globally speaking, things were moving in the right direction. During the coup, however, we felt much more connected to folks and weren't nearly as scared for ourselves....

Except that, even though everyone was saying the coup had no popular support and couldn't last, it was absolutely unclear how the big-picture situation was going to develop, whether there would be any sort of battle for the city, how long the situation of lockdown would continue. Although we were on the other side of town from any of the main areas of concern (government offices and the RSP base), a main road into the city passed just two blocks north of our house. So the given moment felt OK, but there was always this threat that things could go very, very wrong.

Adding to the pressure on me, we had a consultant in town to work on a project proposal. She was staying in the house of a coworker who was on vacation, so it worked out great, until he couldn't come back and she couldn't leave because the airport was closed. Poor Mitch was relocated from his holiday location to Dakar, our regional hub, where he was supposed to work from his hotel room. The consultant, I'll call her Rachel, was also supposed to be working, as we were still on a timeline for the proposal. It was a global call for proposals, so there would be no extensions just because one country happened to have a little security hiccup.

Now, Rachel had not planned on being caught up in a coup d'état—I know, who does? But it's different when you move to a country and you know certain things are on the horizon, as opposed to dropping in for a few weeks and then skedaddling again. So she was a little nervous and found it hard to work, and of course we were desperately trying to find a way to get her out. Her, and her *two enormous dogs*, which she had brought with her, unbeknownst to me. The problem was that I'd been pretty unhappy with the work I'd seen from her so far, and felt that there were a lot of excuses coming for this and that.

So now. It's bad enough I've got to figure out how to get her out, but the dogs as well? The airport was closed. Then it was open. Then it was closed. Then it was open but there were no flights. It was closed but there was a plane, belonging to Macky Sall, the Senegalese President, who had come to "mediate".

Since our house was pretty much directly under the flight path for planes coming in to Ouaga, if we ran out to the porch in time, we could usually make out the design on the tailfin of a passing airplane and know who was coming in. We'd then run in and post it on Ouagamamas, though I feel like the information should have come with a health warning like they do for stocks or mutual funds: A history of arriving in Ouagadougou is no indication of future continued travel. I grew to find the sound of planes overhead, even as they make you pause the TV very comforting in later years, as a sign of normalcy.

The other wrinkle with all this is that work had to pay for Rachel's plane ticket, which meant following procurement rules and involving our procurement manager. Our office was officially closed during all this time, but I'm fairly certain he went in in order to work on Rachel's case and the later relocation of the expat staff to Dakar.

One evening he called me and said he'd found a ticket on Air France for the day after tomorrow, but they couldn't guarantee that they could take the dogs—did I want to buy or not? Well, I wasn't prepared to be responsible for the dogs, and I wasn't prepared to just let them die, so I made the unprofessional choice and told him to pass on the ticket. I think that when the time came, the airport was closed again anyway, so it wouldn't have made any difference, thank goodness.

As the crisis carried on, despite some signs that a political settlement might be in the offing, people in the regional office and HQ were becoming increasingly agitated at having expats and their families in the country. I heard that the President of my organization asked, "Why do we have expats with children sheltering in place for the second time in 12 months in Burkina

Faso?" So, we started making more concrete plans to relocate expatriate staff outside of the country.

For a while we thought about going to Ghana by road, and it's a good thing we'd learned our lesson after the last incident and gotten visas for everyone because there was absolutely no way to get the visa at the border, no way, no how, not even in light of what was going on in Burkina. But we were eventually informed that the road was impassible anyway, so the point was moot. In the end, everyone who left went out by air.

A day or so before they all left, Rachel called me.

Rachel [in Eeyore tones]: Hi, Carey.

Me [as cheerful as I can manage]: Hey Rachel, what's up?

Rachel [mournfully]: I think Mitch's rabbit is dying.

Me [inwardly laughing and crying at the same time—what *else* is going to happen?]: Oh, really? Um, that's too bad.

Rachel: Yeah, it just kind of hopped up into the air, and now it's lying there in a really weird position, and its eyes are kind of buggy…. I think maybe it had a stroke or something.

Me: Wow, yeah, that sounds serious. You should probably tell Mitch.

Rachel: Oh but my Internet's not working, so could you write to him and see if there's anything in particular he wants me to do?

Hmmm, Internet not working………… I've heard that one before.

Me: Uh, OK, let me talk to him and call you back.

Upon which I Skyped Mitch at his hotel room and informed him that I wasn't calling about his house or the relocation or the coup or the proposal, but that his rabbit was dying and did he want us to do anything besides the obvious, which was to stand by helplessly and watch the rabbit die. Thankfully, his emotional attachment to the rabbit didn't run too deep.

We finally decided that all the expats would go to Dakar as

soon as we could find a flight for them. I was allowed to stay only because school had started up again, so I was able to make the case that our children's education would be interrupted if they were abroad. It's true that things were seemingly calming down and it was looking like the DWGs were going to stand down, so it was kind of an ironic time for the expats to leave. But it was felt that they needed to get out from under the pressure, and I think it was important for us to show that we weren't just leaving people in potentially dangerous situations. The other expats weren't all that happy to leave, but once they came back they told me that in the end, it was only when they got to Dakar that they realized how much stress they'd been under, and they were just as happy to have gone, after all.

I was just as happy not to go, in part because, like the others, I enjoyed the feeling of solidarity with the Burkinabè people during this time and didn't want to miss out. To be honest, though, a lot of it was because I didn't want to leave our dog, and because I really couldn't handle the idea of leaving and coming back to a trashed house, or even worse, never coming back at all. These last being, of course, exactly the scenarios that are why you are supposed to leave when you can. As they say: when there's only one road out, use it.

In the bigger picture, in contrast to October 2014, the resistance was felt not only in Ouagadougou, but in secondary cities as well. In fact, given how difficult it was to move around the capital, it's probably true that most of the resistance in the street was not in Ouagadougou. This also gave the people heart, as they saw their cause taken up nationwide. While the majority of the rural population probably couldn't care less who was in government, since they see so little benefit from the state anyway, the urban classes could clearly see that they were part of a bigger movement (thank you, Twitter).

Along with the aforementioned economic pressure, the

continuing roadblocks and demonstrations showed that the coup would not be accepted by the population, assisted by the intrepid and thoroughly wonderful US Ambassador Tulinabo Mushingi.

And finally, about ten days in, something snapped. Suddenly there were reports of secondary army bases mobilizing and sending soldiers marching on the capital. In the South, the West and the East, army commanders loyal to the transition made the decision to jointly bring the situation to a head: either coup leader General Diendéré and the RSP would give up and step down, or—so the implication—there would be armed confrontation.

Boy did this bring up mixed feelings. On one hand we were thrilled to see the regular army taking a stand and forcing the hand of the illegitimate government—and on the other, we were terrified. Remember I said a main access road passed two blocks from our house? In fact the military prison just half a kilometer or so down the road would have been an obvious place for a choke point into the city. Friends of ours lived between presumed points of entry by the loyalist forces and their targets, meaning that anything explosive that missed its target was liable to wind up in their back yard.

I'll admit that at this point I started thinking that maybe staying in town hadn't been such a hot idea, after all. This all lasted two or three days, during which the tension mounted like a rubber band fit for snapping.

After the whole thing was over, a colleague of mine told me she'd taken a bunch of those big cans of tomato paste and used them to elevate her daughter's bed by a foot or so off the ground. She then drilled them: "When I clap my hands like this, you don't ask questions, you don't fool around, you just go straight under the bed and wait, you understand?" Her description of her fear during those days gave me goosebumps—and pointed out how privileged we were, again, to be in a neighborhood relatively away from the action. How positive that word sounds until you are part of it.

Faced with a potentially bloody and destructive battle for the capital, Diendéré finally agreed to step down and that the RSP would hand over their weapons. The regular army would be allowed to take up positions to secure the city while the details were being worked out and the RSP was disarming. Things were still dicey, but the upshot was pretty much that the coup had failed.

This is when you start to realize how hard you were holding your breath.

As the army began deploying throughout the capital, shops started to open and people began to poke their heads out of their shells. Don't tell my boss, but I snuck out despite the continued "shelter in place" status to hit Bingo supermarket for some groceries. I certainly wasn't alone.

On the way home, I pulled around a roundabout to go back in the other direction, and was so intent on missing the traffic coming in from my right that I totally missed the huge APC that was rolling in right in front of me. It gave me a small heart attack, but then I knew what they were doing, and they were definitely "driving casual" (à la Han Solo), so I didn't actually freak out. Still, in some ways it was the clearest demonstration to me of the reality of our situation.

Thinking things were now basically under control, the school and our office reopened the following Monday. The atmosphere in the office was jubilant, which much laughing and back-thumping, and of course lots and lots of venting. The boss called an all-staff meeting for 11:00, where we all got our "*gâteau*" (pastry) and welcomed home the staff who had been trapped outside the country for the duration. (Besides Mitch, three poor guys had been caught in Dakar attending a training and had to watch from afar as their loved ones prepared for the worst.) The CR had been given a small award for his handling of the crisis, which he made a point of sharing with the whole office. After a morning of catching our breath, we all trickled back to our offices to start figuring out how to get things back on track after two weeks' total work stoppage.

And by 1:30, we were back in the boss' office. Diendéré was hesitating and the disarmament wasn't going according to schedule. After a brief conference among the senior staff, the decision was reluctantly made to close the office again and send everyone home. So after a morning of freedom, I was faced with three more days of what felt like house arrest.

To top it all off, the deadline for that darn proposal was approaching, and so we finally had to buckle down and start finalizing things. Poor Carole, the budget manager of the current project, had been valiantly trying to put the new budget together (a feat so complicated and yet tedious that if I tried to explain it to you, you'd feel like I was pulling your hair out one by one) at home, with her small children climbing all over her, sending the enormous file for review via Internet dongle with a crappy connection.

The flaky consultant had finally sort of done her bit, and Mitch had been powering away in Dakar—so there really was no way I was going to not get this thing finished, though it was about as fun as putting on a wet bathing suit. That's the thing about proposal work: so much of it can be torturous, but when your colleagues have put so much time and energy into their part, common decency dictates that you have to do everything you can to get a good product in to the donor.

Finally, the RSP started handing over their weapons, and we were able to go back to work for real. The kids went back to school, the relocated expats came back, and things slowly returned to normal. As with the previous event, it surprised me (less this time) how long it took me to relax once it was over. You really don't realize the stress you're under until it isn't there anymore. Thankfully the whole thing didn't leave much in the way of permanent consequences, though the main streets remain potted with scorch marks where people had burned tires. These are now, predictably, fast on their way to becoming potholes.

51

THE NIGHT WE ATE SHOES

Ouagadougou, October, 2014

When we first moved to Ouagadougou, Eddie stayed behind to finish his contract with his employer of the day, so it was just the kids and me for about six weeks. We stayed in a furnished flat walking distance from the office. It was OK in the sense that the kids each had their own room and there was a pretty decent kitchen, but the first week the kids didn't have school yet and there was neither TV nor internet, so you can imagine how much fun they had all day, every day. All. Day.

I'd found a house some months before when doing my handover visit, but when I arrived and the office tried to seal the deal, the landlord backed out. So now I was forced to look under pressure, which was tough because all the houses seemed too small, partly a product of coming from spacious Lusaka, partly because of how much stuff we had, and partly because the houses were genuinely not huge—or had just one bathroom for a family of four—really? I picked one that I liked because it had a huge porch area and a pretty garden, and thought we were all set.

Except first, the house had to be repaired and spiffed up

before we could move in. And we were playing to a deadline. Mid-September, Eddie was coming, and he wasn't coming alone —he was bringing our beloved Seamus doggie as well, the first and only time we ever moved with a pet. Obviously, Seamus could not stay in the flat two stories up all day while all the people were away, so we absolutely had to be moved in by the time Eddie arrived.

The day grew ever closer, and the house still wasn't ready. The whole situation was greatly exacerbated by the poor communication skills of the particular staff member who was assigned to monitor the whole thing (let's call him Mr. K). The whole concept of getting back to you with progress updates never quite made an impression, despite several imploring salvos to that effect lobbed in his direction. Also, when you say one thing one day and then the exact opposite thing the next day, the resulting mental whiplash is not good for one's credibility.

I did not acquit myself very well during this time, I have to confess. The stress of knowing that Eddie was coming with the dog so we *had* to be in the house, coupled with the slow pace of the work and the unreliable communications, turned me into one of *them*. I became one of those horrible whites who harps and harries and loses her temper—though I never actually shouted, and I'm pretty sure I managed not to cry in public. Let's just say that the stress showed, and it's a wonder poor Mr. K even spoke to me again after the whole thing. Clearly, the staff had plenty of practice dealing with expats who'd fallen prey to the new-posting crazies.

So the big day finally arrived: all the work was allegedly finished and we could move in, all of two nights before Eddie was supposed to arrive. I'd spent some time looking at white goods in different stores, and had finally settled on a vaguely posh and definitely overpriced shop, but one where I could get a nice big fridge, a necessity for our foodie and leftover-loving family. The day before the move, I went to the store to order a fridge and washing machine, picked out the ones I wanted, and was all set to have them delivered the next day, when I found out they didn't take credit cards.

So in something not at *all* resembling a panic I went to Marina Market, one of the more upscale grocery stores that also sells furniture, kitchen goods and some toys, and picked out a much smaller fridge, a washing machine, mattresses, and a water-cooler stand. I was told to come back the following morning to meet the woman who could give me a discount, and they promised me I could have the goods delivered that same day.

This I did, among many assurances that yes, she really would be there and yes, they really would deliver later that same day. I remained doubtful. But I came back the next day as instructed, and lo! met the very nice Ukrainian woman who was apparently co-managing the store, which itself was run by Middle Eastern Christians who I supposed to be Lebanese (but they might be Syrian).

I got my 10% discount and paid with a check. (Which, in and of itself, was a learning experience… but I digress. But, while I'm here, listen: is it my fault they have the payee where the amount should be and vice versa? And when, in English or French, for that matter, does one have to write out large numbers except when writing a check? It's arcane).

In the early afternoon, then, I went back to the flat and brought all our luggage down, unplugged the fridge, packed our cold food and leftovers into a plastic bucket, and drove over to the new house. But as could have been expected, they were still working on the windows and some other last-minute repairs, and most pertinently the new screens weren't up on the porch yet. We hadn't yet taken delivery of the master bed, the dining table, or the coffee table and chairs, so things were pretty minimal, but we were prepared to make due—just get us into the house already!

In the afternoon the guys came to deliver all the stuff from Marina. They'd cut it close to 5:00 pm, but *quelle miracle*, I'd only about 30% believed that they would come at all. This is when I found out that you have to leave the fridge to settle for 24 hours before you can plug it in, or so they said. Now remember that the ambient temperature in October is pretty high, even for Burkina (probably high 90s F and high 30s C), so you know I was bidding my milk and leftovers goodbye—but at least we could eat some of the leftovers for dinner, so we wouldn't have to chuck that much out. At one point I tried to plug in my phone to charge it and the socket didn't work, but I assumed the power was off because they were still working on some electrical stuff in the house.

The kids had walked to the new house from school, so they were around from about 3:30, doing homework and generally trying to stay out of the way of all the hustle and bustle. 5:00 or 5:30 arrived, and the workers packed up for the day. Alone in the house with all our suitcases and a couple of boxes, we started to think about settling in for our first evening. It was starting to get dark, so I went to put the lights on, and—nothing. I checked the socket again where I'd tried to charge my (now dangerously low) phone—nothing. Now my sense of panic was not so mild. So I did the obvious and called Mr K.

Me: We're in the new house.

Mr. K: Yes, yes.

Me: There's no power.

Mr. K: Oh, yes. They said the account was still in the previous tenants' name, so they took the counter away and they'll bring it back when they get your name on the account.

Me [small volcano of panic building]: So why didn't you tell me the power was going to be out?

Mr. K [heavens these white people are dense]: Because they only took the counter away today.

Me [slowly, enunciating carefully]: Ye-es, but you knew the power was going to be out tonight as soon as they took the counter away.

Mr. K: Yes, but they only took the counter away this afternoon.

Me [abandoning this line of reasoning]: You realize we can't stay here with no power, right?

Mr. K: Oh, you can't?

Me [trying to breathe]: No, not with no lights and no fans to keep the mosquitoes away, especially since the screens aren't done yet and the house is heaving with mosquitoes.

Mr. K: Oh, well, whatever you say. The counter should be ready tomorrow.

Me: Good, because you realize Eddie is arriving tomorrow with the dog, so we absolutely have to be in the house tomorrow night.

Mr. K: Oh yes, no problem, Madame.

We really couldn't stay there with no power. The house had been open for weeks while they were doing all the work on it, and it really was full of mosquitoes, carriers of evil strains of malaria and the dreaded dengue fever. There were no nets hung in the rooms, and indeed indoor mosquito nets seemed to be pretty much nonexistent in Burkina, not least because there is usually a fan mounted in the center of the ceiling, right where you might otherwise hang the net. But without a net and nothing to blow the air around to hopefully keep the mozzies away, it would be major buffet time for them all night. Plus, my phone was running on the phone equivalent of fumes. Phone fumes.

So, nothing for it: I told the kids to dig out something to sleep in and a change of clothes, and we were going to go back to the flat for one more night. I grabbed the bucket with the leftovers and off we went. At that hour, it took us a good hour to cross town, and it was pretty much dark when we got in. We went to the back of the car to get our stuff to carry upstairs again, when I noticed that the bucket I had put in the car was not, in fact, the one with our leftovers in it, but another one containing our shoes. And at this time of night, there was no way I was going to drive all the way back to the house and then back again to the flat with the long-suffering kids in the car. They'd been super patient all day, but everyone has limits.

I looked in my wallet and found that I had 2,500 F CFA, or about $5 to my name. I should have had more, but I was waiting for the check with my initial payment for living costs while we settled in. This, it turned out, had been transferred straight to my US bank account, which is why I had been waiting rather a long time for it. So. Kids tired and hungry, all of us exhausted, looking forward to an uncomfortable night basically camping on our former beds, and I've got all of $5 to feed three people dinner today and breakfast tomorrow (good thing the kids could buy lunch at school using pre-paid tickets).

It's possible that I cried just a little at this point.

I drove us down the road to a little market and bought a can of beans with sausages and bread, and then bought eggs for 100 F CFA each until I ran out of money. At this point I had 70 F CFA left, about 12 cents. On the way home we passed the "maize lady", one of the women who grills maize at the side of the road for sale as a snack. It's starchier than the corn you'd get in the US, so not as sweet, but quite more-ish in its own way. The kids loved the stuff, and they begged me to buy one cob on the way home.

The thing was, the maize cost 100 F CFA and we only had 70. So I did what every self-respecting rich, white expat would do and sent our little, blond, angelic Marion over to basically beg a cob of maize for 70 F CFA. The presumption, honestly. It would have been like a game except that we were depriving this woman of an amount of money that would be throwaway for us, but represented something meaningful for her. Sigh.

So, that became the infamous night we ate shoes (and beans and sausages and bread, with eggs and bread for breakfast).

Sadly, the adventure didn't stop there. The following day Eddie arrived with the dog as advertised... but the power still wasn't ready at the house. So despite having packed everything up again and left the flat for a second time, we now had to grab our things and go back to the flat for a second time, leaving the poor dog in his carrier with some water and food.

The third day, we again packed up all our stuff and went to the flat—and this time were able to stay. But the back and forth nearly killed me. I think it all took a couple of years off the life of my poor heart—and then, after the popular insurrection just two months later, we had to move again.

(In my boss's defense, when, several years later, I told him the story of running out of money that first night, he was horrified and asked why I didn't call him for help. Honestly, the thought never occurred to me.)

52

CRAZY WONDERFUL THINGS

It's easy to moan about a lot of things in the expat life: you miss friends and family (not just at home, but those from past postings now strewn all over the world), can't find some favorite or culturally important foods, have to endure sometimes very uncomfortable weather with threats of disease, accident, snakebite, not to mention the day-to-day struggles of navigating between the organizational culture of your employer and the local culture, which you only poorly understand… And then there are what I can only call flat-out adventures: things you'd normally never get to experience, or maybe only one in a lifetime, that you get to squeeze into a long weekend or are just part of the job. I've been ludicrously lucky on this front. Here are some highlights:

- The sound and light show at the Pyramids in Giza. This was on a random Tuesday evening: one of the local finance staff had offered to take one of the expat regional staff in the Cairo office, and they invited me to tag along. The show itself was pretty kitschy, but who was I to argue? It was the freaking pyramids. I also got a chance to see how truly in the middle of Cairo they are, at least on two sides. This was epitomized by the guidebook that comforted any tourists unlucky enough not to get tickets for the show by noting that they could get a very good view from upstairs of the KFC across the street.

- I was once tragically forced to fly in a four-seater airplane up into the mountains of Lesotho, to visit some project sites. The view was truly spectacular, and there's something special about being in a small airplane like that, so much closer to the scenery than in a bigger plane. Unfortunately it was too windy for us to fly back down again, so we had to make the journey back, on roads consisting mostly of slabs of rock, in a pickup truck. My tush was mad at me for three days.

- I went a couple of times to Victoria Falls, one of the natural wonders of the world. If you think you've got an idea of it because you've seen photos, forget it. The real thing is so wide, you can't really get a feel for how huge it is unless you can walk up and down it to get a sense of the scale. People fight about whether the Zambia or the Zimbabwe side is better; I think they both have their charms. The Zambia side is fun for getting very, very wet from the spray, which comes down like sheets of rain. My dad and I went out to the promontory once, eschewing the ponchos for rent—and boy, did we get soaked. I might as well have jumped fully-clothed into a swimming pool.

Fun post-script to this one: A couple of months after I first went to Vic Falls, some friends and Eddie and I went to Niagara Falls, which I had of course heard about my entire life. In the event, I spent the whole time chuckling to myself, because the word you're supposed to be thinking when you see Niagara is definitely not "dinky".

- A week talking about bee products in Hanoi: visiting old embassy friends, taking a field trip into the countryside and meeting beekeepers. A friend of Eddie's back from Hong Kong days, who had also worked in the Vietnamese refugee camps and then settled in Vietnam, took me out to dinner. The only problem there was that I had to ride on the back of his moped, which I thought looked liable to either fall down or fling me off at the first turn. In true expat fashion, I was terrified and sure I was going to die, but did it anyway.

Perhaps the best highlight was going out to dinner at a vegetarian place run by Buddhist monks, where their tradition had it that the original monastery of their order used to house travelers. Not wanting to put their omnivore guests off with a diet of vegetables and tofu, they created meat substitutes using soy. The menu was even divided up into "beef", "chicken" and "pork", but it was all mimicry. We were the little African node in what was otherwise a very Asian and European conference: An American consultant and proponent of beekeeping as a livelihoods strategy for the rural poor; the wonderful Bob Malichi, middle-man between virgin-forest beekeepers in northwest Zambia and the buyer in Aberystwyth; and yours truly.

I still chuckle over the memory of poor Bob, this big African guy, gamely trying to tame a pair of chopsticks into conveying the strange food to his mouth. You have to hand it to him; he was a great sport about the whole thing. I confess to a certain amount of pride that we were able to carry on a very interesting conversation about the goat trade between Rwanda and Zambia, which required knowledge of the latest goat prices. I enjoyed the sense of street cred I got out of knowing the prices for the different kinds and ages of goats.

• Seeing lemurs in Madagascar—along with less-famous but equally wonderful leaf-tailed geckos and tiny little chameleons that just look like a curl at the end of a leaf. The first time I went, we were joined by two members of national staff. One was a doctor by training and great patriot, in love with the uniqueness of his country, and the other was a former employee of the World Wildlife Foundation.

As we toured around the forest, my other colleague and I kept losing these two. Once I went back only to find them marveling at a tree. It looked like a pretty normal tree to me, but apparently it was a very special *kind* of tree. I just loved their child-like enthusiasm for their own culture and natural environment. Given that most Africans will never see a safari park in their lives and are as likely as not to view animals as pests (which, to be fair, they often are), it was a real joy to see them relishing the natural richness of their home.

The lemurs themselves are a delight to see, but the best thing is when you hear them. The indri (whose name means "up", because "Where are the lemurs?" Answer, "up") have this thing going on where they establish their territory early in the morning by calling out. It's not a howl and it's not a cry, just an eerie, rising "ooop". And when this call is repeated throughout the forest, sometimes close, sometimes far, before you, behind you, above you… it's magical.

• Walking out my back door and gathering fresh oregano, marjoram, flat-leaf parsley, rosemary, dill and mint without needing to take more than a few steps.

• A week in Quito, Ecuador, my first time in Latin America. I couldn't get over the mountains. The gym in the hotel was nearly on the top floor and was built with big panel windows around nearly 180 degrees, so instead of CNN while you bike, you can just enjoy the spectacle of morning clouds moving in over the mountains. I promise you won't get bored.

I loved Quito because there was actual shopping. It sounds dumb, but after years of variations on the same crafts everywhere you go, it was so refreshing to be in a place where I could actually buy things I was looking forward to giving people at home.

After the workshop a couple of us went up to a nearby volcano. We toured the hacienda up there and it was really

strange for me to see the Spanish architecture I'm so used to
from California in non-US surroundings. Of course logically I
understood why it was there, but my brain still wasn't ready
for it.

The Spaniards had found an old waystation built by the
indigenous peoples way back when: the walls were two-feet
thick, solid rock. The building was constructed of hand-hewn,
slightly irregular stones, fit together with no mortar. Let me just
stress this again: indigenous peoples, no known magical way of
hewing rock, building and transporting two-feet cubed chunks
of stone, which have been hand-crafted to sit in one particular
place only, and be secure there with no glue. Having tried and
spectacularly failed to destroy this little fortress, the Spaniards
thought better of it and turned the room into their chapel.

We went up the volcano and I got my one and only chance
to try coca-leaf tea, which I liked a lot more than I expected to.
Then we tried to walk up the volcano. Emphasis, in my case,
on "tried". I made about five seconds and then decided that
coming back down the shale slope wasn't going to be any fun,
and since I felt like I was running up against a brick wall at
every step, I beat my retreat to the waiting car.

This is no exaggeration. You'd take a small step up the
mountain, and actually feel as though you'd hit a wall. Two or
three breaths to acclimatize, and then one more step, and
wham! The wall again. I couldn't understand how people were
hiking up the mountain looking vaguely relaxed.

While my friends were up the mountain, it started to snow.
It was fascinating how clear the snow line was as we drove
down, and then the different strata of vegetation as we
descended further. I was fascinated by the plants at some of the
higher altitudes, which reminded me a lot of the proteas in
South Africa.

- Goat racing in Malawi. No, really. I think this was

supposed to be a fundraiser but I'm not sure many of the guests knew or cared. Dress code was pure Kentucky Derby: tuxes and big hats. Mostly it seemed an excuse to drink since the betting took a good 15 minutes between races. After much build-up, the races themselves were over in about three seconds. Perhaps the inventor of goat racing didn't realize that goats are pack animals and so all run together.

• Attending a peacebuilding training in Kenya's Aberdaires National Park, with none other than John Baptist Odama, Archbishop of Gulu, one of the religious leaders who tried to mediate with Joseph Kony of the Lord's Resistance Army in northern Uganda, plus two bishops and three priests. The hotel set up a tent outside so they could say mass every morning.

I went once or twice just to check it out. It was a little bit like being behind the scenes at the theater, seeing all six men putting on their vestments and getting the communion stuff ready. They took turns presiding over the mass and doing the sermon, but they would all put out their hands to bless the host. I'm not Catholic, but seeing all six of them gathered around, there was definitely a special energy to the sight.

• Going to the opera in Sarajevo for all of eight dollars per person. Cried every time.

• Eating leftover pizza in full view of a couple of harems of zebras (hey, don't look at me—that's what they're called). In Nairobi National Park, there aren't any big predators, so you are allowed to get out and have a picnic at certain areas.

• Watching the sun set over the Zambezi river while the hippos grunt away. The hippo call has to be one of the best sounds ever.

• Finding out that cows can swim. No, really.

• In the late afternoon, swimming out into Lake Kivu from the lodge at Kibuye, far enough in that the voices from the shore sound in your ears much less than your own breath, the water smooth against your skin, the shiver of tension that comes from not being able to see the water around your feet, and the golden light of the sun playing against the deep green of little waves on the water's surface. You tread water, hearing just your breath and perhaps the odd wave lapping; go up on your back and float, eyes closed, feeling how much you are in the middle of nature and away from needing to do or be anything in particular.

53

YOU KNOW YOU'VE BEEN IN AFRICA TOO LONG...

When you start preferring Nido milk powder to real milk in your tea, and:

• You think room-temperature sodas are actually not that bad, and (brace yourself) maybe even better than cold ones.

• You pour out the Uncle Ben's rice on the kitchen table to pick through it for stones before cooking.

• You start to say "pick" instead of "pick up", and "shift" instead of "move". "I'll pick you at 3:00."

• You swat at flies and mosquitoes that aren't really there.

• You're prepared to have an impassioned argument about whether maize or cassava ugali/foufou/paap/sadza is better.

• You're in the middle of a work presentation, the power goes out (plunging the room into darkness, and killing the PowerPoint presentation), and both speaker and audience carry on without missing a beat.

• You think it's really normal to wash and re-use Ziploc bags 20 or 30 times, until they're positively dead—and can't understand why not everyone does this. You seriously consider (and possibly do) diving into the waste basket to retrieve that perfectly good Ziploc someone else threw away.

• You think nothing of smuggling a salad into another country for dinner.

• Before swimming in a moving body of water, you ask if there are crocs.

• Before swimming in a stationary body of water, you ask if there's bilharzia.

• If the answer to either of these is positive, you have a beer instead.

• When you pass someone and they ask you how you are, you answer as if they actually want an answer.

• You carry mosquito repellent in your handbag. Always. (Unless you're my friend Ms. Bonkers, in which case it's hot sauce.)

• You think 85F is a comfortable room temperature.

• You see a scene of "Africa" in a movie, some filthy, sewage-filled street with equally filthy children begging on the side of the road, people milling about in every direction—in short, a scene designed to show you the misery of the African Capital City… and your reaction is homesickness.

• Your child learns to count in Swahili before English, and asks Dad to read a book like this: "Daddy, book! Soma!"

54

BUGS

Any self-respecting description of African bugs of course needs to start with mosquitoes. Annoying little shits. When you first get your house, you have to make sure all the mosquito netting is up and watertight: no gaps, no holes. If you've got a really well-built and maintained house (i.e., you're a diplomat), you may get away with this. For us mere mortals there will always be a bit of ripped netting on the bathroom window, or a door next to shoes (which attract mozzies by the ingenious feat of smelling like people), or a screen door that isn't flush to the floor.

There are actually two kinds (in real life, of course, there are many more than two): *Anopheles*, which everybody knows as the carrier of malaria, and *Aedes*, which carries dengue fever. You know about *Anopheles* and how it bites from dawn to dusk, so you put your spray on in the evening and sleep under a net, blah blah blah. What they don't tell you is those little harbingers of doom, the *Aedes*, bite in the *daytime*. In the shade, to be precise, which is exactly where every person would like to be standing. They're striped, so they're a real bugger to see in the shade. We used to get positive swarms of them outside the house in Ouaga. They are fast, and their bites itch so much it hurts.

In most places we actually didn't have to worry about dengue, and even when we moved to Ouaga the word was "well, maybe a few cases a year, no big deal." That was fine and dandy until around 2015, when all of a sudden there was a dengue epidemic in Ouaga and a little bit in other places. We knew of two or three teachers who had to be hospitalized, including a good friend of ours, and I had a few work colleagues who were likewise struck by the disease.

Some fun facts about dengue fever: there is no treatment and no vaccine. Each time you get it, it feels worse. Which is not fun, because what one experiences with dengue is pain. And it's when you are starting to feel better that is the real danger zone (and this is the real reason for people to be monitored in the hospital). If you've been really sick, your platelets can crash and then you are in trouble. One of the missionaries in our extended circle of acquaintances died in the 2015 outbreak.

On a lighter note, let me give you the humble caterpillar. A usually unnoticed creature, unless one starts to crawl on you and you need to flick it off. This is fine except in Rwanda, where you first have to assess carefully whether the caterpillar is furry or not. Bald caterpillars are fine, and may indeed be your friend.

The fuzzy ones, though—now you have to pay attention. The fuzzies are actually little spines that can get into your clothing and will certainly stay on your skin if contact is made. The fuzzies look sweet but they sting, a bit like poison nettles. Also, the cater-pillars have a tendency to come down from an overhead branch —so again, if you're trying to sit in the shade, you're screwed— what is it with these little dudes?

Now our friend the Nairobi fly may be named for one city, but it's pretty ubiquitous around Africa as far as I could tell. Nairobi fly is what first taught me the Grand Rule of Tropical

Insects: flick, don't squash. You don't know what that thing is going to do to you if it dies. In the case of Nairobi fly, recognizable for its distinct stripes of red and black, otherwise looking just like a small bug, upon violent death will exude an acid that creates pretty severe burns and can lead to scarring. Definitely not fun if it's near an eye.

Sitting around on a Thursday night in the living room in Kigali while Eddie was away, and it starts to rain—first rain of the year. As the downpour gets more serious, I spy flying creatures above the lawn. They increase in number, and then I notice that they are coming into the house through the front door, which is again not flush with the floor.

So suddenly I've got things that look vaguely like termites, but bigger, flying all around my living room, and I can't prevent more from coming in. And then I see that there are termites crawling on my floor—they are dropping their wings and wandering around seemingly aimlessly. I honestly felt like I was in a horror film.

I looked outside and the number of grounded termites had become very large, indeed. The crows were coming down and eating some, but obviously they couldn't get everything. Eventually the termites stopped emerging from the earth and I was able to breathe again. Later I learned that the termites are a prized treat, which makes sense, really. And no, I never tried them. But at least I was mentally prepared after that for the invasion that comes with the first rain.

This is the squeamish one. Just skip down three paragraphs if you don't want to read it.

I always wondered why the housekeeper would iron my underpants and socks and things. I asked her about it once and she said it was because of the mango fly. I asked around and was told that indeed, if you are hanging your washing out, a mango fly might come up and lay its eggs in the seams of your clothes.

This larva could then transfer itself to a person's skin and grow in there.

I could never really imagine it but was convincingly told that the same thing existed when we moved to Rwanda and then Zambia, where it was called putsi fly, so we always made sure to iron our clothes well. Unfortunately, this protection was not fully extended to our poor Guinea pigs, Batman and Wildman, who at one point came up with putsi fly larvae in their feet. I took them to the vet and witnessed the removal. It surprised me how big they were, like a large peanut. I never did knowingly see the fly but it must be huge.

Oh, and here's a nice one to congratulate you for getting through the rest. One day in Kigali I was washing the dishes and I kept noticing teeny little praying mantises on the window sill. Finally, I realized that a mother had laid her eggs in the little squares of the mosquito screen, and they were hatching! So I got to watch this procession of inch-long praying mantises down the screen, and then their take-off into the air and praying-mantis-dom. Much nicer than reaching into a lettuce and being bitten by one.

IT'S A SMALL WORLD...

Seven degrees of separation, and all that. I figure everyone in the international aid business is like a supernode for connections across the world; I mean, I connect Bill Clinton to an art therapist in Germany and a goat herder in Rwanda. So it shouldn't be surprising that there are some pretty amazing or funny coincidences in terms of who knows whom, but some beggar belief or are just particularly humiliating....

• When Eddie and I were first together, we didn't really tell many people, though of course Eddie's flat mates knew because I started staying with him rather than at the BPT flat when I was in Prishtina. And from there I suppose the news traveled fairly quickly through the expat community, which wasn't hard since there were only about 15 people in that group.

One day I had a work meeting with one of the NGO crowd, so it was one of those weird-but-common situations in overseas development when you're sitting across the desk from and exchanging business cards with someone you may have been drinking beers with two nights ago. In this case, the man I was meeting (let's call him Bob) was not one of the super party set, but would definitely hang out with people and was a casual friend of Eddie.

About 20 minutes into the meeting, he kind of stopped and said, "You seem to have something there on your cheek." I rubbed my hand across the spot and it came back with a black smudge. "Oh," I said, and after some brief reflection, remembering Eddie getting ready for work in the morning, "it's shoe polish."

Bob heaved a sigh of relief and said, "I've been sitting here for 20 minutes wondering if I should say something. I'm thinking, is Eddie beating her? [nervous laugh] But I finally thought I should just get it out of the way." Upon which we had an awkward chuckle and carried on as if nothing had happened.

• Another time I didn't need to be anywhere until like 10 am, so Eddie just went to work as normal and left me in the flat to do my own thing until I needed to leave.

When the time came, I found that the front door was locked, and without the key there was no way to open it. I tried everything I could think of, but there was no way. I went out to the balcony over the road, trying to see if I could catch the attention of anyone in the Save the Children house across the street, or of anyone passing by. Since I was on the second floor, this wasn't particularly effective. This being before the days of ubiquitous mobile phones, I couldn't even call my colleague and tell her I wasn't going to make it to our meeting.

Eventually I gave up and started reading a random book I picked up, thinking that I would have to wait until the end of the day to be rescued (and feeling much like Rapunzel all that time). But suddenly there was a noise at the door, and Eddie walked in—accompanied by the rest of the senior team in his office, including his boss. Eh heh, err, I introduced myself and sheepishly made myself scarce.

• One of the fun details of NGO work in Kosovo at that time was that the Serbian government would not allow the international NGOs to register. This meant, among other things, no radio licenses and hence the need for aid convoys to be accompanied by UN cars that were allowed to sport the big Codan radios. Fortunately, this book is not a memoir of UN-NGO relations.

Anyway, this lack of registration also meant that all international NGOs fell under the auspices of the Serbian Red Cross, which loved nothing more than to assert its authority by laying down all kinds of bureaucratic controls on things like bringing money and goods into the country or making payments.

One of the people Eddie complained the most about during his time in Kosovo was the head of the Red Cross at that time, who seemed to take perverse pleasure out of doing his best to block just about anything.

One day I had my own meeting with said human, just an informational thing to find out what the Serbian Red Cross' activities were. We'd only gotten about 10 minutes into the meeting when he started to rail against the NGO crowd and especially "that Mr. Eddie", who was such an unreasonable pain in the butt and whom he would quite obviously have loved to see the back of. "You should hear what he says about *you*!" I thought, though I did manage to suppress a smile and refrained from telling him that he was slagging off my boyfriend.

• I once wrote a somewhat (ehem) nasty letter to the Economist, complaining about the spelling of an Albanian activist's name. I'm not sure why I put on the snotty tone with the letter; I think I was showing off that I knew something better than the editors at the Economist. That and maybe trying to stand out, which I'm sure I didn't mean to do through being rude, but may have done nevertheless.

About six months later I met a journalist who was writing primarily for the Financial Times about Serbia, including the conflict over Kosovo. I don't even remember now how we met, but he was interested in talking to me because I had a lot of political background on the main players in Kosovo that most people didn't have. He never formally interviewed me, but at one point did say that a well-known BBC journalist wanted to do so. I was pretty chuffed at the idea, but it never materialized.

One day we were talking and I said about reading the Economist or something, and he suddenly stopped in his tracks. "Wait a minute," he said, "did you once write a really snotty letter to the editor about somebody's name being misspelled?"

"Err." [Cue Carey sinking into the ground just a little bit.] "Yeah, that might have been me…"

"We do read those letters, you know."

So now you know.

• Eight years after first leaving the Balkans, I was hired on with a new organization and our family moved to Sarajevo. From there, I was covering the entire Balkans region, eventually also covering our programs in the Middle East. My first trip in the region was to Belgrade, of which I had very fond memories from when I lived there for BPT, even though the part of town we'd be in was pretty far from where I'd lived. This was something like my first week on the job. We flew to Belgrade from Sarajevo and got to the hotel in the late afternoon. Once I got settled, I decided I had better get some money, so I left the hotel for the bank we'd passed about two blocks down the street.

While standing at the sole traffic light between the hotel and the bank, I thought I heard my name—though no one knew me in Belgrade anymore, so I assumed I had misheard. Still, I turned around—only to find Renate, my BPT colleague from back in the day, standing there behind me. Not only was it crazy that she was passing by the same corner five minutes after I'd come back to the Balkans, but she was leaving in a few days to go live in Croatia. Seriously, what are the chances? We went and had a drink, and it was lovely.

• When Eirwyn was in high school, in Ouagadougou, we decided it would be helpful for him to have a math tutor. Jeff was a trailing spouse, a mathematician and former professional tutor, originally from Texas. He was a math geek in the best sense of the word, being into math and gaming but also kickboxing and motorcycles. We persuaded him to tutor Eirwyn, and he was wonderful: he didn't let Eirwyn slack off but was also really supportive, and Eirwyn did really well with him.

One day I mentioned my friend from high school who is a math professor at San Francisco City College. "That's where I got started loving math," Jeff said. "The advantage of the city colleges is that the teachers aren't doing research; they're really there for teaching. I had the best instruction there out of all the higher institutions I attended." So did he know professor X? "I think she only teaches evenings, and I attended during the day," he said, "but I definitely know the name." Does this mean there's a wormhole between San Francisco and Ouagadougou?

56

THE DANISH CONNECTION

Pomona College, ca. 1990; Ouagadougou, 2016

Some Danish friends of ours in Ouaga had an old friend of theirs to visit for a week or so, and they invited us over for an afternoon to meet her. The friend herself was American and had met our Danish friends overseas. We got talking a little bit about small-world stories, and I told her the following tale:

When I was studying Japanese language and literature at Pomona College, one of the long-standing professors there was Professor Stanley. He was definitely old-school, and one got the feeling he'd been delivering essentially identical lectures for twenty years or so (hence the yellowed pages in his notebook), but he knew his material really well.

One day his son came to speak at a brown-bag event in the foreign-languages dorm, which is where I resided. The son was a photojournalist and had been all over. He talked about the "most important organization no one has ever heard of," which was the CSCE, now OSCE (Organization for Security and Cooperation in Europe).

That organization wound up sending military observers to

Kosovo around 1998—armored personnel carriers painted orange, which were immediately dubbed "pumpkins"—and they've done a lot of election observation in places like Serbia, so I've had plenty of reason to pay attention to the them in the intervening years.

But the really interesting story he had to tell was about his reporting from Tiananmen Square in 1989 (which was only a year or two before this story happened). He'd been there for a couple of weeks photographing the action, but as things started to really tense up, he was compelled to stay in his hotel room. From this spot he couldn't see the square, but he did have a view of one of the roads leading into it.

This road happened to be the site of the famous stand-off between a lone Chinese citizen and a string of tanks that were heading into the square, an event captured in the iconic "tank man" photograph that is one of the most frequently used images associated with the events of the time.

The younger Stanley also took some photos. After the crackdown, he knew that the Chinese authorities would be trying to confiscate any film that foreign journalists had. Stuck in his hotel room as he was, what to do? In the end he found an air vent in the ceiling of his bathroom, into which he deposited all his film and notebooks—for his notes could also be used to implicate individuals. When he later had the film developed, though, there was nothing that could beat that famous tank-man photograph. Or so he thought.

A good ten years later there was a story in the *Pomona College Magazine* about the younger Stanley and Tiananmen Square. What really caught my eye was the reference to hiding the film in the ceiling vent in the bathroom. Hey, I remember this story! And it was this film that was the central attraction, namely:

Some seven or eight years after the crackdown in 1989, a group of journalists got together to catalogue all the photographs taken of the events, including ones that hadn't previously been published. So the younger Stanley dutifully sent in copies of the photos he had, including the ones from the street heading into the square. Immediately the archive team knew they had something special on their hands, which the journalist himself had not been able to recognize in his own work.

The photo in question captures that same stand-off between the lone citizen and the line of tanks, only some seconds beforehand, so the tanks are still 100 meters or so away. Presumably it was this lack of immediate confrontation that made Mr. Stanley think that his photograph was not worth much.

What the archivists recognized, however, was the incredible power of seeing this man, shopping bags in hand, *already standing* in the path of the tanks even when they were still some distance off. It poignantly demonstrates the courage of this man, who easily had time to get out of the way, but took his ground and held it.

The part of this photograph that always gives me goosebumps is in the upper left corner, where you can see another man on a bicycle, frantically pedaling away and throwing a panicked glance back over his shoulder. The contrast between his desperation to get away and the calm premeditation of the "tank man" shows just how courageous the decision was to stand his ground.

"Oh," said the friend of the Danish friends, as I finished my story, "How funny you know Professor Stanley. He is a good friend of ours!"

57

MEANING WELL

Croatia, ca. 1996

I don't want to tell too many tales here that I heard from other people, but this one just tickled my fancy. It was relayed to me by a BPT colleague from our Split office. At the time, the Croatia team was traveling into the Krajina zone to check on the few Serbs who remained there. The Krajina had been the Serb breakaway area from Croatia as it was fighting for its independence from then-Yugoslavia. The Croat armed forces re-took the area in 1995, expelling the Serb population and provoking what was at that time the largest human migration in Europe since WWII.

Many of these people settled in Bosnia, but some went on to Serbia, where they were largely denied humanitarian assistance because (rump) Yugoslavia considered them internally displaced persons (i.e., not having crossed an international border). They used the prospect of aid as an enticement to get the refugees to settle in Kosovo and thus boost the number of Serbs there, where they were largely housed in collective centers. This was the population that Eddie's organization originally came into Kosovo to serve.

The BPT team (called *Otvorene Oči* or "open eyes" in Croatia) would make a small tour through the Krajina, visiting those who stayed at their homes, checking on whether everyone had received the assistance they were due.

Now these folks, who were largely elderly, didn't have much social contact now that the area had been cleared of almost all its people. So inevitably the team would be offered some kind of schnapps (usually *rakija*—a bit like ouzo but pleasantly free from any aniseed flavor) at each place they stopped, from first thing in the morning right through the day.

One time they stopped at the farmhouse of an old woman, who welcomed them into her house as usual. When asked whether she was getting any aid visits, she began to complain about the various soldiers who had come through. From her description of the uniforms, the volunteers were able to sketch out a rough timeline of who had come by: first the Serb Krajina troops, then the Croatian troops, then peacekeepers from various countries.

And then she described the Americans: "All those other soldiers, they helped me by chopping my wood for the fire. But then these ones [the Americans] came, and they chopped my firewood, and they chopped it into these little, tiny pieces, look! Look how they ruined my firewood! Now it is all going to burn so quickly and it won't last the winter. What am I going to do?"

58

THE SIEGE OF SARAJEVO

Sarajevo, 2007-2009

If you're any good with dates then you know the siege of
Sarajevo was not in 2007, but over a decade earlier. What I
found interesting was the way people would reminisce about the
war or weave memories of it into their everyday experiences in
2007. At first I was a bit taken aback, to hear these things
discussed so matter-of-factly, but then I decided it was a sign of
having incorporated those events in a way that honored them
without being ruled by them. And folks were surprisingly willing
to reminisce.

"Ever since the war, I can't stand waiting in line."

"If there's one thing I can't eat since the war, it's rice."

"Oh, yes, we all know how to knit. It was one of the few
things you could do during the war when the power was out for
days or weeks at a time."

My friend Alma (a saint among women, who took any excuse
to show up at the office with homemade baklava) even told me
that she kind of enjoyed the war, in a way. Everyone was pulling

together, and there wasn't much to do so they'd get together and just hang out. I got the feeling that if you could get over the basic fear that was part and parcel of the situation, there was a certain quality to the time spent with friends and neighbors that was lost once the hustle and bustle of regular life took over.

59

WHY SARAJEVO IS NOT A HUB AIRPORT

Sarajevo, Vienna, and beyond, 2007-2009

When I was first hired by my organization, I was based in Sarajevo (airport code SJJ) but also covering Serbia (BEG), Albania (TIR), Kosovo (PRN), Moldova (KIV) and Bulgaria (SOF). I got to almost all of these destinations with Austrian Airways, through their hub in Vienna (VIE). And if you care to look at a map, you will see that Vienna is in the *wrong direction* when trying to get to countries *east* of Bosnia and Herzegovina.

Though later, when I started also covering Lebanon and Egypt, I had the great pleasure of transiting through Istanbul, which would have been fine except that the flights out of Beirut (BEY) and Cairo (CAI) generally left at oh dark thirty.

The thing about Sarajevo is fog. The city sits in a big bowl surrounded by mountains, which in turn are surrounded by bigger mountains. Besides making it ideal for a siege, this structure aids navigation in the city enormously, because you can always just head downhill and you'll find the river, which will orient you.

When we moved into our house, Eddie being a keen gardener, we asked about the growing season. Since we were up the slope a bit, the landlord said something about not seeing the sun for four months come winter. How wistfully I remember that I first took this to be an exaggeration.

That bowl landscape of Sarajevo brings two phenomena that are not great for aviation: thunderstorms, and fog. The fog is actually insane. Being from northern California and having spent time in San Francisco, I thought I understood fog, but in Sarajevo it was so thick you couldn't see the next lane over in traffic. I heard stories of people needing to guide in the pizza-delivery guy in by flashlight because the visibility was so poor. The thunderstorms seemed pretty normal from the ground, but apparently if you are in a small-ish plane trying to fly through one, they are not fun.

They can also start and stop pretty suddenly. So Option #1 for Making Air Travel Fun is the threat of thunderstorm. It might be raging at the time you are scheduled to take off, or you might have been in the air for an hour when they announce that the weather has changed (or not changed as hoped) and the plane would be returning to VIE.

At times passengers would do this three or four times over the course of a day, each time hoping for a window in the weather that would allow them to land. You know you're in trouble when the ground crew take your boarding pass with the words, "Bye, good luck! We hope we don't see you again!" The alternative was to land in Skopje (Macedonia) or Dubrovnik (Croatia) and be bused up, which, taking easily eight hours, probably took longer than waiting for a break in the weather would have.

Option #2 is pretty much the same as Option #1, only the cause is fog rather than thunderstorm. At the time, the Sarajevo airport did not have the radar to allow planes to land in fog; it was visual only. So every time the visibility wasn't great, the planes were stuck. Nothing out, nothing in, sometimes for a whole day if the fog was feeling ornery. This leads to—

Option #3 is being left to sleep in the airport. You'd get a sandwich and a bottle of water, and then try to bed down on the seats. These were those molded-plastic things all joined up in banks of four or five, i.e., not quite the bed with slightly too-soft springs that I could look forward to at home.

Option #4 was the leave-at-three, eight-hours-in-transit scenario. A typical flight from Cairo might have me trying to sleep at 8 or 9 pm, waking up just in time to be picked up at midnight, driving an hour to the airport to check in and then sitting for an hour after that. You'd get to Istanbul around 6 am, and the connecting flight to Sarajevo might be at 2:30 pm.

There was a particular bank of seats just below a Starbucks where there generally weren't many passengers and you could get a good couple of hours in if you played your cards right. A couple of colleagues of mine who also worked a lot in the Middle East had found other gates that were quiet at that time of the morning. At some point you'd give up and be "awake", trying maybe to read but not succeeding much. And at 1:30 you'd trek over to the gate for the Sarajevo flight, only to hear that the flight was delayed because of Option #1....

60

IN WHICH I TAKE THREE DAYS TO TRAVEL FOUR HOURS

Lusaka, Johannesburg, Antananarivo, ca. 2011

I promise I won't regale you with too many travel stories, but this one is special. I was supposed to go to Antananarivo (Tana), Madagascar, a week or so before Easter. There are a couple of ways to go from Lusaka to Tana, but the most straightforward one is to fly to Johannesburg and then take an Airlink flight on to Madagascar. However, Airlink does not fly every day.

The thing was that if I was going to take Airlink and work a full Monday-Friday week with the Mada team, I would be traveling back on Easter Sunday, which seemed unfair to me and my family. So instead of flying Sunday to Sunday, I decided to go on Saturday, which meant taking Air Madagascar from Jo'burg to Tana. The flight down from Lusaka was normal enough, and I got in at around 9:00 am. I had to get my second boarding pass in a little transit area, and when I arrived the flight wasn't posted yet, so I sat down to wait.

I waited, and I waited. There were two gentlemen next to me who were, I was pretty sure, speaking Malagasy, so I introduced myself and asked whether they had any news on the flight. They told me they'd heard it had been canceled, so they were trying to figure out what to do. I went and asked around, and basically got the idea that someone from the handling service was supposed to come deal with us. So we waited a bit more, and a bit more. Apparently, there weren't many passengers caught in limbo like we were, so we weren't the priority.

My new friends were from the agriculture ministry in Madagascar, and had just been to a workshop on conservation agriculture. This was something I knew a little about, so we chatted a bit about that. Then the topic turned to our current predicament. One of them had traveled on his diplomatic passport, but the other had casually left his at home and used his personal one. Unfortunately, this meant that in the absence of a transit visa, he could not leave the airport.

Some two hours later, the handling-service guy arrived and escorted us to the transit hotel. Somewhere along the way we were given to understand that the President of Madagascar had commandeered Air Madagascar's only airplane, which is why we were stuck. An Air France plane was supposed to land in Tana the next day, and would be rerouted to then come pick up the stranded passengers and take them on to Tana.

Airport Guy brought us to the hotel and told us to sit tight for a few minutes and he would be right back. But I'd overheard his conversation with the hotel receptionist, who had clearly said that they were no longer accepting his company's vouchers. They went around and around for a bit, and the receptionist was holding firm, so I suspected it was going to be a while before we'd be getting our rooms.

The Malagasy colleagues asked whether there was a phone they could use to call home and tell their wives what was going on.

"Oh," sighed Airport Guy, "There are no public phones here, and we don't have a way to charge you on ours, so that would be really complicated." In exasperation, I let them use mine.

By the time Airport Guy came back, more like an hour had passed rather than 20 minutes. Somehow, he had sorted out the voucher issue, but now there were no rooms left in the transit hotel. At this point it was after 1 p.m., and we'd had nary a crumb to eat nor a drop to drink. Couldn't Airport Guy help us get something to eat? And the airport was hot; I was starting to shrivel. Nope, he said, he wasn't authorized to give us vouchers or anything.

So, now that we couldn't get rooms in the hotel, what was the plan? Well, the two of us with the good passports would be able to get vouchers to allow us to stay at a hotel in Jo'burg, but Mr. Regular Malagasy Passport was just going to have to overnight it in the airport. It made me feel sick. All night, in the Jo'burg airport? How depressing was that? But apparently there was no other way.

Mr. Diplomat and I were then taken to a back room where Airport Guy prepared our vouchers. It seemed to take forever. Again I asked for some water, and was told that the people who worked in the back there brought in their own water; there was no fountain or sink or anything.

Eventually Mr. Diplomat and I were about to be carted off to the hotel, when Airport Guy asked whether we wanted to pick up our suitcases. Well, given how much confidence this person inspired in me generally, there was no way I was leaving my suitcase to the vagaries of his company's bureaucracy. So I asked for it to be brought up, a process that took about another hour.

At this point it was about 6 pm I'd had nothing to eat or drink since the plane from Lusaka to Jo'burg that morning, and had been waiting around basically all day. As a last piece of information before I got on the shuttle, Airport Guy told me that we'd been booked on a special Airlink flight at 7 the following morning, and so should be at the airport by 6.

Now the really surreal part started. We were put up in hotels that are part of a huge gambling complex just outside the airport. Convenient for the airport dudes, I suppose, but a serious culture shock. We're talking gold on white, marble everywhere, huge mirrors, chandeliers, the works. But my room was decent and not too tacky, and there were a number of good restaurants to choose from (in a gallery with a ceiling painted like the sky). I had Italian and paid with my voucher, so all was good.

The next day I took the bus and got to the terminal at 6 as directed, but couldn't find my flight. I walked between A and B terminal a couple of times, and then finally just walked up to an Airlink counter to find out what was going on.

"Oh, that flight? It just left."

Turns out they had pushed the departure time forward and not informed me. "We tried to call you, but you weren't in your room," they said. Well yeah, because I was out eating dinner. Imagine! And they couldn't have tried again an hour later?

"It doesn't matter, anyway," I was told, "there weren't enough seats for everyone in your group. We'll call someone from the handling service for you."

And so I waited, and waited, for about an hour, at which point I was approached by Airport Guy #2. In his defense, he was much nicer than #1 had been. He seemed to actually care about the inconvenience we were being put through, and the ping-ponging with the information.

"Please tell me that that Malagasy man who slept in the airport got a seat on that plane," I said.

"I don't think so," he replied, regretfully.

A bit more waiting around and then we were sent back to the same gambling complex for the second night. It was a different hotel this time, but the same idea. This was when I found the true value of my Kindle, as I had a huge selection of books to choose from, and no danger of running out of reading material.

The following day (day three, Monday), I went to the airport as instructed and checked in to my Airlink flight. And who should I see as I headed down to the gate, but our old friend Mr. Normal Passport! He was sitting on the floor leaning with his back on a pillar, looking like he'd had time to get used to the pose.

"It's not so bad," he said. At least the second night they'd taken pity on him and given him an emergency transit visa or something, so he could at least get out of the airport and sleep in a bed. But he'd not retrieved his luggage, so he'd not been able to change his clothes or brush his teeth, poor guy.

Our flight was delayed, but eventually we were able to board. We'd gotten all settled in our seats, when the pilot came on and told us there was a fault with the plane, and we'd have to get off while they made their repairs. So off we came, and we sat around for another two hours or so, and finally at about 11:00 we were able to depart.

And so it was that I landed at the end of the working day on Monday, exactly as if I had gone Airlink to begin with.

61

HOW I SAW "CHESS" THE MUSICAL LIVE

July, 1988

S ome travel stories stick with you because they were particularly hideous or funny, and then there are the ones that form you, the ones that teach you that you can get through anything. My first such experience was the summer I graduated from high school. The youth orchestra I played in was doing a tour in Austria and Germany, for two weeks after graduation.

Then, instead of going straight back home, I was going to meet my wonderful dance teacher and a bunch of her students for a dance camp near London. And after that, as my graduation present from my dad, the two of us plus my newly minted stepmom were supposed to go to Scotland and romp around the lands of our Scottish heritage, nosing about in local church records and such to find out more about the bits of the Mackintosh clan that we were related to.

As it happened, though, I got a phone call from my father about halfway through the Austria-Germany trip, saying that Bea had had to have surgery on her knee and she wasn't going to be able to walk well enough, so the Scotland trip was off. Now remember that it was 1988 and I was still a kid, so I didn't have a credit card, and it was the days before electronic tickets. So Dad promised he'd sent a new ticket and some cash, which I received a few days before my flight to London.

When the day came, it turned out that a couple of other kids from the orchestra were flying home via London, so one of the chaperones asked if I didn't prefer to go with them. I said sure, not because I was nervous in particular about taking the flight alone, but it seemed like it would make the grownups happier. The chaperone went off and changed my ticket, and I duly flew with them to London.

This is where the real fun starts. The day before I was due to fly back to the US, I called the airline to confirm my ticket— remember those days? There was a lot of silence coming at me from the other end of the line, and she confirmed my name a couple of times.

Finally, she confessed she had no record of me on that flight. I said something really intelligent like "wuuuuh?" We went around in circles a little bit, until she realized that I'd changed my flight and never told the airline I wasn't taking the flight I'd originally booked to London. At this point, deciding I was a flake and not actually doing my trip, the airline had canceled all forward reservations, i.e., everything my father had organized as the backup plan.

"Oh," I said. "Oh." A pause while I take this in. "And what do I do now?"

There was a ticketing office in London somewhere, so the thing to do was find it the following day and use the ticket I had to get a new reservation. I jotted down the address and, with the help of the concierge at the lodge where we were staying, figured out roughly where it was.

And then it turned out that Margaret, another girl in the group, also had to stay an additional day before heading back, so we agreed to stick together. We found a youth hostel and threw our bags in, and then it was only 4 pm or so, so we decided we might as well see a show. We went to a little kiosk thing where you could buy tickets, and looked at the posters advertising the shows on offer. We hemmed and hawed a bit, and then decided on *Chess*, knowing nothing about it at all.

So that was how we wound up, on a day when I should have been in the air on the way home, not entirely sure where we were or whether we were going to get any sleep that night, watching a really rather spectacularly wonderful musical. And if you've never heard of it, don't feel bad: you're in a big club. There's a song, "One Night in Bangkok", that you might recognize if it was played at you, but I don't think the musical made that much of a splash, which is too bad.

It's one of those things that never became widely known and yet is exceedingly popular in the circles of "those in the know". I absolutely loved it, and was momentarily comforted by the thought that I wouldn't have had this special experience, had our original plans not gone haywire.

After a dodgy night in the youth hostel, I was now truly ready to go home. I'd been away for three weeks, and although at least during that last bit I was able to navigate in English, the whole situation was wearing on me. So I headed out on the tube toward the airport, leaving what I thought would be enough time, because I just couldn't believe it could take over an hour. Well, anyone who's been to London is now laughing at my innocence, but there you are. So I arrived at the airport technically within the window to check in, but sufficiently toward the end.

As I was working my way toward the front of the check-in line, I came to understand that they had overbooked the flight (shocking, I know) and were asking for people to volunteer to travel the following day. I have to say it never even crossed my mind to step forward, even though there was nothing waiting for me per se. I was done with the uncertainty and having to pretend I wasn't scared out of my mind at some level.

So when I finally got to the front and they told me there was no seat for me, I fought to hold back tears. I was just so done: the cancellation of the Scotland trip, the changed flight to London, the shock when I realized I didn't have a reservation to get home, and now I had a reservation and still couldn't get on the bloody plane. Were the fates just against me?

In the end they put me on another flight to Portland and then down to San Francisco, and the super catch was that the Portland flight also didn't have a lot of seats, so they put me in first class. The first benefit of this was that I could use the spiffy lounge, but even better than that, they let me use their telephone to call home and alert them I was coming in on a different flight.

In the actual airplane, I mostly felt embarrassed, showing up in the poshest part of the plane in my jeans and tennis shoes, and not being exactly freshly washed. Having more space was great, and the food was good, but for some reason the seats up on the second floor didn't have the entertainment system, so no movies! But I think I slept a lot of the flight, anyway. After this everything went smoothly enough. I don't even remember the transfer to the Portland-San Francisco flight. But my mother was there to pick me up, and finally I was home.

62

IN WHICH I HUMILIATE MYSELF IN JAPANESE

July, 1990

The summer after my second year at college I went to do a 6-week intensive course at the International Christian University in Tokyo. I tried to pack fairly lightly, but I was also trying to test out of a music-history course and so had a bunch of books and scores with me. Not so light. I had to arrive the day before registration for the course because of how the planes landed, but a Japanese student at Pomona had given me her phone number and said I could stay at her place that night. I just needed to call her when I landed.

Which I duly tried to do—and got ringing and ringing. So I figured she'd stepped out, no problem. I picked a seat and waited about half an hour, and then called again. Same thing. I waited another hour, fighting off jetlag and the urge to sleep, and then tried again: still nothing. At this point it was getting on towards four or later in the afternoon, so I gave up and decided to get a hotel for the night.

I went to the tourist bureau and asked for help booking a room. They asked what kind I wanted, and I asked for a *ryokan*, or traditional Japanese-style inn, since they were cheaper than a hotel. Rather than booking the room on my behalf, the tourist helper dialed the number for me and then handed me the phone. Gulp.

I did just about well enough to order a room without a bath (the cheapest), at which point the woman on the other end of the phone says, "*matte imasu*" [I'm waiting]. Rather desperately, I'm trying to figure out what she's waiting for, but she just keeps repeating, "*matte imasu, matte imasu.*"

In desperation, I pass the phone to the tourist-bureau lady, who jabbers something quickly into the phone and then puts it down. I think she just said I was an ignorant foreigner and one had not to pay attention to my strange behavior. And then she explained to me that "We're waiting" is just a phrase to end the conversation, in the sense of "OK, we're waiting for your arrival." Oh. You couldn't have helped me a little earlier?

I then had to take a train out to the neighborhood where the inn was. I left the station, and was hit by a wave of hot, humid air. They'd said to head straight for a bit and then turn left, but nothing was matching the description they'd given me. Instead, I was in the middle of pachinko madness; every shop I was passing seemed to be a pachinko parlor. Lots of neon and flashing lights assaulted my eyes, though this being Japan, it didn't feel particularly seedy. I walked around the block probably about three times, lugging my super heavy suitcase behind me, and for the life of me I couldn't relate what I was seeing to the directions I'd been given.

Feeling foolish and miserable, I went back inside the train station, where I figured out that I'd exited from the wrong side. Coming out the other direction, I was greeted but a much more rural view, and *there* was the bridge I was supposed to cross. Again, I hauled my suitcase up the hill to the inn, my arms quite sore at this point and rather covered in sweat from the exertion in the humidity.

I'd love to say that the inn folk welcomed me warmly, but the only heat involved was coming from their reaction to my bedraggled state. Of course I'd not intended to stay in a Japanese-style inn, and so had not worried about my footwear, which is why I had rucked up wearing only Birkenstocks and—crucially—no socks.

I knew I couldn't wear my shoes on the tatami mats, so I made to take them off, which brought forth gasps of horror from my hosts. My knowledge of Japanese having pretty much flown out the window and their knowledge of English being essentially nonexistent, the main hostess was reduced to crying "Japaneezu stayru! Japaneezu stayru!" Wow. So helpful. Because I had no idea that you were supposed to do things "Japanese style" in a Japanese-style inn.

She motioned at me to wait and then dashed off into the bowels of the inn, coming back some minutes later with a wet dishcloth in her hand. She then had me sit down on the couple of steps leading up from the entrance to the tatami mats, removed my shoes and started cleaning my feet like a child, all the while repeating her "Japanese style" mantra over and over. I thought I would cry from the humiliation.

Finally I was shown my room and left to my own devices. I hadn't eaten or drunk since the plane, so I was hungry but even more urgent was the thirst. There was a thermos of hot water to make tea with, so I kept filling the little teacup and waiting for the water to cool some before drinking it.

At some point another one of the *ryokan* staff came and beckoned for me to follow him. He took me to another, empty, room, one with a shower and *ofuro*, the very hot bath that one traditionally enters after one has washed off—and I mean really, very, ouchily hot. It's brilliant and definitely one of Japan's best inventions.

But I had asked for and wanted to pay for a room without a shower. When I protested, the staff member protested right back at me, and basically made it plain that I was considered too filthy to be allowed to sleep on their floor. So once again I swallowed by pride and took a shower, and went in the *ofuro*, allowing myself to feel my body finally relaxing after the long flight and all the tension since.

Making my way back to my room, I had a few more cupfuls of water and then decided to turn in for the night. The bed was also very Japanese style, a thin futon on the floor, and another thin coverlet. It wasn't uncomfortable, but I had trouble falling asleep out of jetlag, a mixture of replaying the day I'd just had and knowing I had to figure out the busses the next day. Finally, in the wee hours, I managed to drop off into a light sleep, only to be jolted awake at around four in the morning by a decent-sized earthquake.

Now, being from California, I am used to earthquakes, so they don't usually phase me. But I wasn't prepared for the Japanese earthquakes, which are caused by subsidence rather than two plates rubbing together. The action of one plate passing under another one causes earthquakes that are more like rolling waves, rather than the jolty kind you get in CA. They also, in my opinion, last longer. There were certainly several per day, which was a totally different experience. Anyway, this was my first one in Japan, and it really did startle me. I lay there with my heart pounding and feeling grateful that there weren't any high shelves in the room.

The following day I managed the busses, no idea how, and made it to the program on time.

My roommate was nice enough, a woman in her early 20s

married to a Marine. She was from Florida, but there were program participants from all over the world.

This made for a rather interesting atmosphere when Iraq invaded Kuwait, around the middle of our time there. I think what hit me was that everyone really felt it, even if their country was not at risk of getting embroiled in any kind of counter-action. It was so weird being outside of the US while the discussion there was so hot about what should be done.

And what then brought it all home was the reports my roommate was bringing me from her Marine husband. He was gearing up to be deployed, and he used their code word for when things are really hitting the fan. It felt like having a little window into what was happening behind the scenes, even as the possibility of a military response was in early discussions among the international community.

And then there was the time my friend Amy and I traveled to Yokohama to visit her old host family in a typhoon...

63

IN WHICH I PRACTICE MY CROATIAN

Split, Croatia, ca. August, 1997

B alkan Peace Team was not really an organization in and of itself. It was a project formed by a bunch of peacebuilding organizations such as the International Forum for Reconciliation, Peace Brigades International, War Resisters' International, a couple of church groups, that kind of thing. There was a kind of steering committee made up of representatives of these organizations, to which we sent our regular reports and generally justified how we were spending our time.

We did send regular updates and sometimes special messages if something really important came up, but even with some basic writing in code, there was a lot we felt we couldn't say via e-mail, because for all we knew the Serbian state was monitoring us. This wasn't a completely self-important idea: the first volunteer to go to Kosovo had been interrogated by the police, declared persona non grata, and deprived of all of her notebooks, some of which obviously contained sensitive information. So everybody understood that regular face-to-face meetings were very important.

One such meeting was in Split, on the Croatian coast. It's

actually a beautiful little city, well worth a visit. Anyway we had our meeting there over three or four days. The problem started on day one when we realized that the secretary, the one person paid by BPT, had canceled at the last minute because she was sick—and so no one had brought our money!

Normally, she'd bring a couple thousand deutschmarks for both the Croatia/Krajina team and us, the Serbia/Kosovo team. We'd spirit this money into our respective countries and then use it for all of our expenses. The countries were not really using credit cards yet, and Serbia at least was cut off from the European banking system because of the sanctions. Anyway, suffice it to say that we were operating on a strictly cash basis, so the expected transfusion was very necessary.

And so the following plan was hatched: Each member of the steering committee would go to the ATM every day and take out the daily limit their card would allow, which would unfortunately all be in (Croatian) kuna, so then Team Belgrade would have to use the kuna to buy dollars, which we could use in Serbia to buy dinar.

In this way, over the course of the workshop we quietly built up quite the mass of kuna. It then fell to a colleague and me to go change the Serbian half. It turned out that the maximum dollars you could buy from any one exchange agent was $3,000. I remember it exactly because this is the sentence I had to have ready for every exchange agent we went to: "I want to buy $3,000."

Sounds straightforward enough, right? I mean, I was allegedly working in Serbian. Ah—but here's the catch. What used to be the Serbo-Croatian language has now split into essentially four constituent parts: Serbian, Croatian, Bosnian, and Montenegrin. Believe me when I tell you that the differences between the four are less than those between US and British English. It was all politics, and countries wanting to establish their own sense of identity separate from Serbia and separate from the former Yugoslavia.

The point of all this is that it was going to be very uncool for me to speak Serbian in the exchange agent's. I would have said: *Hoću da kupim tri hiljada dolara.* But the Croats would say: *Hoću kupati tri tisuća dolara.* Maybe the difference doesn't look that big to you, but it's big enough when you're nervous and unsure how exactly you are going to be treated if they identify you as a Serb…. Who knows, maybe I was exaggerating the danger, but it still made me really nervous.

And then there was the factor that we were trying to amass pretty large sums of money, maybe $15,000? for Team Belgrade to take back with us. We were probably breaking some kind of law, and I definitely did the next day when I smiled sweetly at the customs officer and said I had nothing to declare. It's amazing how well you can lie when you have your story all set up ahead of time.

So there go my colleague and I, into the first exchange place. I duly stumble over the request, but it's OK. We've prepared the kuna ready to go—and of course I am only allowed to buy *deviza* or hard currency because I'm a foreigner, so there were forms and things to be filled out, my passport number to be taken down.

But finally we were done, so we moved on to the second exchange agent. And then the third. At this point my colleague's bag was getting pretty full of money, so when I brought out the $3,000—in 100-dollar bills, mind you—and she tried to put it in her bag, she shoved her hand in and a huge waft of kuna came flying out all over the street.

We did eventually get it all, and I did my juju thing with the customs official on the bus, and back we came to Belgrade, with coffers replenished.

64

HAPPY BIRTHDAY TO THE RESCUE

November, 2012

My wonderful friend and colleague, Robert, is a bit of a conundrum. He often walks around with his passport in his pocket, which is a good reminder that he is, in fact, American, even though he doesn't sound like it. Having been raised mostly in southern Africa in a missionary family, he didn't have the full-on White African accent, but his speech was definitely influenced by same.

Robert does agriculture, and in such a way that in order to be able to conceive and write good funding proposals, I essentially deputized myself to him for about two years. We had an awful lot of fun together, also with his wife and mother-in-law.

One of the interesting things about Robert is that while quite the pacifist in some ways, he is an avid hunter. Certain rooms in the house have very large deer and buffalo heads mounted on the wall. It's surprisingly un-tacky, but intimidating as hell. Those heads are *big*. The family also has an ashtray made from a buffalo testicle—you're welcome.

The year Eirwyn turned 13 was a bit of a Charlie Foxtrot, to be honest. He'd invited a select few friends over, and in the end none of them could come. The last person canceled the morning of, so we were left pretty high and dry. The only thing I could think of that would be fun for him was to go shooting with Robert for the first time. Thankfully, said shooting master was available and we heaved a sigh of relief.

So that weekend our whole family piled into the car and followed Robert down to the shooting range. As Robert was setting up, he was also giving Eirwyn a lesson in gun safety. This is why, if Eirwyn was going to learn to shoot, I wanted him to do it with Robert—he is all about safety. He'll even leave the range if other patrons are behaving too dangerously, just to get out of the way. So he gave Eirwyn all the rules, things like 1. Never put your finger on the trigger unless you intend to shoot, and 2. Never point the gun at something you don't intend to kill.

Now Eddie and Marion were not keen on the loud noise and the general shooting thing, so they went to a hut some distance behind the shooting stands and drank tea. I, however, was not to be outdone by my punk son, and so stuck around with the intention of getting a few shots in myself (having never shot a gun before in my life). We started with a small rifle, a .626, at 100 meters and then 200. Eirwyn of course went first, and acquitted himself very well. Robert was super patient and calm, just the thing you want when handling live ammunition.

I should note here for the record that the only thing we were killing was pieces of paper. Later, when we felt like going shooting again, Robert and I would say, "I think those pieces of paper are multiplying; time for a cull," and nod knowingly at each other.

Eirwyn and I both got to take home our bits of paper, with the cluster of holes clearly marked. This was apparently the thing to look for, not making bullseyes, but being a consistent shooter so that the three bullet holes were nicely close together.

After the rifle, we tried a handgun. Good heavens, that thing was heavy. And you start to appreciate how inexact they are at any real distance, so all those cop shows where you see someone aiming really well with a handgun while driving and smoking and calling his mother at the same time, fuggedaboudit. Our mission was to shoot little plastic bottles filled with water; this made them suitably spectacular when hit. I liked the rifle better, though.

And now I have to say that through this exercise, I got a different idea about hunting. I'm still not sure how I feel about shooting wild animals, though as Robert points out, if you do it responsibly (only if there is a male you can target, and then only if that animal isn't sitting in front of another animal in case the bullet goes through, and only if you can get a good heart shot where you can be relatively sure of killing the animal more or less instantly), you are taking down an animal that has lived a healthy and happy life, and which experiences no stress prior to being killed—which are certainly not things you can say for our "modern" meat industry.

The permit costs a fair amount of money, which goes toward keeping the nature reserve free of encroachment and also supports the villages surrounding it. Once you've killed an animal, you're allowed to take the head and a few choice bits of the animal, but the rest also goes to the nearby villages.

Doing the actual shooting, I gained an appreciation for how still and calm you have to be to pull off a good shot. I took forever lining up just to take one, and that was with bean bags to support the gun and relatively little in the way of distractions such as wind. Then I imagined tracking a group of animals for two or three days, camping in the wild wherever you find your-self, trying to come up on the group from the right direction, finding a target that matches the constraints above, and then having to get super calm and still in yourself to be able to squeeze the trigger and not jump at the loud noise and the recoil.

Now, I might still prefer to go through all the steps outlined above only to "shoot" with a camera instead of a gun, but my point is that I came away kind of understanding why (responsible) hunters do it.

And then, of course, there is the meat. When we arrived in Lusaka, Robert's wife kept mentioning the buffalo leg in her freezer and how it needed to get eaten one day. A couple of years later, the day had come: I think they'd intended to do steaks, but they did brochettes (kebobs) in the end. In my veggie-ness I did not partake, but everyone said it was wonderful. Even Marion, who was often only so-so on meat that needed chewing, munched with gusto.

In case you were wondering, Eirwyn's birthday turned out great. After the time at the range we went to a beautiful house owned by some friends of Robert. Instead of being one building, they had separated the kitchen and living room from the bath and also the bedroom. And all the rooms were open at the top: they had a thatched roof but there was a significant gap between the walls and the roof. We worried about mosquitoes but they assured us that mosquitoes don't generally fly that high. We had hamburgers and such, and a cake, and sang happy birthday, and in the end it was a wonderful day for all of us.

Marion and Eddie never did shoot, but Eirwyn and I went back a couple of times. I think Robert had more fun teaching Eirwyn than if he'd been shooting, himself.

65

MEET YOUR INTREPID WILDLIFE HUNTERS

Kiambi, Zambia 2009

One thing we never got to do in Rwanda was camp, in part because there was only a tiny part of the country where you really could. But Zambia, now that is a country that knows how to do its natural parks. It is home to the South Luangwa National Park, a vast area where you can see just about every wild animal on the map, and even the North Luangwa, which is supposed to be even more beautiful but requires a very sturdy 4x4 and some serious survival skills to enjoy.

Wanting to start small, however, and not knowing how the kids would react to the sleeping in tents and such, we decided on the Kiambi National Park, which is a smaller one down by where the Kafue and Zambezi rivers come together. There aren't huge amounts of wildlife, but it's easy enough to camp there and there are little tours and things you can do. And the campground is right on the river—though up a steep embankment, which is good for not getting stomped on by a hippo or eaten by a croc in the middle of the night.

So looking forward to this trip, I tried to keep my expectations low. No broken bones, no snakes, and the kids having a decently good time. That's it.

Down we drove, then, about 3½ hours, and got to the campground at around 12:30. Taking the temperature of the group, I proposed that we eat our lunch first before setting up the tents, which was a good move. We spread our couple of blankets out on the lawn and put all the food out that we'd packed for said purpose up in Lusaka.

We'd been sitting there for all of five minutes, maybe not even that, when I looked up and saw the head of a snake traversing the spot just behind Eddie. "*Seriously?*" I thought. "I ask for three simple things, one of which was NO SNAKES! How hard can it be?"

And now I had a dilemma: I needed to let Eddie know of the snake in his proximity, but I risked startling the bejeezus out of him and scaring the kids, who were only 8 and 10 at the time. Also, I was a bit extra nervous because the snake was moving with its head held high, which is traditional black-mamba behavior. Black mambas, as I'm sure you know but I'm going to tell you anyway, are, famously, not black but green. The name comes from the black inside of their mouths. They are also very fast, can easily outrun a human, have a tendency to leap at people and attack before being provoked, something unique to this species.

In other words, they are some bad juju.

They're also not that common, so prudence told me it was probably not, in fact, a black mamba, but something more innocuous. Unfortunately, I was not well-versed in the snakes of Zambia and did not have the ability to calm myself with a reasonable assumption of an alternative. And I wasn't even sitting two feet away from it; that was Eddie.

I made some "subtle" motions to Eddie indicating that he should turn around slowly, which he did. Obviously, trying to get up and move our picnic would be a stupid idea, as it would attract the snake's attention and probably make it feel more threatened. So we had to just kind of sit there and watch it go by.

"Oh, look," I said now for benefit of the kids, "a snake. Isn't that cool?" (Because actually, I do like snakes and would normally be chuffed to have one so close, if only I knew it wasn't poisonous, which I didn't.) "Oh and look, it seems to be hunting that chameleon on the tree." And indeed, there was a chameleon on the trunk of a small tree, just a few feet high, next to our picnic area.

So we sold it as our very own episode of Animal Planet: Snake v Chameleon. The snake made a few lunges at the chameleon, which promptly climbed up the tree trunk a bit and then fell to the ground. "See? The chameleon is playing dead," Eddie said. And indeed, the snake went over and kind of poked at it, but the chameleon appeared to be dead. I guess snakes like to do their own killing, thank you very much. No prepped chameleon steaks in vacuum packaging for them.

Anyway it really was very entertaining, and the snake seemed sufficiently focused on the chameleon that we could relax a bit and eat our lunch.

After our picnic I went over to the office to tell the receptionist about the potential black mamba. "Ach no," she said, "it was probably just a tree snake. They are a little bit poisonous but they're pretty shy, and they don't usually bite." I tried to convince her about the way the snake was moving, but she was not to be perturbed. So I gave up and went back to our campsite, where we went ahead and put our tents down.

Quite common in the camping area were water monitors, which look vaguely like Komodo dragons but are much friendlier and less disgusting. They came up because of the sprinklers, which created pockets of cool moisture that they obviously liked. We christened our favorite Mathilda. Mathilda, the water monitor. She seemed to like the name; at least, she didn't object to it.

Our first night there we made our food, and the campground staff made us a bonfire, which was a thoroughly delicious thing, so the plan was just to sit around the fire for the evening and enjoy the outdoors. We weren't allowed to eat at the main restaurant (lodge guests only, none of this backpacker riffraff), but there was a little clubhouse where you could get chips and play pool. And, they had beer. So we ordered a few to take back with us to the campfire.

Well, we thought that any cold beer was a right luxury while camping, so imagine our pleasant surprise when the guy hauled out a small cooler and *chilled glasses*.

What I'll also always remember about that evening was that Marion picked a stick out of the fire that had just the tip glowing orange. In the dark, she started waving it around, making designs and writing words. It was just dark enough that you couldn't see the rest of the stick, just the orange glow at the tip, and the streak of orange it made when she moved the stick quickly. It was a bit like a 4th of July sparkler, only way, way cooler.

After our trip, when I was back in Lusaka, I looked up Zambian snakes on the Internet. A tree snake our friend was not: wrong color and wrong head. I looked through all the snakes, and the one it fit best, based on head shape and the moving with its head a foot off the ground, was no other than…. The black mamba. It is, of course, possible that I misremembered the snake's appearance (no, I didn't), but at any rate we could be very thankful for that courageous chameleon.

66

STUPID ANIMAL STORIES

W hat would tales of Africa be like without some fun with animals? OK, maybe some are not so fun. But many of them leave an impression.

Actually, the first one I want to tell you about is not an Africa story at all. When we lived in Sarajevo, we'd often sit outside when the weather permitted, drink some wine, and chat. Well, it transpired that a hedgehog or two lived somewhere close by, and if we paid attention, sometimes we could see them coming down the little hill to us. Sometimes they would get really close to us, and we could hear their little rustle as they walked around. It always felt like a benediction from nature, that the hedgehogs would feel comfortable enough in our garden to come out and play.

Also in Sarajevo we had fireflies, which I had never really experienced before, nor have since. It all seemed so terribly civilized and European.

In Kigali we had the friendly and the not-so-friendly. Baby praying mantises just being hatched are completely adorable. The problem is when they hide in your lettuce and you figure it out only when you stick your hand down there and it comes back out with a praying mantis' jaws clenched tightly around your finger. Those suckers can draw blood.

Part of the soundtrack of our lives in Kigali was this bird that would come and sit every morning on the bars on the window in the play room, see his reflection in the window, and tap at it. Bong, bong. Bong, bong, bong. Booong, bong, bong. A very unwelcome alarm clock.

Those were the friendly ones. Around year three of our five in Rwanda, a troop of vervet monkeys moved into our neighborhood. Now vervets look kind of cool: they have pale blue genitalia, and they have nice long tails and all that. I laugh now when I remember that a vervet monkey was the first animal I saw the first time I went to Nairobi National Park—and how I sat in awe and watched it for the longest time.

Well let me tell you, when they move into your neighborhood it stops being funny. A grown male vervet monkey is easily as tall as a three-year-old child, and about a gazillion times more powerful. When you have a three-year-old child in the house, you really don't want your kid running up against Mr. Monkey in any kind of confrontational way. And yet, although the monkeys moved into *our* neighborhood, they quickly decided they owned the place. It's a bit like Godzilla coming in and deciding he owns Disneyland.

Seeing as how monkeys live in troupes, it's not just one or two that come to hang around, it's several family groups. They moved around the neighborhood, so they weren't on our property all the time, but they liked the trees between us and our friends up the hill, and would sometimes come down into the trees by our front fence.

Once a medium-sized adult came up to the house and sat on the windowsill to the kids' playroom. I walked up to take a better look, and the monkey just sat there, looking at me. You're not supposed to anthropomorphize animals' behavior, but I swear this monkey was saying, "Go on, I dare you!" The only thing keeping this monkey outside was the mosquito screen which I'm pretty sure wouldn't have kept him out if he'd really wanted to get in.

The kids got so freaked out, if they saw monkeys, they'd run inside screaming, "the monkeys are coming, the monkeys are coming!" They never attacked any of our people, but they did harass the dog we briefly had. I think they were trying to play with him, but he wasn't having any of it, and, frankly, was no match for their superior numbers and agility. Or, he just didn't quite understand what they were aiming at.

The really annoying thing was that they ate our garden, specifically our guavas, and they went after our bananas as well. It should be noted that I am not a huge banana fan (especially if they are at all mushy or too sweet), but I really liked the bananas that grew in our garden. In fact, they were the only bananas I'd eat. They were small, just a few inches long, and even when the skins went yellow they had a kind of tangy flavor and firm consistency like a slightly under-ripe banana. Yum. We'd have to harvest the whole bunch of bananas a few days before they were ripe, and let them ripen in the garage, where we could close the door against monkey invasion.

At least they never made it into the house. There were some baboons that lived close to friends of ours in Nairobi, and if they ever left the window open, shwoop! any fruit on the counter would be gone, which you might kind of predict, but they'd also go after bread and other things.

There was a lodge in Akagera National Park in Rwanda, which at the time was nearly the only nature-touristy place in the country. The Akagera Lodge was abandoned and partially destroyed during the genocide, and sat unused for about ten years. During that time, a troop of baboons moved in and pretty much had the run of the place.

Then a South African company bought the lodge, renovated it and reopened it to the public. The renovation was nicely done, and the lodge started doing a pretty solid business. The only problem was those baboons. I guess no one explained to them that their home was now off-limits, so they hung around and had a habit of coming into people's rooms if they didn't leave the door locked. Again, not so much fun if your kids are roughly baboon-sized.

The epitome of scary for me was a field trip for the whole grade one in Eirwyn's school: that was about three busses full of six- and seven-year-olds. Never mind that one of the busses got stuck in the mud on the way down there. The kicker came when the teachers said it was time to start distributing chocolate croissants to all the kids. They had decided to do this in the parking lot, in full view of the baboons, who watched very carefully from the lodge's roof. I honestly thought there was going to be blood, but maybe for once the humans had the edge in terms of numbers.

Another touristic close encounter was with the relatively (at least locally) famous Fanta elephant, so called because he supposedly happily drank soda pop. There was a guy who wasn't his keeper, exactly, but could (sort of) handle and mollify him. The thing was, this elephant was one of those bulls that roams around in solitary, with no family group and no troop. This is known for making many bulls depressed and often a little bit loopy, and honestly Fanta doesn't help this situation. We stopped for the "show" once but felt so bad for the elephant that we kind of avoided him after that.

And that was just as well. We heard from some friends that they had been charged by the Fanta elephant, and their British diplomatic car had sustained some damage. They'd been really afraid because of all the kids in the car. Some time later, the US Department of State put out a travel warning for all US citizens, not exactly advising no travel to the park, but to avoid the area that the elephant was known to frequent. At that time (and it may still be the case) that was the only travel warning issued because of a wild animal in the history of travel warnings.

Another rather habituated animal was Hugo the hippo, who defied normal hippo behavior by coming out on the shore in broad daylight, at Eagles Rest resort. Hugo could often be seen wandering around close to the campsites, not lolling about exactly, but showing no urgency for getting back into the water.

My mother and I once stayed in a lodge just outside of South Luangwa National Park, where like the lodge in Akagera, the monkeys pretty much ruled the roost. Every mealtime the workers would chase the monkeys away by any means necessary (including slingshot), set the tables, and then after the meal immediately clear the remains away so as to save them from monkey attack. But in-between meals, it was monkey territory.

Said dining area was on the top of an escarpment, and looking down there were often entertaining scenes of elephants bathing, antelope scrapping, your basic wildlife show. One day a few of us hung back after lunch to enjoy the view. After we'd been there for about 10 minutes, one of the monkeys came down and made off with another guest's room key. The keys were on keychains made from palm nuts, which are light brown and roughly the size of a golf ball, with the room number inscribed into the nut. So that was annoying, because it was actually "siesta time" (they assume you'll want a nap in the afternoon after having risen early for the first safari of the day), meaning there weren't that many staff around.

And now this guest couldn't get into her room. We tried enticing the monkey down from the tree, but that was nothing doing; the monkey knew when it had a good snack on its hands. Eventually they found a replacement key.

Also potentially obnoxious are elephants, wonderful as they

are to watch. My mother and I were once mock charged while trying to get back to the lodge at the end of the day after a driving safari. In a mock charge, the elephant doesn't intend to actually ram into you; it just wants to scare the heck out of you so you'll go away. Well, at least with people, it's pretty darned effective. The problem in our situation was that we had to get past the elephant to get to the lodge, but the road passed too close for her comfort to her and her baby.

I have to say I was rather proud of myself for not panicking, or at least not allowing panic to rule my actions. Instead of backing up at top speed, which was tempting but I figured would be an invitation to run after us, I just carried on our path at a moderately slow pace. I hoped that would show that we were in fact getting out of the way without making it look too much like we were making a hasty retreat.

Our friend Robert (of shooting fame) took great delight in warning us about adolescent (male) elephants, who apparently like nothing more than a little mock charging at everything that moves, just to prove their mettle. He told us this while Eddie's sister and her partner were visiting from Belfast: they already thought it was impossibly hot, and now they were being warned of adolescent elephants that wanted to charge them!

In the event, we did come across one such. We rounded a bend and there the little guy was, and sure enough, he gave us a real send-off! Of course the really little ones are achingly cute, especially when they haven't learned to use their trunks properly yet and so kind of fumble all over everything. They're also a little scary because they're so curious, they'll come right up to your truck, and you never know how Mama is going to react to that!

The downside in the Madagascar forest, I discovered, was leeches. The paths are pretty uneven, and then sometimes you are asked to go off the path and into the forest, which can be quite steep. So the natural thing is to hold on to the trees as one passes by. Only the trees have leeches. And they're teeny little things, just a little string, so they're easy to miss. And one thing you don't particularly want to discover is a leech that's been hanging out on you for some time.

Then there's when the wild things come find you closer to home. One of the wonderful things about the streets of Ouaga is that while donkeys are the main work animal, you are fully likely to see a random camel wandering down the street (with an owner, for sure), or sometimes a horse being trotted around the neighborhood.

Another one we got our fair share of was bats, foreign and domestic. In Rwanda they would hang around in the trees and come out at nightfall, occasionally whizzing past you if you were sitting outside. The ones in Lusaka were really big; you could be excused for thinking they were seagulls. The Ouaga bats were a little smaller, but what was weird about them was that they'd come out in the afternoon, when it was still really light. Not at all bat-like behavior, as far as I knew.

Then there were the ones that made a nest in the attic of the house where some friends of ours lived. They were small and could pass through a circular hole maybe an inch and a half wide. Every day at six they would emerge to go feed, and it was like nothing I'd ever seen. They just streamed out of these little air holes in the attic, and the sound of their radar was a bit overwhelming. We were told not to get too close because if you were standing where they emerged in great numbers, you risked getting anointed with some nice guano. Good fertilizer—not so nice on your clothes.

In Kigali we really wanted to have bunnies, especially since Eddie had had some as a kid and was very enamored of them. So we got some raised boxes (so they couldn't dig their way out) and put a couple in with the idea of getting bunny babies. We got a couple of litters, but every time they all died, and initially we couldn't figure out why. Then we noticed that ants were climbing up the legs under the boxes, and they were able to get in with the bunnies. Somehow, ants and baby bunnies didn't mix, and it was the smaller animals who won.

Finally, we gave up and just made an enclosure in the garden, and allowed the rabbits to dig themselves a burrow. And, voila! Some weeks later, out popped six wee bunnies, all black and white. High adorableness factor. And they all got names like One Spot and Two Spot based on the patterns of the fur. We could sit on our porch and watch them hopping around and nibbling the grass and being generally full of cute bunniness. Yay!

Also cute were the guinea pigs we had in Lusaka, Batman and Wildman. Wildman was so called because he had a hair lick, and Batman, well, he was just Batman. They did all the usual squeaking that guinea pigs do. Until one day they mysteriously died without warning, surely unrelated to the whole putsi-fly thing. I guess they just don't last that long.

I'm just not going to tell you about the roaches. You're welcome.

Another personal favorite of mine were the crocs that lived in the forested areas around the Zone du Bois, the part of Ouagadougou we lived in. There were some over by the university, and some in the big park across the road.

One day there was a blockade of the main thoroughfare on my way home. Since it was by the university, I assumed it was something to do with the (genuinely appalling) conditions there. But no: it was a protest by people in the neighborhood because the rains had encouraged some of the crocs from the forest by the university out into drainage ditches and other puddles of water around the neighborhood. They wanted the city to come and remove them.

This became an even greater problem when the city cut down a swathe of trees in order to widen the Fada road, the big road into the city just by our house. Having lost their habitual digs, a lot of crocs started wandering around the Zone du Bois looking for a place to hang their little crocodile hats.

One night we came home to find that a "croc" had been spotted in the drainage ditch just in front of our house. Apparently it had just gone into the sewer, but was still hanging around. Later that evening, the guard called us to say that it was on the move again. Funny what you learn about people when you see their reactions to news like this: do they run away from or towards the croc?

Well, our croc was a caiman, which is like a croc only much smaller, maybe a yard/meter long in total. Still able to pack a punch if it really wanted to do so, but an unlikely candidate to go after a human. It emerged again from the gutter and started sauntering along the street towards climes unknown, so we had plenty of time to study it. Truly, it was a beautiful animal. Its skin was a kind of yellowy green and brown, and easily half its length was taken up by a rather powerful tail. Granted, anything of the croc variety is going to be ungainly when walking on land, but this one was more dainty, in its way. It moved off into the dark and we never saw it again.

67

IN WHICH A BEAR IS ENTERTAINED

Sarajevo, 2007-2009

One of the best things Eddie found to do with the kids in Sarajevo was go to the zoo. It cost very little for us, and was a pretty good zoo, considering how small Sarajevo is. They never visited the llamas much, cute as they are, because they'd just as soon spit at you as look at you. They also didn't smell all that great. But there were peacocks and other birds, and some monkeys, lots of goats, ducks, and geese. There was also a very good park for the kids to play in, with the kind of play equipment that wasn't really available elsewhere in the city.

They'd spend some time in the play area, and then eventually it would be time to go get some lunch, so they would exit via the bear enclosure. Please don't ask what kind of bear it was. I just know that it was big. The fence on the enclosure wasn't very high, but they'd lowered the floor so that when he wanted to roam around he was too far down to "interact" with any humans.

But there was a central area that was more on sidewalk level, and here the bear used to sit, people-watching. This bear was doing a pretty solid impression of Dad on a Sunday afternoon, beer in hand, watching the game.

Then Eddie and the kids would go to Pizza Popeye, which had nothing to do with the cartoon character, as far as I know. Their signature pizza was (wait for it) the popeye, which had mushrooms, spinach, and an egg in the middle. I know the egg is not really an American thing, but it's very common in the Balkans, and I'm telling you, it's *good*. The story was that the Pizza Popeye people (say that fast 10 times) were mafia, and that the restaurant was just a front. Then again, you could probably say that about pretty much any successful retail institution in Sarajevo, so we chose to close our eyes and keep munching.

68

SONJA

Bonn, St. Petersburg, Belgrade, 1993-1997

Truth to tell, Sonja was not an easy person to get to know. She is a bit distrustful by nature, and doesn't choose to reveal much to people she doesn't really have confidence in. I think what saved me is that I recognized this fairly early on, and never asked about her upbringing unless she started us on the topic. And because I didn't push, she very gradually opened up and told me her story. I won't repeat it here because it's not mine to tell, but suffice it to say that she had quite a rough childhood and was now standing pretty much alone. The contrast with my privileged position, having easily enough money to draw on to live as a student in Germany for essentially as long as I wanted, was pretty stark.

One of the constants about Sonja was that she hated wearing her glasses, and so was liable to walk around half-blind most of the time. You'd greet her from across the street and she wouldn't know who it was, so you'd have to wait until you were quite close before her face would suddenly open up and she could greet you by name. She's also on the shorter side and has a lisp, all of which contributes to a vibe that she is not to be taken that seriously—and yet she is very smart and has accomplished a lot since university.

After we'd been taking Russian for all of a year, we decided to go together on a program of 6 weeks' immersion in St. Petersburg. We were both thrown into very welcoming but (to us) baffling host families. My host mother kept asking me, "do you understand? Do you understand?" It took me an embarrassingly long time to realize that *"ponyimayesh?"* was the equivalent of "you know?" and was thoroughly rhetorical. So my attempts to answer "no" had been thoroughly irrelevant.

I had also failed to pick up on the fact that the water from the tap was not to be drunk—oops. I had confiscated a large plastic soda bottle and just filled that sucker from the tap, merrily drinking from it for a good three days before I heard the bad news. Ironically, I was the only one in our entire group not to have stomach issues, so I figured I'd just made such an assault on my gut flora that they'd packed in all resistance. So I kept drinking the bad stuff. The African in me cringes at that now, but I guess I got lucky.

Sonja made a very important discovery about learning Russian. Taking the bus, we quickly learned that people ask "Are you getting off?" and if the answer is no, they'll maneuver a bit forward, and so come to stand by people near the door who are also getting off. This makes for constant rearranging, but less danger of being stranded in the bus because you can't squeeze yourself out in time. Thankfully, the answer to this question relied more on body language than actual words spoken, and anyway *"da"* and *"nyet"* aren't that hard to say or understand.

The problem with the question, though, is that it's an actual sentence. I tended to stumble over it and get some weird looks, but poor Sonja couldn't get people to understand her at all—until she learned the secret. The magical thing was to… mumble.

Yes, ladies and gentlemen, the way to be best understood by actual Russians is to speak their language as indistinctly as possible. Well, maybe not really, not all the time, but I think there's something about muttering a bit that actually makes the sounds flow more naturally. At any rate, once she figured that out, Sonja had no more difficulty on the bus.

One year I had a little birthday party in my 6m2 room, nice and cozy. Sonja brought me a really nice flowering plant for my room, which I appreciated a lot since the only other green thing I had was cut tulips. These I kept in a white and blue milk jug that lent the ensemble a vaguely Dutch air (or so I hoped). Then Sonja told me the story of how she bought the plant.

"I went into the store," she said, "and had a look round, and decided on a particular plant for you. And when I went to pay, I asked the lady if there were any particular care instructions for the plant. At this point she considered me with a perplexed and condescending look, and then said, 'Madame, all the flowers in this shop are artificial!'" At which point Sonja mumbled her embarrassed thanks and exited the shop, sans plant.

69

IN WHICH I EAT AND AM MERRY IN TWO CULTURES

Kosovo, January 1999

Y ou may know of cultures that celebrate a name day or saint's day, which can often be more important than a birthday. In Serbian culture, each family has a patron saint, and on that saint's day, the whole family celebrates. They make huge piles of food and of course have the mandatory booze at hand, and people just stop by throughout the day. There's no start time and no invitations are issued; it's simply known that if such and so a family is having their saint's day, one should stop by and help them celebrate. This fete is known as *slava*, which is related to the word for celebrating, so I suppose it's a bit like saying "The Celebration".

Our Dejan, being pretty much the youngest in the office and entertaining everyone with his happy and generous nature, evoked a fair amount of parental feeling on the part of the other staff. This was also because he lived in the flat under the house that was the IRC office. Although he shared the flat with Mahmoud, the 40-something ethnic-Albanian engineer, I think people felt it more keenly that Dejan lived away from home, since he was so much younger.

One day two things coincided: Dejan family's *slava* and the handing-over of some toilets we'd built in a school to the school authorities. Of course we all wanted to go to the *slava*, but we were going to pass through Dejan's village pretty early in the morning if we were going to be at the school in time for the ceremony. You might think that his family would tell us thanks but no thanks for showing up at that hour, but in fact they got up especially early so that a full feast would be ready for us when we arrived, at something like 8 am.

Now, I ask you to picture this scene: roughly 10 ethnic Albanians and a couple of Americans sitting around a table, eating and drinking to help a Serb family celebrate their patron saint's day. At the same time, tensions between the Kosovars and Serbs were getting serious. Clashes between the KLA and the Serbian special police were becoming commonplace, and by this point I think everyone knew there was going to be a war. You could just feel it coming.

All the Albanian staff hauled out what Serbian they knew, and the older ones (who experienced a united Yugoslavia into their 40's or 50's) regaled the company with jokes that were either anti-Milošević or good old standards from Yugoslav days. It was a group that was safe in the knowledge that they were all friends despite the politics, where simple human decency and the rules of hospitality set the tone.

Plus, we were rather enjoying all the food—and yes, the *šlivovic* (a local liquor)—so we were hardly going to say anything that might offend our hosts, though I would say the joy of helping our Dejan's family celebrate was genuinely felt by all those present. This was evident in the number of toasts the ensemble proposed, and a glug of *šlivovic* for every one.

And there was Dejan's grandmother. She can't have actually

been this old, but from the lack of teeth and heavily weather-beaten skin, you would have had my permission to think she was at least 80. She was also thrilled to have us in her home, and especially the Americans. She walked up to me, took my hand in hers, and said something very sweet that I couldn't understand. I'm told it was "peasant Serbian", more or less, so let us call it an "earthy" accent. Anyway, on top of that she mumbled and didn't have many teeth, so we pronounced her to be the test of Serbian comprehension: if you could understand her, you were sorted. I, clearly, failed this test.

And so we toddled merrily on our way, a few brain cells lighter but stomachs heavier.

About two months later, NATO started its bombing campaign against Serbia.

70

IN WHICH I GO TO OBSERVE BUT BECOME
THE OBSERVED

Ulcinj, Montenegro, ca. April 1997

As things were slowly starting to shift from the stagnated "situation" (how I came to hate that word) that dominated the years between 1986 and 1996, someone had the bright idea of convening a peace conference. The idea was to get NGOs and peacebuilding types from both sides together, and see whether some confidence-building measures couldn't be agreed upon. In the spirit of wanting the event to have some heft and therefore actually produce something useful, I imagine, journalists and diplomats came, along with observers from a few international NGOs. Plus, li'l ol' me.

I don't really know why. BPT (by design) wasn't particularly well known, and we weren't registered in Serbia as an NGO or anything. But it's true that there weren't really any other foreigners who had their ear to the ground as much as we did. So I guess someone somewhere across the line decided we would be useful—or at least that it would be nice to throw us a bone.

The train ride down was spectacular. We went through more tunnels than I cared to count as we wove our way around and through mountains worthy of Switzerland. I remember my first Serbian-language teacher waxing poetic about the coastline of Montenegro (the "black mountain") and the great mountains that come down straight into the Mediterranean. Well, I've heard people go on and on about the beauty of their home country, so wasn't counting on too much, but for once she had not exaggerated at all. The peaks loomed; the descent was precipitous; there was hardly anything between where the mountains hit the sand and the sea began. It was truly spectacular.

The conference itself took place in Ulcinj, south of Podgorica, the capital, also known to my friends as "the Pod". Ulcinj was a smaller town that seemed to live pretty much off tourism—as far as I could tell, since we were in the hotel most of the time. I barely remember the actual conference, mostly that it was a lot of making of speeches rather than peace.

I did make one friend. We'll call her Amanda. She was interning or something at the embassy but had spent time in Albania, and so spoke the language passably. We were kind of the only two younger, more Western women amongst the observers and so pretty much stuck together.

We met a bunch of people but in particular there was Glen, the head of a peacebuilding NGO in Macedonia. It was a well-known and respected organization among those who know, so I was mildly excited to meet him (not least because I thought I might try for a job with them after BPT). I asked him about his work in Macedonia, where tensions between ethnic Albanians and Macedonians were also high, if not as fraught as in Kosovo. We exchanged other pleasantries and he told me about his wife and kids, normal stuff.

Amanda also met Marko, a journalist from Belgrade. So the four of us started hanging around a bit, not all the time but enough.

On the second day of the conference, Marko and Glen

suggested we go to a nearby beach instead of sitting through all
the boring speeches. Amanda and I thought it over. We hesitated
a lot—really, go play hooky—but in the end we decided to go.
Why not see more of the country while we're here, and the
prospect of the meeting yielding any excitement while we were
gone was pretty slim.

So imagine my surprise when, upon arriving at the beach,
Marko and Mr. Family Man removed their clothes (and I mean
all their clothes) and ran into the surf. I turned to look at
Amanda and was relieved to see the same shock and discomfort
in her face that I felt. And then the boys invited us to come join
them, presumably in the same state of undress. Uh, no thanks.
They pressed. Amanda and I exchanged more glances. No, we
would rather go take a walk on the beach.

And so it was that I saw Albania from close up: our little
beach walk took us right up to the border. I took a good look at
the "motherland" (so called by Kosovars). And thus Albania
entered the list of countries I've seen by land but not entered, or
landed in but not left the airport, which currently also includes
DR Congo, Hungary, and Thailand.

After some time Amanda and I wandered back to join the
boys, who made rather a big deal of what we'd missed by not
getting in the water. Nice try, dudes.

Now in my innocence I was still kind of debating whether
they were making a pass at us or genuinely just being very "free"
(and it's true we didn't have any kind of bathing attire with us, so
it's not like they had the choice to wear something other than
their underwear, and I honestly doubt I would have preferred
that to the *à la nature* version we got). You may laugh at my
naïveté, but I'd never traveled in the circles of casual sex, and am
generally speaking not the person who gets hit on.

That evening Glen and I had discussed something about
work because yes, we were still talking to them even after the

strange beach escapade. I can't remember the exact issue, but we left it that a bit later in the evening I would pass by his room and drop something off. He gave me his key so I could get in even if he were momentarily busy with something else.

You've probably seen this coming for a mile, but call me crazy; I didn't, OK? I knocked, he said something about come in, so I used the key he'd given me and…….. he was half sitting, half lying in bed, with no clothes on the bits that I could see. And based on our earlier beach adventure I had the distinct feeling that there wasn't any other clothing going on lower down.

Despite my thoughts of his wife and what she would say if she saw her husband like that, I decided my best strategy was to feign indifference and basically pretend he was sitting on his bed with his clothes on. So I walked in, left the papers behind, greeted him politely but perfunctorily, and made my exit.

I think I can safely say that, aside from an abiding appreciation for the Montenegrin landscape, the one great thing I got out of that whole experience was meeting Amanda. No matter what else happens, "We'll always have Ulcinj!"

71

SOME PEOPLE GET ALL THE FREQUENT-FLIER MILES

Kosovo, 1997 and Rwanda, April 2004

Now there's one public figure I did come across a few times, and that is Richard Holbrooke. Don't get excited (if you even remember who he was); I never actually met him, though I was close to two of his visits overseas.

The first one was Kosovo, during the build-up of tensions that would later explode into full-blown conflict. You may find this strange, but I've always considered it an honor to have been in Kosovo while everything was breaking down, essentially watching a country descend into what amounted to civil war.

We aid types typically come in when the shizzle has already hit the fan, and most of the time we've already decided who we think are the good guys and who the bad. But watching the dial get turned up, bit by bit, and—what I found so crucial— watching the doors of opportunity close, one by one, that's something else. It was a gradual process, for sure, but there were certain times when you could hear a big steel door slamming shut: one possible opening for reconciliation and preventing a war, gone. And then another.

When Holbrooke, who was famous for having brokered the Oslo Peace Accords that ended the Bosnian war, and then Secretary of State Madeleine Albright visited Kosovo, I heard such a door close. And of course I don't really know what their official reason for coming was, or what their policy goals were and whether they felt they had achieved them or not, so I'm not trying to make any big judgment of their visit. But there was one group I was familiar with, and that was the Albanian Students' Union.

This was after the march that had ended in tear gas and my friends getting beaten up, so clearly someone at the State Department had decided that the Albanian Students' Union, which organized the protest, were good people to talk to if Holbrooke and Albright wanted to get a more granular sense of what was going on.

The problem was that Mr. Holbrooke and Ms. Albright were really well known in the region, and our little band of students was suddenly to be honored with this high-level visit. Unfortunately, my colleague Renate and I were able to see pretty clearly how the whole thing went to the heads of certain people, in particular Albin Kurti, the President of the Union.

Albin was already on the more radical side of politics, supporting the Democratic Party (PDK) rather than the big mama on the scene, the Democratic League of Kosovo (LDK), led by Ibrahim Rugova. Rugova, who famously wore a scarf every day and said he would never take it off until Kosovo was independent, had led the Kosovars in peaceful resistance though the parallel system of government and public services for the previous 10 years. Now younger folk were becoming impatient and counseled more direct action against the Serbian government. The PDK wasn't yet directly threatening the LDK's supremacy, but they were becoming ever more influential.

Albin was in the minority even within the Students' Union

with his allegiance to the PDK. It was a bit challenging for Renate and me, because if anything we wanted to help them think of ways to continue their non-violent resistance. Around the time when we brokered the direct talks with the Serbian Students' Union, we were arguing that real change would come when they got people from the "oppressor" on their side. As in, change would not come directly because of what they did, but if they could make a sympathetic case to average Serbs, *those* people might actually have the power to change something from within.

And it was this window that closed with the Holbrooke and Albright visit. Where once the leaders had listened, perhaps skeptically, but attentively, to our arguments, after the bigwigs had been in town and asked the Kosovar students' opinion on things, the decision for more direct action was pretty much a done deal. Not that direct action has to be bad, but in this case is usually meant some level of violence.

I'll be the first one to say that our influence on the Albanian Students' Union was relatively minor, and I don't mean to imply that if they'd just followed what we were saying, the war wouldn't have happened. That would be ridiculous. What I do think, however, is that we were proposing a potentially effective form of advocacy and that among students it might have been easier to forge some kind of contact that could act more in favor of peace than the other way around. But after that visit, that possibility no longer existed. And I do believe that the trajectory ending in war is fed by a series of seemingly small events that together lead down only one road.

Albin, at least, came out of the whole thing OK. He was imprisoned for a while after the Kosovo crisis for wanting to destroy the Serbian state or some such; he described himself as Europe's only political prisoner. He never really left politics, and now heads the Vetëvendosje (self-determination) party, which came in 3rd in Kosovo's 2017 general election.

The next time I was in the proximity of Mr. Holbrooke was in Rwanda, for the 10th anniversary of the genocide. We'd been in the country for about two years at that point, in fact just about exactly two years, since we had arrived in Rwanda on genocide-memorial weekend. That whole event was so weird; all that protocol and the events and national mourning over a horrific event ten years in the past. Anyway, this is when I was working for the US embassy, and although his visit had nowt to do with my role there, when you get a big visitor it's all hands on deck.

What I really remember about his visit is that he visited the genocide memorial, though he didn't really go inside. Instead, there were three open graves dug and ready to receive human remains. I found it poignant that even ten years later, they were discovering bodies and laying them to rest at the memorial.

Our friend Dick (surely crossing paths on two continents brings us to first-name terms?) read a speech standing at the foot of those graves. I don't remember much about it except that he assumed a fair amount of blame on behalf of the US, and basically said that they (he, Clinton, other senior White House staff) were so preoccupied with what was going on in Bosnia at the time that they basically failed to realize how important the killings in Rwanda were. I thought it was a brave admission, even if it only confirmed what many people had suspected for years.

And where do I fit in to all this? My role was to stand over in the corner, top right from Dick's vantage point. I wasn't security because duh, just being ceremonial by giving the whole scene some visual harmony. I vaguely recall something to do with my clothes that was irritating me; I think it was my heels being unsteady on the grass we had to walk on.

So did I actually meet said Mr. Holbrooke? (We're back on formal terms to emphasize his importance.) Truly: no. He certainly saw me but I'm sure I didn't particularly register.

Still, a week or two later he made an address (I can't

remember where—in front of the UN?), which I didn't hear, but based on the coverage of it, I was 90% sure that it was the same speech he'd made in Rwanda. It makes sense, really. Why waste a really good speech on a couple of Rwandans and a handful of embassy employees? I understood then that we'd been the dress rehearsal.

The other thing that happened during the 10th anniversary of the genocide was at the official ceremony, with high-ranking Rwandan officials and also ambassadors and such from different countries. Our friend HEPK (His Excellence Paul Kagame) delivered a scathing speech in which he said that Rwanda didn't need international aid, and he made some particular criticisms of France. Upon hearing this, the French ambassador and his entire entourage left the ceremony, which caused quite the buzz around town.

Things deteriorated from there, and in the end Rwanda cut diplomatic relations with France and ordered the embassy closed. The Ambassador was given 24 hours to leave the country, and other diplomats 72. The French school and the French Cultural Center were also closed.

We felt the closure of the school because the Belgian School, which was much bigger, agreed pretty much without question to take in students of the former French School. So classrooms got a little more crowded, but I think everyone agreed that there wasn't an alternative.

Some time afterwards, we spoke with a friend who had been working as a local hire in the French embassy. Since she was not a diplomat and not French, she didn't have to leave the country. But she did have a front-row seat to what it was like for the people who did.

As soon as the rupture of diplomatic relations was announced, the Rwandan staff stopped coming to work. Which was understandable, but it put the embassy in a tight spot. For one thing, there was no driver to take the Ambassador to the airport, so our friend wound up driving him.

Another problem was that they didn't have the staff to access the safe, which meant they couldn't pay people, our friend included. On the other side of the coin, the remaining diplomats were desperately looking for what to do with all of their consumables (household goods that diplomats can bring with them to their post, when the local stuff is considered too inferior). So an offer was made to pay our friend in toilet paper!

72

THE MOUSE AND THE ELEPHANT

One of the most challenging but also fun things about doing the kind of work I did overseas is meeting everyone from the wrinkled old lady who's growing maize for her family to cabinet ministers, from ambassadors to unemployed youth with limited prospects. Sometimes you might meet two or three of those in the same day. Honestly, if you'd told me 10 years ago that I would feel comfortable meeting with ministers or the equivalent of a president's chief of staff, I definitely would have said, "who, me?"

It gets doubly weird when you're meeting an ambassador and maybe one of his staff, and they're people you know socially. Hanging out at the softball game one day, meeting them again in suits, with full ambassadorial protocol, two days later. But we just go with the flow.

Cabinet ministers are sometimes funny, too. I've met people whom I knew when they were in a lesser capacity, and then meeting them again it can be hard to know how friendly to be. Some are very formal and, I should say, they are helped in this by having posh anterooms and then often couches so huge they are kind of hard to sit in. Others, though, will joke around and do everything to make you at ease. One minister took a selfie with my colleagues and me and delightedly informed us that he was going to put it on his Facebook page.

In the first seven years working for CRS, I didn't have all that much contact with our Catholic-church partners. Maybe the rank and file of the folks who carry out our joint programs, but not church dignitaries.

Then I went to Burkina and joined the country office, where among other things it was my job to help maintain good relations between us and the Catholic church, in particular the Bishops. Then Christmastime arrived, and suddenly I was joining a delegation to go see the Cardinal. Uhhhh, OK! Bishops, I mean, they're not exactly a dime a dozen, but they oversee what might be a couple of counties in the US. The Cardinal, on the other hand, now this guy is a big deal. Remember the dudes with red hats who elect the Pope? Yeah, that kind of cardinal.

So you can imagine that I was the teensiest bit nervous, being a non-Catholic and so not the strongest on church protocol, about to meet someone who is basically just below the Pope. We were all terribly formal, and some kissed his ring, though not everyone because besides me we had several Muslims with us. But really, once we started talking, Cardinal Philippe Ouedraogo was a very humble and easy man. He even served us cake, rummaging around to find a cake slicer and then forks (we met at the Archbishop's place, so it wasn't his home), cutting everyone a slice and bringing it over. That really impressed me since there were household staff around who could have done it just as easily.

Another person who really impressed me was Bill Clinton. People who've been in the room with him will already know this, but it's one thing to hear in the media how much the guy loves to meet people, and it's another thing entirely to feel the electricity dart through the room when he walks in. He is a true rock star, no two ways about it.

He came to Rwanda for something to do with the Clinton Foundation, of which I happened to know the country manager. I saw her pass by one day and, rather cheekily, I said, "I want to meet him! I don't care that I have no legitimate reason to be at that reception, but I wanna meet him!" She laughed and said OK —but I never guessed she would actually follow through with it.

So imagine my surprise some weeks later when I received an invitation to a reception at which President Clinton (at that time three or four years out of the White House) would speak, followed by general mingling. I was more curious than anything; I certainly didn't expect to be witness to what it's like when a rock start enters a room, but I wasn't even looking at the door and I could feel the change in mood immediately.

Clinton's speech was primarily about his foundation and what they were doing for HIV in the country. At least, I think so. Mostly I was fascinated by his hands and how graceful they are.

Afterwards, people went up to try to shake his hand and bask for a moment in his sunshine. It was impressive to see how he found something to say to everyone, even if it was just, "I like your tie." And of course people frantically worked to say something that would single them out a little bit, or give him an opportunity to ask a question. I, feeling particularly inept at such things and a bit put off by all the people standing there at the rope line waiting for their chance, retreated a bit to the back of the room. I had a little glass of wine and some nibbles.

After a while, though, I watched all these people have their moment with him, and he was obviously enjoying himself, and I told myself I'd be really cross if I didn't at least try to get a photograph of myself with him. So I sidled up to the rope line, kind of on the margins, and was waiting for a moment when I could interject, when he saw me. "Oh, you want a photo? Come on!" At which point he grabbed the camera out of my hand and stuffed it in someone else's, and said, "Here—take our picture!"

So yes, I have a photograph of me with the former president.... and L. L, who managed to photobomb my photo and stick her head between the two of us. Some time later my husband had a meeting with L in her office, and he saw that she'd cut me out of the photo and was displaying herself with Clinton alone. Boo, hiss.

The other thing I want to share with you is something I didn't experience directly, but that was relayed to me from an embassy colleague who'd had the job of accompanying Mr. Clinton around all of his visit.

When it came time to leave, of course Clinton was like an hour and a half late, because, Clinton. His handlers were going nuts. Waiting for the former president, lined up along the tarmac from his car to the door of the plane, were US military personnel who were in-country to ferry Rwandan peacekeepers to Darfur. They'd been standing in the hot sun, in full uniform, for at least an hour and a half.

And instead of rushing through to get on the plane and get to Uganda, his next stop, he stopped and greeted every single soldier down the line, giving each one a little compliment or an encouraging word—and making him even later. You don't have to like Clinton as a man or a president, but this seems to me like a moment of true personal respect.

But the person I most want to tell you about is not a minister, or a Cardinal, or a president. In fact, I don't even remember his name.

For you to understand this story, it would be helpful for you to understand one activity that CRS does in Burkina, and that is called SILC. It's often called "microfinance", but it really isn't that: no one comes and puts money in a pot, and they have no forms to fill out for a loan. The participants (who are usually women) pay their own money into the pot as a form of savings, and they put in as little or as much as they can afford.

Once the pot is big enough, the group starts giving out loans. To get a loan, the participant needs to explain to the group what she wants to do, and they vote on whether or not she should get the loan. The loan is paid back with interest (not some outrageous amount that is going to bankrupt anyone), and this further grows the pot. At the end of a cycle (9–12 months), the money is shared out to the group members according to how much they've paid in.

SILC is great for providing people with small loans that they can use to do some petty trading, start a little business, pay school fees, whatever. But much more important the groups build what we call "social cohesion"—basically, a sense of community and trust between people. To be a member of a SILC group, you have to trust the other members.

But not only that, in places where women don't often get out of the house, the meetings might be one of the few times they get to socialize with other women. And what happens is that they start to really support each other, visiting one another if they are ill, even making a long trip to a hospital to do so, hearing each other's problems, and sharing in each other's joys. It's especially great for women, since they tend to be in an all-female group and so hold all the leadership positions. It's empowering.

We see the evidence of this when we go to the field. Understanding that field visits are 80% theater, but there are certain things you just can't fake. We see crowds of 1,000 people coming to tell the donor how much they appreciate SILC, and practically ripping the microphone out of each other's hands for the chance to talk about how much SILC has changed their lives. They write songs about their SILC group, and get matching skirt wraps made.

One woman told us of how unhappy she was in her household growing up, and then she got married. But "the misery followed me to my new home," she said, describing how she subsequently became so desperate she wanted to end her life. And then a few friends convinced her to try SILC, and now she has a new sense of agency and is actually happy.

We visitors tend to get drafted to come and dance with the women. There's a hip-bump thing they do that looks easy but is kind of tricky, because they have a tendency to smash into you pretty hard! So you have to bump back equally hard, and it can leave you feeling a bit bruised. But it's a lot of fun to get in there and dance, and you can just feel everyone kind of relax and really start having fun when the whitey guests start dancing.

One visit, after we'd done the whole official program, the emcee approached us with a young man—a kid, really—who was holding a chicken. He told us, "This young man insists on telling you his story. As you can see, he is handicapped [he was blind]. He says no one used to talk to him and they all thought he was worthless. He had no way of earning money and was just there all the time.

"But then, a SILC group decided to take him in. He was able to save like everyone else, and then he took a loan. He now raises chickens, and he wants to give you this chicken to show his gratitude. He now has something to say in the group and people treat him like a human being."

I hate crying in front of project participants.

So I went up and took the chicken, and probably embarrassed the hell out of him by giving him a hug, and then proudly stood there and insisted that they take some pictures of the two of us together. In that moment you don't care that his teeth are bad and that his heels are cracked from walking around in the heat and dust all the time, that he doesn't smell all that great; it's such an amazing privilege to be part of something that you can be sure has done some lasting good. I always come away very humbled from those experiences.

BLOOD, SWEAT AND TEARS

Lilongwe, Malawi, January-March, 2014

And how, you ask, does an organization get the money to do all these great (and sometimes very stupid) things? We write proposals, that's what!

It's hard to describe in a way that won't put you to sleep just how tricky these proposals can be. Coming up with activities is usually the easy part. But they all have to fit into a certain logic that explains the theory behind what you want to do, and then why the activities will get you to a certain set of goals. Then you need to say exactly *how* you are doing to do the activities (who, where, what, when) and how you are going to monitor and evaluate what you've done so you can make sure you're on track and prove that you have actual results.

Once you've done all that, you cost it out and find out how much over budget you are, and then you start cutting. And if you're working together with other organizations on the same project (which CRS almost always is), you have to define roles and responsibilities, and work out who gets the budget for what bits of the project, and how the different organizations will work together and make decisions while they're implementing it.

And then, you cut the budget some more.

And then you have to *write* the bleedin' thing into a project proposal that usually asks you to answer a gazillion questions in like 20 pages. Let me tell you, those pages fill up *fast*. I'm like the queen of squeezing a document down to size.

So that's your average proposal...and then we have Food for Peace. This office gives out US money for a couple of different things, but the really juicy ones that for sure you want to win are big programs over usually five years, worth tens of millions of dollars.

So these mega-proposals tend to take on a "must-win" quality, which is great if you need to leverage help from HQ, but not so great if you're on the actual proposal team trying to do incredibly complicated versions of all the steps outlined above. And since we usually started drafting the proposal when the draft Request for Applications (RFA) comes out, which can be over a month before the final RFA drops, we might be working on one of these suckers for a good three months non-stop, 100% of people's time (plus the 25-30% they add on to keep their regular jobs ticking over while they're gone). After I'd been explaining these big proposals to my kids for some time, my son came out with: "it's like the Olympics of what you do." Which is a perfect description —only there's no silver or bronze medals; it's gold or bust!

So in the early months of 2014, back when I was a technical advisor for proposal development (among other things), our office in Malawi was working on one of these monsters—5 years, $60 million. And they were struggling a little bit: everyone was doing their best, but they were kind of missing someone who could steer the ship and make sure that everything got done as needed in the time they had. So, guess who was drafted to basically move to Malawi for three months and steer said ship? Yours truly, that's who.

I do have to put in a plug for my family right here, because the experience nearly drove everyone mad. While I was testing my leadership qualities in Malawi, my kids were missing me, and my husband was suddenly a single parent (and also missing me), and it wasn't really something they had any say in.

Luckily I had a really good team to work with. People were very committed, and we came together in that way you do when you're working intensely toward a common goal. And as you will in these cases, we started to develop our own language. In our case, a lot of it was based on the *Lord of the Rings*. Sasha, our budget magician, declared that he was going to get in all the partners' budget managers and lock them in the conference room (thereafter nicknamed Mordor) until the budgets were finished according to his specifications.

There was also a partner organization that had been given a particular role, and we felt they were not really holding up their end of the bargain. (They of course have a different side of the story.) So, they were Boromir, who tried to take the ring from Frodo, but eventually they fell on their sword.

Then there was Meredith, who first was down with malaria, then found out she was having twins, and then caught a case of bronchitis so bad that we could hear her coughing from all the way across the building. But she stepped up amazingly, taking on double the load that she should have had to without any complaint.

I think emotionally the low point came when one day two people stuck their heads in my office to say, "You are saving this proposal," and on the same day I tried to do my daily check-in with the family and talk about possibly coming home for a long weekend, and my husband said, "I'm just so tired and fed up; I really can't talk with you about this right now." That ripping sound you hear is me being torn in two.

And then there was the night I was walking from my car to the entrance of the hotel where I was staying, and I was walking kind of fast because we'd worked till 9 pm and I just really wanted to get home and have a glass of wine, and the road wasn't well lit and I forgot about the speed bump I'd just driven over. I went down so fast I don't really remember falling; I just know that I was shouting for help because I wasn't sure I could get up on my own.

The poor hotel: there I was, bleeding profusely from my chin on their front doorstep. What an advertisement. I think they thought I was going to bleed out right there in front of the hotel. Anyway, they found a taxi willing to take me to a local clinic, and on the way I sent a text to my friend and colleague Jennifer, with whom I worked most closely on the proposal.

Imagine her horror when she walked into the clinic and found me covered in blood. Those chins, man, they can bleed. I got some stitches for the chin and they told me my left wrist wasn't broken, though it hurt like a monster.

The next day I walked into the office and you can probably guess the reaction. I had raccoon eyes from the bash to my head, the nerves in my jaw were so swollen that I couldn't really open my mouth, certainly not enough to eat anything but very mushy food, and I had an Ace bandage on my hand. That sprain took a really long time to heal, and I figured out only much later that it was because I was still typing through the pain. Still, I credit the sprained hand with sparing me a broken jaw, which would have been much worse.

So, you see that this whole adventure cost us actual blood, sweat, and tears.

Happy post-script: After you submit the proposal, if you're in the running to win, you get what's called an issues letter, meaning the donor asks for clarifications or sometimes changes of approach on certain things. We got a pretty friendly issues letter for this proposal, confirming our gut feeling that we'd done a good job on it. The team had been great and worked together well, and it showed.

This also highlights one of the more frustrating aspects of this whole theater, that the process by which you find out whether you have won or lost is so gradual, there's often not really an obvious moment when you get to say, "We won!" You can have a nice thing to celebrate submission of the proposal, but if you want to wait for the signing of the agreement with the donor, it can take nine months or more, by which time everyone's attention is elsewhere.

A couple of team members participated in the issues-letter phone call from different locations. Only Jennifer and I were in Lilongwe, so we went to the USAID office. There we sat with the person who was the donor's point of contact for the preceding project. We did the phone call, which was fine, and then Mr. USAID broke the connection.

And then he started telling us about how proud he was to have worked on the previous project, and how good this proposal was. Of course, he had no idea he was sitting across from two of the most central people on the team, and the one who'd written the final draft of almost the whole proposal. He said it was one of the best proposals he'd seen. Rachel and I just sat there in shock, and nodded our thanks.

When we got back to the office, we danced around singing "Hava nagila" and saying "We nailed it!" That moment of unsuspecting feedback was super gratifying.

And yes, we did win, and the other most gratifying moment was when I was invited to do some work with the project team after they'd been up and running for a few months, and got to meet all the people who had a job because of the proposal I'd helped to write. That was an awesome feeling.

IN WHICH I GO TO PRISON

Transdniestria, 2008

Never heard of Moldova? Yeah, didn't think so. It's one of the former Soviet republics, nestled in there right by Romania and Ukraine. Moldova was actually one of the breadbaskets for the Soviet Union, with very fertile soils and pretty nice weather. They're also notable wine makers; in fact, most houses, at least in the countryside, seem to have grape vines in the back garden the way we might have a couple of tomato plants or basil on the kitchen windowsill. And do look out for Moldovan wine; if you can get some, it's likely to be a bargain and very tasty to boot.

Besides relative poverty and high unemployment, the fly in the ointment is a strip of land called Transdniestria ("across the Dniester [River]"), which is pro-Russian and is ostensibly agitating for independence. I say "ostensibly" because I rather got the feeling that the current arrangement suits people just fine, but let me not pronounce too much on things I don't know that much about.

All of which is to say, even for people who come to Moldova,

Transdniestria generally remains off-limits. Now, CRS' Moldova country office was providing some support to the Caritas office in Transdniestria, which they used among other things to support an orphanage in Tiraspol, the capital. We'd been giving this money for a while, and folks at HQ were starting to wonder whether we weren't doing more harm than good.

Orphanages have become quite controversial in the development world, as large percentages of children who live there often have living parents or other relatives who maybe just don't have the means to care for the child. So there is a growing sense that the emphasis should be on keeping children in their own families, rather than bringing them to institutions. Also, with those pictures in the back of people's minds from the Romanian orphanages with the malnourished kids who'd been tied to their beds, there were some obvious questions about the conditions in the home we were indirectly supporting.

And so, a small delegation of us was to go to Tiraspol and see for ourselves. We took only international staff, who could get across the border more easily than Moldovan nationals. And to help us get in and navigate around, we were graciously invited to piggyback on a trip by a representative of Caritas Czech.

For his part, he was accompanied by two Ukrainian doctors, who were doing the actual work in the field with Caritas Czech support.

I remember that we needed our passports at the border, and that all the infrastructure of a true international border was there, albeit on one side only. It felt surreal.

We started at a clinic that was offering HIV tests. They talked about the horrible stigma that was still attached to HIV there, and how difficult it was in the beginning to get the doctors to be willing even to touch a door handle that a person with HIV had just used.

To my delight, there was a Ugandan doctor there, whose job

was to advise the local doctors on the protocols for testing, confidentiality, and stigma reduction. I was so happy just to see an African face again, and I just loved that an African had come to do capacity building in Europe. Ha! Of course, in some ways this was a dubious honor, considering why the good doctor was so far "ahead" with the protocols and such. But still, I couldn't help but relish the role reversal.

After the clinic, we went to the prison. It was a women's facility, and overall the conditions looked as OK as a boring institution can look. Later I commented to one of the others on how normal it all felt, and he said that this was one of the distinguishing things about prison life: it's a lot of normalcy and boredom punctuated by the occasional sudden outburst of energy or chaos.

We went in and split up to accompany the Ukrainian doctors to the rooms where they would carry out the examinations. I came to understand that they'd started their HIV work with drug users, and when some of those were sentenced to prison, the doctors couldn't leave their patients untreated. So they followed them into the prison system.

The first patient came in, and with her the first surprise. "She is HIV positive," said the doctor, "and she also has xyz." Um, sharing the woman's diagnosis, isn't that against patient confidentiality? Then she asked the woman to remove her blouse. Mr. Caritas and I looked quickly away. "So," I said, covering that side of my face with my hand, "what did you do last weekend?"

I just couldn't believe that the doctors would do these exams with us in the room, and take no precautions at all to ensure any kind of confidentiality or even basic human dignity. At least, that's what it felt like to me. It seemed like a holdover from Soviet times.

After that embarrassing episode, we went to the TB wing. Again, if you want to create stigma and isolation, you can hardly do better than by putting people in a physically separate wing, with the words "inmates with tuberculosis" hanging prominently over the entrance. At that point we knew better, and refused to go in while the women were being examined—which thoroughly perplexed our Ukrainian colleagues.

After the prison, we visited the orphanage, the purpose of our visit. I can happily say that, although we may have had reservations about putting children in an institution, this was a very well run place. The children went to school, and they had art and play activities; the structure was clean and warm, and the children obviously felt well there. So we were able to go home and give a positive report, leaving out the prison bits.

75

IN WHICH I GET BOOKED BY THE POLICE
(JUST KIDDING)

Sarajevo, June 2009

When we moved from Sarajevo to Lusaka, I had to provide all kinds of information for my visa. The Zambian government is not keen on being told that whitey from Wichita or Stuttgart can do any job better than a Zambian, so expat positions are limited and closely monitored. You can't even volunteer without a work permit.

One of the things I had to send in was my fingerprints. Well, OK… but where do you actually go to get fingerprinted? It's not like you can just walk into a police station and ask them to take your fingerprints. The US embassy was at a bit of a loss when I asked them. Their system was all electronic, and there wasn't really any way to give me a copy of my prints that I could stick in an envelope.

They were sympathetic, though. You know, one of the most difficult things that embassy folks have to deal with is that a lot of people seem to think the embassy should be able to help them out with any problem. There are, of course, certain times when the embassy can pitch in. (If you get arrested or detained by the police, for example—but even then all they can do is make sure you have a toothbrush and try to make sure you get a fair trial. It's not like they can spring you from prison.) But they really have a limited mandate of consular services they can offer, and anything outside of that is pretty much at the discretion of whoever you happen to land with.

So the person I got foisted upon was very nice and said she would consult some people—and lo, in a few days I received a communication saying that the Regional Security Office could help me. It seems they had a full set of all the stuff you need to do fingerprints old-style, with rollers and real ink and the little card you have to roll your fingertips over to transfer the prints. Just like getting booked! Ehem—or so I'm told.

I believe we were quite the sight, hanging out in the consular waiting room, while he squeezed the ink onto the plates and rolled it thin. And then the tragicomedy of me trying to actually do the fingerprints. You have no idea how tricky this is. You have to roll your whole finger so that the ink gets on the whole pad. And then you have to roll your whole forefinger onto the card, *without smudging*! I had serious trouble with this maneuver, and I was sober and willing. I can't even imagine what it must be like to try to print someone who's under the influence or not happy about the process.

Also, I can't imagine what people thought we were doing....

76

IN WHICH WE NEARLY FREEZE (BUT SEE PENGUINS)

Pretoria to Kleinmond, August 2003

One year when the kids were still pretty small, we got it into our heads that traveling to South Africa in August would be a good idea. It's not that we didn't realize that it would be winter, more that we just couldn't conceive of the cold on the African continent. What can I say; we were newbies.

We initially went to stay with some friends my father had made years before when he was doing some work in South Africa. They very generously put us up for a few days, and we got to see some of the sights of Pretoria, including a monument to the Boers' trek and, very entertainingly, the zoo. We enjoyed watching the people at least as much as the animals, especially since we'd seen so many of the animals in the wild that it was less exciting to see them in their enclosures. (Does this make us zoo snobs?)

After that, we intended to go down to the Cape for another week or so. Our hosts were building a house in Kleinmond, a little town on the Cape. So we rented a car, and, armed with a map and a vague sense of the overall direction we wanted to move in, we took off.

We'd decided to take things easy and use three days for the drive, which would give the kids a little time to run around and me some time off from driving. Rather than planning where we would stay, we decided to just wing it, looking for places as we went. The optimism of the young.

But being stupid is apparently not all bad. The first day, when the shadows were starting to look a little long, we realized places were a little fewer and farther between than we had anticipated, so we turned in to the first place we saw. It turned out to be a thoroughly delightful guest house, with a common dining room and a sitting room with a great log fire.

We'd just about arrived and gotten settled in when the power went out. Not an uncommon occurrence in Rwanda, so it didn't faze us too much, except that the owner came by our little bungalow to tell us that while she could cook without power, she was going to have to stoke up the fire in the oven and that might take some time.

So we had quite a wait for dinner, which we decided would be most comfortable sitting by the fire in the main hall (especially since our rooms were pitch black). There we met the only other guest: a Dutch truck driver who'd lived for a couple of decades in Zimbabwe. He described how his kids loved to get on the phone with their friends from "home" and speak Shona. Although they had moved "back" to the Netherlands, he still mostly made his living from doing long hauls in southern Africa, so he was gone for long periods of time. But what did the kids want when he got home? Mealie [maize] meal!

The power eventually did come back on, so we were able to get ready for bed without any trouble. We slept well, though we woke up early because the morning light was coming into our little bungalow. I looked outside and beheld magic: there'd been a frost overnight and so we were surrounded by a carpet of silver. We hadn't seen frost in years. And the birds were out, singing to their little hearts' content. It was splendid.

The second day was probably the longest drive, and we were out on the Karoo (in winter), so the view was pretty boring. There was a particular kind of cracker that you could get easily in South Africa but only sometimes in Rwanda. The kids loved them, so we had a good stock in the car. And a good thing, too. Marion wanted to nosh on them non-stop. The sound track to that drive is a little ET voice coming from the back seat saying "mo kecka mo"! and "mo kecka mommeeeee".

That second night we found out the disadvantages of not booking any places in advance. Not to give any bad reputation to Bloemfontein, but after our trip some folks did tell us that it wasn't perhaps the most salubrious town in which to try to find a place to stay. ("Oh, yeah, it's a dump.") Anyway, after some searching and not finding a whole lot, we landed in a place called the Wagon Wheel.

It would have been funny if it hadn't been so darned uncomfortable. It was the type of place where you can put change into a slot by the bed and it will give you a "massage". The real problem was that the room was really, really cold. And the heater was so loud there was no hope of sleeping with it on. But before going to bed we did go to the restaurant, which had a wagon-wheel motif and red-checked plastic tablecloths. We ate our heated-up frozen meals and retired back to our room, where we duly froze the whole night.

The third night, we got lucky again. We found a little gem of a guesthouse in Oudshoorn, having taken the Garden Route over the mountains, about a half-day's drive from Kleinmond. Our room kind of reminded me of the family room in my house growing up, I think because of the sliding glass door to the outside. It was very comfortable, and the hostess was lovely.

So the place was perfect, except that they didn't have a restaurant. The hostess recommended a Ukrainian place not far away, so that's where we went. It turned out to be this very charming, tiny establishment with maybe four tables. That evening it was just us and one other couple, roughly middle-aged. Of course the children, being one and three, and having spent the day in the car, had, er, some energy to burn off.

At one point we apologized to the couple next to us about the noise. "Oh no," they replied, "we have four children ourselves, and we remember what it was like!" We wound up chatting with them and had a delightful conversation. They'd been overseas for years themselves, and the husband was the director of an international school in Ukraine—hence their hankering for some Ukrainian food. They knew about NGO work, and one of their daughters was working somewhere for an NGO on small-arms reduction.

The one thing they said that I'll never forget was that when the children were little, it was easier just to have the mattress on the floor and at leave the baby with them in bed, so mama could just sort of roll over when the wee one wanted to nurse. But even as they outgrew that, the kids generally stuck around on the bed for a couple more years, until they each eventually decided that they wanted to sleep in their own bed and would wander off to do their own thing. What touched me was when she said that when the whole family is together now, the kids (now grown, obviously) say, "Let's take all the mattresses and put them down on the floor like when we were little!"

The next morning we drove on and finally arrived in Kleinmond. We installed ourselves in the house as best we could, which was still unfinished, and then went out to find some groceries and have a look around. We soon realized the mortal peril we were in: the temperatures were near-freezing, a frigid wind was blowing, and the kids in particular didn't own clothing for this kind of cold. We went to one clothing shop and found a good jacket for Eirwyn. Unfortunately, they only had it in size for age 5, and Eirwyn was maybe 3½, so he did an excellent scare-crow impression for the rest of the trip.

The only other really annoying thing was that there was a strip of wood or something on the house that wasn't nailed down properly (remember the house wasn't finished), and it flapped in the wind. And what a wind it was: that kind of vicious one you can find along the seashore just about everywhere. So all night, up in the master bedroom, we heard this sound, something between a smack and a rattle. Suffice it to say we didn't sleep very well during those few days.

We never made it into Cape Town that trip, mostly because I was intimidated by the thought of driving in a bigger city I didn't know at all. We did try to go to a mall out in George, and were rather disappointed to find a dinky, run-down and thoroughly unimpressive place. We braved the rain, which was pounding down on our poor little under-dressed selves, to go in one shop and verify we were in the right place. "Ah no," the storekeeper said, "you'll be wanting that big mall across the street."

And indeed, there it was, waiting for us. To give you an idea of what this mall wanted to be when it grew up, its slogan was "Simply the Most". The most stores, the most restaurants, the most useless stuff to buy… it was overwhelming. But we did get some good things, including a very nice shawl that I still have. And don't go thinking of some thing out of the 1970s: this mall could fit into any place in the US and feel at home. Actually, it's probably nicer than quite a few American malls.

Another thing that was really great about that trip was the arboretum, which had loads of local plants that don't exist outside of that area. If you've never heard of a protea, they are very distinctive South African plants, kind of a cross between a flower and a succulent. Real gardeners will tell you I'm not describing it correctly at all, so all I can say is it's worth looking up if you're curious.

Out in Hermanus we got to enjoy one of the best whale-watching places in the world. In the winter, it's right whales who are on display (though I have never heard of a wrong one? or a left one?). We headed out there and had a good hour of just watching the whales do their thing: swim around, come up into the air, spin around, all that stuff. And then to the other side of Kleinmond, near the arboretum, was a great little site for seeing African penguins. We went to see them a couple of times. The walk down from the road is a little tricky, but it's well worth it to see them up close and watch all what they get up to.

All in all it was a great trip, though next time we'll go in January!

77

IN WHICH WE LEARN HOW TO TELL WHO
YOUR FRIENDS ARE

Rwanda, April 2002 to July 2007

We arrived, father, mother, 2-year-old son and 3½-month-old daughter, in Rwanda on the weekend of the eighth commemoration of the genocide. I don't know why we were allowed to do this. We were dropped off in our new house, which had almost no furniture, and were told not to come out for the rest of the weekend. The thing was, aside from the slight detail of no mosquito nets, we also had no fridge and no oven or stove. In a small panic, Eddie called the office saying that this was unacceptable etc., etc. They said, it will need a purchase order and that won't get done till Monday, sorry.

And then, some hours later, came a couple of guys carrying a fridge and a stove. It was like they'd dropped down from heaven. And this is how we met Denis.

Denis was a driver, which is pretty much the lowest status (except for cleaner) in the office—though, to be fair, with their keychains and expensive watches they can generally impress the rural folks just fine. His English was very good, which was a bit of a surprise. We found out later it was because he was essentially trapped in Uganda for several years, and so had spoken English instead of French. He'd never had the opportunity to finish high school, and so couldn't move up much in the office despite his obvious talents.

Our time with Denis really began when his wife had their third child. Eddie went over to see him at the house and got to hold the baby, whose real name was Mohammed but was universally known as "Boss". The following year, they invited us to their house for Eid. Denis' home was in the middle of Kimisagara, a high-density and rather informal part of Kigali. So we put on what vaguely African clothes we had (my standby was the jelabya Eddie'd had made for me in Khartoum) and tramped our way down between the houses to his. It was just a little mud path down from the main road with some mud stairs, which were a bit tricky to negotiate while wet from the rain, especially while carrying gifts.

More Eids followed, and gradually the rest of the family began to get used to us. One year we brought some colored pencils and paper, and you should have seen how the kids just threw themselves at them. Another year we brought a bunch of *Pingu* videos. You probably don't know *Pingu*. I'm sorry. It's a bunch of stop-animation penguins and the odd seal who speak gibberish that you can kind of understand. What can I say; it's just cute. We thought the videos would keep the children occupied, but in the end the adults watched, too.

One of the things that made me really admire Denis was when I asked him whether he'd had a good Ramadan. "Yes," he said, "I was able to pay school fees for a couple of children in the neighborhood, so it was a good Ramadan."

His children also grew to love our family, Eddie in particular. This is not surprising, because he is the baby whisperer. Denis told us once that Boss, now a few years older, would tell the family that Eddie was *his* and no one else was allowed to even use his name!

One of Denis' children seemed to have some developmental issues. At age 10 she still wasn't talking, and she was having trouble keeping up at school. That said, she was friendly and outgoing in her own way. I asked a speech-therapist friend of mine to do an assessment with her; she couldn't find anything specific but gave the parents some ideas of how to vary teaching methods in the hope that something would stick.

That year, Denis wanted to give us $50 to buy toys for his kids while we were on home leave. He was scrambling around to get the money together. When we said he could pay us when we got back, he was so happy. "OK then buy for $100!" he exclaimed. He later told us he had to keep the toys under lock and key so that his daughter could use them and not be trampled by the boys, never mind she was the eldest.

The speech-therapist friend of mine went to the school and explained different learning styles to the teachers there. Even the idea of some children learning by reading and others by writing was completely new to them. Our special case aside, the teachers were thrilled. They'd never been taught different teaching methods before, and recognized that this information could be useful for all of their pupils.

One year over Christmas Eddie borrowed the projector from his office, and we showed a couple of films like Cars and The Incredibles on the wall of our living room. The kids were completely enchanted—by the films, and also by the house with all its "stuff". Denis' wife, who spoke no English or French, demonstrated how she felt about our house by falling asleep on our couch.

At the office, Denis continued to be very reliable, and also helped us out as a family if we needed it. We grew to feel that at any time of day or night, if we called him, he would drop every-thing and come to our aid.

I can't describe how much that mattered in a society that values not revealing what you're actually thinking about someone, and where it seems people are out to get each other all the time. People say you can know someone for years, he'll buy you drinks, you hang out… and secretly he's just waiting for the moment when you are weak to strike. It can make you pretty uneasy when you stop trusting your guards and your house help, and don't know what the neighbors think of the *mzungus* in their midst. It can make you really paranoid, when you don't feel like you can trust anyone.

I wondered a lot how Rwandans actually survive in this atmosphere. How do they cope with having no one they trust, and thinking everyone they know could be plotting to hurt them? This was a great mystery to me for a long time.

Finally, as Denis gradually introduced us to his family and close friends, I started to understand it: people have these little islands of a few friends and family with whom they are close. That little group practices mutual defense and is where you can share your actual thoughts, even on taboo subjects like ethnicity and politics. Having thus circled the wagons, they are equipped to face the rest of the world.

And the thing was, we were let into Denis' close circle. It took a good four years, but when it happened I lost a lot of my Rwanda fatigue. In many ways I feel like our time in Rwanda truly began then.

But sadly, after five years, our sojourn came to an end. I got a job in Sarajevo and had to leave in February, with Eddie and the kids scheduled to come join me in July. I wanted to hire a driver to do the school runs and some basic grocery shopping, and other little tasks for the family as necessary. But to find a driver who would work for only five months was going to be difficult. So when I interviewed a potential driver, I asked him what I would need to pay him for him to promise to stay the whole time. It was a fair chunk of cash, but I was willing to do it if it meant having my kids in safe hands.

And two weeks into the gig, he quit.

Eddie started looking for a replacement driver, until one day Denis came up to him.

"Let me drive your children," he said.

"No," replied Eddie, "I can't use a work vehicle to take the kids to school, and it's not your job."

"Please—let me drive them."

"No, I really think it wouldn't look right."

"Mr. Eddie, you are vulnerable right now. Everyone knows that Madam Carey is out of the country and that you are alone with the children. Please let me drive them. It will be safer."

And with that, it was decided. We had to admit he was right. The end of contract was known for being a time when you are particularly vulnerable, as you try to wrap up your life and prepare for the next one. I heard stories of house help who'd worked for the same person for five years, never complained, and then at the very end accused their employer of never providing vacation time and sued for significant back pay.

In July, when I came back to fetch the family and we did our definitive pack-out, we received an invitation. Denis' sister was in town from the Netherlands, the sister he hadn't seen for seventeen years. He'd been in Uganda in school and was caught there during the genocide, at which point the sister fled the country and had been in the Netherlands ever since. It was so touching, seeing them together.

Denis gave a moving speech, saying that it was the happiest and saddest of days. I couldn't believe he was equating our departure in importance to seeing his own sister after almost two decades. I confess I was moved to tears. But it wasn't over. He produced the cake we'd brought (the first store-bought one in all the years we'd been showing up with cakes) and talked about how it takes many different parts to make the cake. He said the whole family has to be involved to make such a cake, which prompted some embarrassed squirming on our part, but we understood the point. He was rather elegantly using our family as an allegory to his own for how people should work together and support each other.

At the end, they insisted on driving us to the airport, the whole family. I think it was the first time I saw a Rwandan cry. There were a lot of words like "we are one family" and "we are always together".

Also at the end, my car didn't sell. After a little while, I realized that what I really wanted to do was to give it to Denis. I knew that he was studying at night and that a car would help him get there, and I also knew that he would make the car available for people in his neighborhood who needed one. Basically, I knew he would put it to good use.

And the best part was, I really didn't care what he did with it. If he wanted to sell it, he could do that. I had no lack of confidence that he would use the car or the cash to some good purpose. Of course he did give me updates—he got the body fixed and made some other minor repairs, and nicknamed it "Impfizi", meaning "strong" or "powerful", like a big bull. I was a bit ashamed, actually, that I'd never gotten those things done. But for me, I was glad to learn what a "gift" really means.

78

IN WHICH I PLAY BUTCHER

Kigali, December 2003

There's one Christmas our family will never forget. Our first Christmas in Rwanda, we were going to have a colleague from Eddie's work over. Johannes was Swiss, and a vegetarian. I wasn't veggie yet at this point.

It was morning, and we were all still in our nightclothes. Eddie reached down to wipe Marion's bum on the potty, and came up with one of those gasps that happens when you know you've just done something seriously bad. Turns out he'd cut his own bum with the toilet-paper holder, which was in reality just two pieces of relatively sharp metal protruding from the wall.

We got him to go lie down, and I took a look. The toilet-roll holder had cut straight through the sarong he was wearing. The cuts were obviously pretty deep, and I told him that I was convinced he needed stitches.

This was, however, a bit awkward since I could hardly drive him and leave the two under-fives at home, and trying to bring them with us would be horrid. Also, Eddie's French wasn't the strongest, and he certainly wouldn't be on top of his game at that particular moment. So now the hard question… whom could we call who wouldn't take a pitchfork to us just for asking if they could take some time out of their day to accompany Eddie to the hospital?

Finally, after some brain-wracking, I came up with Sylvie, with whom I'd occasionally met to practice our respective French and English. Her English wasn't great but she could get the gist of things pretty well, and Eddie would be there to help out. And, being Belgian, Sylvie's French was perfect. Even better, I figured that Belgium would be like Germany and that the main festivities would have been on the 24th, so she might be able to get free.

After a deeply embarrassing phone call, Sylvie agreed, and arrived with her car a few minutes later. Eddie went armed with quite a few towels so as not to get blood on the seats. And off they went.

A couple of hours later, they were back. Eddie looked a bit traumatized and not only from the procedure of getting the stitches. "They were playing French Christmas carols non-stop," he said, "I'm lying there on my stomach and he's doing his thing and there's Christmas carols." Also, and slightly more crucially, the doctor had refused to let Sylvie behind the screen because she wasn't Eddie's wife. So her translation services were provided from the other side of the room.

The next level of surrealism was the turkey. Obviously, Eddie was in no position to stand up and cook. We pulled out a spare mattress and put it on the floor in the living room, on which he lay, face down. Shortly thereafter Johannes arrived, and what a sight greeted him.

But he responded willingly enough when we explained that the two of us were going to have to be responsible for preparing the turkey—which came, like all local birds, with the organs still in the cavity. So picture, if you will, Eddie on the floor reading from a cookbook to figure out how long the turkey needed to cook, and a vegetarian guest working with the former-and-to-be-again vegetarian doing all of the unpleasant stuff with the turkey. Merry Christmas, everyone!

IN WHICH WE SHARE CUSTODY OF CATS

Rwanda, 2003-2007

In countries where there's a lot of social distance between foreigners and locals, as in Rwanda, it can be very difficult to form friendships. Also, the locals have their friends, so why bother with people who are only going to be around for a couple of years?

In Kigali, we had a gorgeous garden out the back, and sometimes the kids would be out there just messing around. After some time, the kids in the house adjacent to ours up the hill would come down and peer over the fence at us. I assumed it was because we were white and they enjoyed seeing us in our "native habitat". I asked them to leave us alone, but their curiosity was too great. I think they treated it as a game. One time I walked out the back door and I heard "I got the mum!" and a head quickly disappeared from view.

We had this horrible generator that was much too big for our needs ("keep the loads up!"). It was also terribly, penetratingly loud, and it blew diesel fumes directly toward our neighbors, something I felt guilty about.

One day, the mother of the obnoxious kids herself peered over the back fence, so I went up to introduce myself. I climbed onto the waist-high bed at the back fence so that I could speak with her almost eye-to-eye. We introduced ourselves, and then she set me right back when she said, "I wanted to apologize. I think my kids are looking over your fence, and I told them it's rude, but they seem to like your kids and I can't seem to get them to stop."

Well now, that's some motherly solidarity, right there.

"Are they bothering you?" she asked.

Now, what was I going to say? Their looking over the fence did irritate me quite a bit, but now that this perfectly nice woman was standing there, I couldn't say it. Plus, I'd begun to understand that our kids were as keen to talk to her kids as the other way around, so it seemed we were outnumbered. At least I got to apologize for the loud generator.

Now, you know how little kids have no sense of when it's too early to bother other people? This was Eirwyn. Marion was still too small to climb up the water tower. Our water was fed by gravity, so unlike many people we still had water, if cold only, when the power went out. Eirwyn would get up there just above the fence, and start to yell, "Kaaa-ren! Ken! Kaaa-ren!" at six thirty in the morning, when it has just gotten light enough to even *find* the water tower. Sometimes they'd be there, and sometimes they'd not, but Eirwyn would just keep calling until either they came out or the mother, whose name was Dinah, came out to tell him they were out or still sleeping.

And so began the merging of our households. The kids began to wander back and forth freely between the two houses, and Karen and Ken would often stay for dinner at our place. We had a fish pilau recipe that our kids kind of liked but they *loved*. We took to making it every Friday, and funny how they always showed up on a Friday around dinnertime.

But our kids were round theirs a lot, too. Unlike in many African homes, where the front sitting room was for guests and you don't go exploring any other parts of the house, our kids made themselves comfortable in Karen and Ken's bedrooms, the kitchen—and even Dinah and David's bedroom. This isn't quite as weird as you think, as David, a big mucky muck in the Rwandan Army, was posted outside of Kigali and so it was usually just Dinah.

Imagine David's surprise, then, when he woke up some weekend morning with wee Marion standing in the doorway saying, "Hi, Dinah! Oh, hi, David!" She was expecting to sit on Dinah's bed and have a story read to her. Dinah had been letting the kids come into the bedroom in the mornings if she didn't yet want to get out of bed. I guess she hadn't warned David!

The other thing we shared besides children was cats. Our guard knew we wanted a cat, as we'd heard that their scent supposedly repels snakes. After having found a few of the serpentine persuasion in our garden, and given my near-obsessive fear of a snake biting one of the children, we were pretty much ready to try anything. So one day our guard appeared in front of the house with a kitten, whom we immediately named "Socks" or "Soksi" because of her white paws. We fed her so she stuck around, though she remained outside, and was too wild to get into a box or anything domesticated so that we could take her to the vet. So she was more a habituated feral cat than a pet.

Soon enough Soksi had made some little ones, so then there were like six of them. And eventually there was another generation… we think all were sired by the same tom who kept hanging around but never stayed. So yes, there was definitely some inbreeding going on, but without a feasible way to get them fixed, what could we do? The children did learn a lot about dealing with animals, though. Eirwyn exhibited unexpected patience and tenderness when he sat down and let the cats come to him, and even fall asleep on his lap.

The cats spent a lot of time up at Karen and Ken's so we definitely had joint custody, though we did most of the feeding. When we left, the cats just migrated up the hill.

There were a few times we really felt that we'd made a special connection with this family. One was an invitation to the engagement ceremony of a niece or cousin. This is when the groom's family is supposed to give the final approval for him to marry his chosen bride. The ceremony consists largely of the groom's family insulting the bride's family, often dredging up (real or imagined) grudges from decades past. Nowadays, the families have given their approval long before spending all the money on the ceremony, and the gibes are all in good fun, but back in the day they were apparently deadly serious.

And so you might hear, for example: "Ho, you there! The second cousin to the bride's uncle! You remember, there was that time 20 years ago when you cycled past me and you failed to greet me!"

And the reply: "But no, that day I was very ill and there were problems with my eyes and I could not see you. This is why I failed to greet you!"

And so on. Har, har.

But still, we were the only non-family members there, which was surely a great honor. We tried to show appropriate gratitude, but Marion (aged maybe three) scuppered that by sitting on Grandpa's lap—this being the patriarch of the whole clan, a well-respected person and former bureaucrat of some high standing. Grandpa was one of the few people so respected that food was brought to him rather than his having to go stand in line at the buffet. (I believe they served us, too; special white-man privilege.)

So Marion, innocent as she was, gets talking with Grandpa and the next thing you know she's sitting on his lap. He gives her a piece of goat from his *brochette* and Marion wolfs it down. Now this is something, because at this age she would not eat any meat that required actual chewing. The exception being, apparently, Grandpa's goat brochettes. Marion said sweet things and looked adoringly at him, and so he gave her all the brochettes she wanted. Typically sweet of people's reaction to small children, but still embarrassing for us, watching our well-fed daughter nosh up all of his meat!

Dinah and I have kept in touch off and on over the years. They have moved, and Soksi is no longer around, but they do have two cats. David is still a big deal in the army. Karen and Ken are about 10 feet tall, and Karen looks the picture of her mother. We always laugh about Eirwyn calling over the fence and poor David waking up to find strange children in his bedroom!

80

IN WHICH I BECOME A FOUNDING BOARD MEMBER

Lusaka, 2013-2014

O ne of the things about being a regional staff member and traveling around a lot is that it's really hard to put down roots in the country you live in. You're gone too much and home too irregularly to join a club or a class, and you're just not around enough to easily make friendships. This is even more true of friendships with local staff, especially in Southern Africa where whites have no novelty value.

In pretty much every country we've worked, there's been some sort of bulletin that acts as a kind of notice board for the expat community. In one of these, I saw an ad for a meeting of Women in Aviation International. This intrigued me because of Eirwyn's interest in being a pilot, so I contacted the person listed and asked whether we could somehow join or come to a few meetings even though I was going to be absent on the day of the actual meeting. I was reassured that there would be other meetings, and that I shouldn't worry.

Imagine my surprise, then, when a few weeks later I opened my mailbox to find that I had been elected to the board in absentia. *Say what?* And then I went to the first meeting, because I kind of felt that I had been Shanghaied, only to discover that they were just launching the process to create the Zambia chapter. Then I understood why I'd been roped in sight unseen: they needed every warm body they could get.

Well, OK, I figured. It was a meeting per month, which I thought I could swing. And the more I found out about WAI, the more I liked the organization. They have chapters that provide scholarships and different ways of getting involved in aviation, and there's a massive connect meeting once a year where women can meet mentors, take classes in financial management, hear speakers who've done great things in aviation, and more. They provide scholarships to help young people get qualified on their plane of choice, or to complete additional certifications so they can do new things.

To be part of the board, I had to become a member of WAI, and I loved reading the monthly magazine, in the way that it's fun listening to any real enthusiast talk about his or her passion.

So there I was, not just interacting with Zambians but Zambians who *weren't in the aid business*. That is part of why I stayed, just a fascination with who these people were—and how they ran their meetings. We were fortunate enough to have as our president the first female pilot in Zambia, and the rest were a number of women (and a few men) who were involved in aviation in some way.

The meetings were all about three times longer than they needed to be, in part because of a stickler's adherence to protocol that I didn't think needed sticking to. I also felt like we went round and round a lot. Lots of talk and no clear commitments. None of this would surprise anyone who's worked with the local staff of many countries in Africa; it was just a really different thing to see it up close and without an expat leader setting the tone, and a different kind of discipline for me to just sit back and do the meeting as they wanted.

But I earned my keep in one fell swoop: we had to pay dues to WAI in the US, and no one on the board had a credit card. They were getting ready to wire the money, at a fantastic cost to the emerging organization's purse, when I said that I could easily write WAI a check on my US account, if the Zambia chapter could just pay me back locally. Well, you'd think I'd handed them the keys to the empire. It was such an easy thing for me to do, and I knew it would make our lives much easier, so why not?

They also knew that I had really joined for my son, who was too young to learn yet but was pretty consistent in saying that he wanted to be a pilot. They named him their "future president".

Then I almost lost all my credibility with them. To this day, I cringe when I think about it. For our registration as a Zambian association, we had to provide completed application forms from every board member with our fingerprints. As the membership chair I had been entrusted with the folder containing everyone's applications. This was no small thing, considering our board members came not only from Lusaka, but also from Kitwe and Ndola in the north of the country. It had taken several weeks to get all the paperwork together, since each member had had to organize getting fingerprints, and then the documents often had to be sent down with a bus driver acting as courier.

Well, if I didn't one day get the little button thingy wrong on my coffee thermos and put it open into my bag. Upon arriving at work, I realized in horror that all the applications so carefully compiled were soaked in coffee. They were all worthless. I was honestly afraid of what my esteemed colleagues were going to do to me.

But in the end they accepted this step backward as just a part of the process, and eventually we all met down at the police office in Lusaka to do the final fingerprinting and submit our application. We impressed the policewoman with the fact that our president was the first female pilot in the country. I think she felt some female inspiration. She certainly wished her daughter could be there to meet Mrs. Ndhlovu.

The best moment for me came when I got to accompany a group of members to a girls' school specializing in STEM subjects. Our president gave a fine speech on her life story and the obstacles she overcame to realize her dream of becoming a pilot. But my favorite speaker was one who worked as a flight engineer, maintaining and servicing airplanes. She got up in front of these girls, who'd received pieces of paper, and started to show them how to make a paper airplane—but at the same time, she was explaining all the aerodynamics of how planes fly, using her own body as an example. She twisted her arms this way and that as she demonstrated the various functions of the wing when the flaps are in different positions. She bounced along as though she were truly in the air, being buffeted by the wind a little bit. I bet they kindled some real interest in aviation for a few girls.

Unfortunately, I had to leave the WAI Zambia chapter when we left the country. In the last few days, we were having some sort of leaving thing with friends, and then the WAI folks said they were doing a big barbeque and could I come? There was just so much else going on that day, I really didn't feel like going, but they were insistent and so I decided to make an appearance. I was running late, so my arrival wound up being right as they were wrapping up.

No sooner had I arrived, though, when they whipped out a bouquet of flowers and a huge card, signed by them all, and then a three-foot high carving of the African continent, with the Big Five safari animals carved around the edge, Eirwyn's and my names carved rather inexpertly into the middle, and the names and date painted with whiteout.

Honestly, I was blown away. I knew they appreciated the

business with the check, but they kept insisting that I'd done a lot for them and they never would have started if I hadn't been there to help them. I surely don't know if that was true, but their gratitude was so heartfelt, I couldn't help but be very touched. I felt awful for almost not coming, and leaving it to the very end. But they seemed happy enough since I had shown up, and I was certainly grateful for having done so.

81

IN WHICH WE ARE FAMOUS FOR A DAY

York, 1999

The place we lived in in York was in a courtyard delightfully named Barleycorn Yard. We were up on the second floor, with windows facing the street, so that come tourist season all the tour-bus riders up top had a great view of our living room. It was quite an old building, and the bit next to the street was slowly subsiding, so the whole living room was pitched slightly forward in that direction. This always gave me a rather slippery feeling, and although I used the room plenty, I always rather felt that my footsteps would cause the whole front of the building to come crashing down. Ah, England.

Now, there was a TV show at the time called Time Team, in which a team of archaeologists scrambled around to find out what they could about a particular site in three days. It was kind of fun, and always gave you a greater understanding of what troves of former buildings, castles, great halls, and burial sites lurk beneath great swathes of the country.

Then one day, Time Team announced that it was going to do a special, live-broadcast episode using three different sites in York:

a Roman site, a Norman one, and a Viking one. Since our street was known to have been erected by the Vikings, it wasn't a real surprise that the Viking dig was going to be in a building site not four doors down from our house.

It was all lots of fun, and I reckon a large percentage of the population of York was watching as everything played out. At one point the lead commentator, Tony Robinson, said something like, "Right, after this commercial break I'll be coming to you again from the Viking site in Walmgate Road." So of course I went to poke my head out and watch him come by—and was met by another fifteen heads at my height, all of whom had the same idea.

What was very cool was that the lots of land on the road were all a Viking unit of measurement wide. As in, the Vikings made the street and then parceled out the land, and those parcels had never changed, for over 1,000 years. They were long and narrow, originally with not much frontage. The building would run at one side toward the back and house animals, with a cooking space, a space for hanging out and a space for sleeping, all open to the empty corridor of land stretching parallel to the building for its entire length.

You could see some of this in how Barleycorn Yard was constructed, with buildings to the left and empty space to the right, though that all stopped not very far back. Behind it was a green area, and then the property had obviously been cut short, so it didn't go back as far as an original Viking one would have.

Our Time Team friend did find some old coins and evidence of habitation, but we didn't really need that. Our lovely street had featured on TV, and we weren't even in London! It felt amazing to live on a street that had been continuously inhabited for a thousand years.

82

IN WHICH WE ARE THE IDEAL TENANTS
WITHOUT EVEN TRYING

August 1998 – September 2000

Said Barleycorn Yard was truly a lovely spot. There was the
main house out front, which still sported frosted glass inside
from when it had been a pub, and then another back building
stretching the width of the yard a good bit behind. There were
businesses in the back house and the other flats in the main
house, and Eddie had rented the one-room flat on the second
floor.

We were a little nervous when I came and wound up staying
on for a while, since the flat was technically let out to one person.
Things got really dicey when we were about to become three. At
this point the landlord and his wife, Tony and Breeda, had
moved from the back house and were living one floor above us.
So it wasn't like we could hide the fact that a little screamer was
on its way.

So one day, Eddie screwed up his courage and went to tell
Tony that there were going to be three of us… and was greeted
with total delight. Phew. Later on we used to visit with Eirwyn
and Tony would bounce around with him, very sweet.

In the meantime, though, the other tenants had been up to no good. One day the guy with the business in the back selling timeshares packed up and absconded with everyone's money. It was a minor scandal, and one time I came home to find the local news filming a report from the middle of the yard. Don't mind me, I just live here.

Then the person from the front room on the ground floor left, and Tony let the room to a woman who was going to do nails or something. I can't remember what the actual front was, but from the few glimpses I got inside there was a lot of pink and soft lighting, and a screen up about halfway back that hid, well, the bed and who knows what else.

Eddie and I didn't think much about her or any of the tenants, to be honest. But then we kept getting strange buzzes at the door, always men, asking questions I could never quite decipher, though one apparently asked whether he was too late for "services".

When we told Tony all this, he got quite huffy. And he thanked us for saying something, because it confirmed his suspicions of what was going on. Pretty soon that particular lady was gone and someone else had moved in. Funnily enough our friend was filmed being arrested for plying her trade in her new location, which happened to be in the proximity of a Catholic school. Oops.

One evening, not long after we'd bade farewell to the woman in question, Eddie and I found Tony and Breeda sitting in the garden at the back of the back house, which was a rather large and wild space. They were sitting companionably side by side, sipping white wine, and watching the bonfire they'd made with the furniture the former resident had left behind. When we asked what they were doing, Tony said, gleefully, "We're burning the tart's bed." What to do? Nothing for it but to sit down and enjoy the fire with them. "Do you think we have time for one more door, darling?"

83

IN WHICH THE HEAD OF HOUSEHOLD
GOES FROM DAD TO PA

Ouagadougou, 2015-2016

Now, I want you all to know that the carrot-cake recipe was *mine* to begin with. Just because Eddie tweaked a few things and then made it for everyone whenever he could get cream cheese, do we *have* to praise him as this amazing baker? Also, for the record: *I* taught *him* how to make bread. And seriously, it's not even that hard, even if it does smell and taste amazing. Just because I was working and didn't have the time or energy to produce a cake every time someone sneezed, I mean, really?

And by the way, until Ouaga I was doing most of the cooking for the family. But that gets no credit—it's just Eddie and the baking. You'd think these people never saw a carrot cake before.

Now, where I will give him some points is the sourdough, especially all the starters he made from scratch. Though I did love the packaged San Francisco starter, and never knew until Ouaga that it was a different strain, which is why his always tasted funny to me. You will allow me, though, that the homemade starters tended to bubble over out of their containers and make rather a mess, never mind it's incredibly fun to watch.

Where he was definitely more mercenary than I was with the flour. Our poor Scandinavian friends who had no idea what hit them. Eddie cleverly let it be known that he would love some rye flour or anything else that was a little wholemeal-y and could make bread more interesting. Again, he shared the spoils, so they were happy to continue giving. He also started buying wheat berries and grinding them in a friend's grinder. So all in that was a pretty healthy trade in cakes, bread, flours, and sourdough starters.

Then came the day that we knew we'd lost him for good. The only milk available in the supermarkets being long life, he started buying a couple of gallons from a guy who would bring the milk up on his bicycle from a farm somewhere. And no, it wasn't pasteurized, so before putting it in the fridge he would have to first boil the skedoodle out of it.

The fresh milk was good, though, for splitting into curds and whey, which you can't generally do with long life. (At least this long-life milk was always OK, unlike the Ugandan stuff we got for a while in Rwanda that was frequently off.) This splitting is good for making *paneer* cheese or fake ricotta, so sometimes Eddie would make a bunch of *paneer* and we'd make a curry. Since the *paneer* only uses the curds, the whey is left over. He would keep it for using in bread, but discovered that he like the taste of it on its own.

And so the day that Pa stepped out of the kitchen with a big bottle and a glass, saying enthusiastically, "Who wants a nice big glass of whey?" Cue groans from the kids. "He's gonna start weaving his own cloth, and making his own clothes and furniture next."

84

AND SOMETIMES YOU JUST MAKE A GOOD FRIEND

Kigali, Lusaka, everywhere 2004-

I met Anna through the Ambassador's Girls' Scholarship Fund, for which I was the US embassy point person for a couple of years. Anna worked for FAWE Rwanda, which ran a model school but also lobbied for girls' education in general and distributed scholarships to keep girls in school if they could. FAWE was our local partner in the AGSF scholarships, as they had the information about test scores and which girls were supposed to be in which secondary schools.

Through that work Anna and I became friendly, and then we discovered that she and her family lived just up the hill from us. We took the kids up to meet her one day, and as she was giving us the tour of the garden, there was a tree with some kind of berry on it. Anna gave Marion one and that's all she wrote: Marion practically emptied the tree. Her face was deep purple surrounding a big fat grin. (So African, to just give the whole tree to a child.)

Anna had lunch with my mother and me when she was visiting us, and now she always asks after her: "How is Mum?"

Anna had been a refugee in Uganda before the end of the genocide, when she moved to Rwanda, albeit briefly. Her husband was named the first ambassador to Japan after the genocide, and they spent a good five years there. (They made some very good friends there who turned out to be cousins of my boss in Burkina—go figure.) Now, her husband was the head of the Post Office, also a decently senior figure in the national administration.

She invited me to dinner with some friends, all of whom were also senior figures of some kind. It was very interesting to hear what they had to say it relative privacy: nothing against the government, but a different spin on things.

After Rwanda, we had the two years in Sarajevo, at which point we came back to Africa, notably Zambia. We hadn't been there a full week when I was sitting at a *braai*, and I got a Facebook message from Anna. Was I really in Zambia, she asked? Because she was, too! She was currently up north on some kind of workshop, but in a month or so she was moving properly to Lusaka. She'd gotten a job with COMESA (the Common Market for East and Southern Africa), which is based in Lusaka, and took a cute little condo for herself.

The one thing Anna knew for sure was that I loved Rwandan beans and *dodo*, aka amaranth leaves. So she used to invite our whole family over for a banquet of Rwandan food. It was heaven. We also had her over to our house. She always brought Rwandan goodies for us. I think these times are what really cemented our friendship. She'd come over, eat, sit around, even swim in our pool, and all the time we were able to speak about all sorts of things. It was just easier being outside of Rwanda. She watched our kids grow and it was like she was watching her own.

Anna and I still keep in touch. She Facebook messages me at random times of the day, just to catch up on how the family is doing. I love how I'll be sitting in a café somewhere, messaging with my friend in Rwanda. I think of all the African friends I made, she is the one most likely to still be in my life in ten or twenty years.

85

IN WHICH (AMERICAN) FOOTBALL TAKES
OVER THE WORLD

I never really thought that American football had any kind of following overseas. But it seems there is one, or the airwaves are just really empty at certain times and the broadcasters need filler.

The first time I ran across it was at least 15 years since seeing it in the US. I'd just brought Eirwyn home from the hospital, and he was sleeping in a Moses basket next to the bed so I could hear him if he got hungry. At some crazy hour he wanted to nurse, so I brought him to the couch in the living room and flicked on the TV just to see if there was anything to keep me vaguely alert. And what should I find, but NFL! And the Niners were even playing! So exciting, only they lost.

Our second year in Sarajevo, we also discovered NFL football on TV. Thankfully it was on around dinnertime, so there was no need to stay up ridiculously late. I want to say it was on Tuesdays, so maybe a repeat of Monday night football. We watched it enough that Eddie started to master the basic rules, and he actually got quite into it.

Probably the most fun, though, was when my employer asked me to go to Quito, Ecuador for a peacebuilding training. Because of the way the flights arrive, a bunch of the attendees were going to be landing the Sunday before the Monday start, which just so happened to be Superbowl Sunday. So someone who knew the town a bit gave us all directions to this one "American" sports bar not terribly far from the hotel, and a bunch of us (exhausted, jetlagged and happy to be there) took over a table or two, got wings and beers, and watched the game.

The fun thing was that there were different groups of people and one or both of the others was rooting for the other team. Thankfully, I don't think there was anyone among our group who really cared that much who won; it was all about the experience and having a chance to get together. Plus, we lost. Again.

86

TERROR, PART 1

Ouagadougou, January 2016

O ne evening after dinner, I got a call from my boss.

"Hi, Carey, how are you?"

"I'm fine, thanks. How are you?"

"I am fine. That is to say, I am not so fine."

At this point I'm starting to register that indeed, he is sounding a bit keyed up. Not in an excited kind of way, a "coming down from lots of adrenaline" kind of way.

"I was sitting in Veranda Café having my beer, when all of a sudden I heard gunfire just a bit up the road. All of the customers who were sitting outside ran inside. We were waiting there but I could still hear the gunfire. Eventually I decided that I didn't like being stuck there in a box, so I made a run for my car and drove back home."

It took me a few minutes to process that he was talking about a terror attack. They'd hit a very popular, Westernized café, Cappuccino, and the hotel across the street, Splendid. This kind of gave me goosebumps because we'd been to Cappuccino several times, and CRS often put visitors in the Splendid precisely because it was across the street from the café.

What incensed a lot of people was that the attackers had apparently been seen in a nearby mosque, and someone allegedly spotted a gun and tried to warn the police, but it was not taken seriously. Also, the police response was very slow, which gave time to the attackers to inflict a lot of damage.

We were touched by all this in a few ways. For one, Eddie and a couple of people I knew had either been in Cappuccino or driven by just hours before the attack. Also, an American missionary was killed whom Eirwyn had met briefly on a service trip. The worst was the owner of the café. He lost something like five members of his family, including his wife and son, in the café he owned. The café itself was totaled. It took him around 18 months to re-do the place and open up again, brave soul.

A café across the street from Cappuccino, Taxi Brousse (bush taxi), was able to reopen much more quickly. The US Ambassador, with his keen understanding of how to hit the popular heart, went down there with a number of his senior staff, ordered great big beers for everyone, and snapped a photo. This photo then went to the newspapers with the caption: "Ouagadougou is open for business!"

87

TERROR, PART 2

Ouagadougou, August 2017

After the January attack, some people started avoiding restaurants popular with expats, and places like the big supermarket installed inspectors at the door who were supposed to wand everyone. They especially avoided going out on Fridays, since this was the day of the previous attack and of course it's the Muslim day of prayer. But with time, people started to relax a bit, and life turned back largely to normal.

That is, until the 16th of August the following year, when gunmen opened fire on a popular Turkish restaurant, killing around 30 people.

One of those people was Tammy Chen, a teacher well liked by staff and students alike at our kids' school, one of those people who was good at getting people to cooperate and bury their individual issues for the betterment of the school as a whole. Tammy had led a trip to Italy for six or seven kids that summer, which Marion had been on. Our kids liked her a lot. She was killed with her new husband and their unborn child.

Eddie and Marion were traveling from the US to Burkina

that day, and got into the taxi to go home, a route that passes very close to the restaurant, right when all the action was starting. They didn't notice anything, so it didn't feel like a really close call, but it kind of was one anyway.

The reaction to this attack was very different than the first one. There are roadblocks and helicopters patrolling all the time now, and the whole atmosphere has changed; people don't feel as safe. A lot of expats have left, though many of those will be replaced. But we are worried for the future of our little Anglophone community in Ouaga.

88

RACE

Something that often shocks people when they newly arrive in a lot of African countries is how openly race is discussed, and in a way that takes for granted that different ethnicities have their own characteristics. There's always a special word for the whites: *mzungu, faranji, toubab.* And it's generally assumed that white people are more delicate than Africans, not being able to handle the sun or rough roads, and of course that they have an inexhaustible supply of money. Some people even express gratitude for colonialism: I had a nanny once who said that colonialism was good because it brought Christianity to Africans. I actually kind of tried to argue the point with her, but the absurdity of the situation overwhelmed me and I gave up.

A lot of people flounder with the whole house-help concept. The visuals of a black woman scrubbing the floors for a white family are a bit uncomfortable. It gets worse when they see that the house help intends to eat on her own at the back of the house. I've known more than a few families who started out inviting the house help to eat with them at the table, which is catastrophic on a couple of levels.

The really bad thing is that it totally upends people's ideas about the natural hierarchy of things. In the house helps' minds, the family is naturally higher on the totem pole than they are, so the family is showing a lack of understanding of the rules when they invite worker to sit with management.

But worse, in a way, is that it brings the house help into an untenable position. They can accept the invitation and be mortified on the inside, or they can try to get out of it and thereby go against their need to please their employer. And so, what is intended as a generous and egalitarian gesture quickly becomes a source of cringeworthy embarrassment. It's certainly not my intent here to justify hierarchy or white people feeling superior; I just mean that we are the guests in their country and we should make the effort to understand the dynamics before upending everything.

Paul Kagame keeps saying that Rwanda doesn't need the stinking foreign powers' aid, but funnily enough he keeps taking it.

I had a friend who volunteered with a local NGO for a while. The colleagues asked where she went to church (not "if"). When she said she was Jewish, they were completely taken aback, having never met a Jew before. They reached out their hands to touch her lightly and asked with awe, "Is it true you killed Jesus?"

I've had mothers hold up their babies to watch me go by in the car. You can just hear her saying, "Look, Junior, it's your very first *mzungu*!"

There are some countries where to be white is automatically to be guilty in cases like a car crash. It doesn't matter how much you were in the right and the other guy in the wrong; it's assumed that as a mzungu you will have the cash to pay and are so a better target for "justice".

We had friends who were crashed into by a car that was going backwards and in the wrong direction on a roundabout, at speed. Unsurprisingly, said driver was very drunk at the time. Unfortunately, he was also a cabinet minister. So when, the next day, our friends went to the police station to helpfully provide additional details of the crash, they were summarily fined for reckless driving. When they protested, they were told they should be happy they weren't fined for the damage to the minister's car and his distress.

I once had great fun with a six-year-old friend of Eirwyn's, who was mixed race. I'd come to the school to do some volunteering with the first-graders. I was wearing black boot socks that were a little bit sheer. Charles looked at the bit of leg showing between the bottom of my pants leg and my shoe, and said, "Why do you have black, there?" Quick as a flash, I answered, "Oh, well you know what? I'm half black and half white, like you! Only I'm white on the top half and black on the bottom half." You should have seen the moment of confusion on his face before he figured out it was a joke.

The other thing is that, as I understand it, many African populations consider lighter-toned skin to be superior to very black skin. Clearly these people have not appreciated the folks from Sudan who have seriously black skin. I've heard it referred to as blue-black. Anyway it looks completely awesome. I don't know if this attitude is a by-product of colonialism's making skin that is closer to white more desirable, but it could be. Ridiculous.

Where it gets really confusing is African-Americans in Africa. This is where my blond, green-eyed, born-in-Nairobi daughter looks at black Americans and says, "I'm more African that you are!" And one must concede that she has a point.

People of African extraction might well be able to pass for local on the street, though there is a definite American way of walking and holding oneself that could still give them away. Anyway they do not necessarily immediately get the mzungu reception, but of course for the most part they lack knowledge of local languages. But they're not white. So are they mzungus or not? No one seems to have a definitive answer, leaving each person to negotiate the situation as they will.

Or, you could be like an African-American I saw being sworn in to the Peace Corps, who came up and spoke from the podium in the most perfect Moore, complete with tonal accents and funky vowels. There was an audible stir in the audience when she opened her mouth. I wonder if she ever passed for Burkinabè.

So, as you can see, race has its fault lines in Africa, just not in the same place as in the US. And of course the situation varies widely, in particular between former French and British colonies, since the home governments had such different relationships with their overseas territories. Obviously there's much more here that could be discussed, ad infinitum. Personally, I would love to set all this aside, but it leaves its imprint on too many aspects of life to be ignored.

HOUSE HELP, GUARD HELP, CHA CHA CHA

Another fraught topic is house help. Love them, hate them, a bit of both, there is one thing guaranteed to get people's blood pressure up, and that is the strangers they invite into their house every day.

As I've said before, Westerners often have a lot of embarrassment about having house help. We don't need it in the West, do we? Well, in the West you don't have to sweep and mop the floors in the entire house every day, and iron all your clothes because you don't have a dryer or you have to make sure there aren't any mango-fly eggs lurking in the seams. Let alone needing someone to watch children after school or take them to playdates if both parents are working, because day care is non-existent, and who can cook meals or (our favorite solution) chop veggies and pre-cook beans so that you can make dinner in half an hour when you get home. Oh, you say—you move to Africa and suddenly you don't cook for yourself anymore? Let me tell you, it's great to have everything so natural and from scratch, but sometimes you'd just like to have a nice jar of curry sauce or some pre-cleaned lettuce.

What's weird and kind of scary is how much power you have

over house help, up to a point. They depend on you for their livelihood. One called me her mother. She wasn't talking about age, but about the role I had in her life of taking care of her. And I did do a lot of things for her. When she told me she was HIV+, I gave her the time to go to all her doctors' appointments (sadly, not a given) and made sure she got enrolled in the national scheme to receive treatment. I could have paid for her drugs, but then when we left she'd be stuck.

I also tried to teach her about savings. I told her she could choose to put aside a certain amount of her paycheck, which I would keep for her, but I would always write down how much was in there so she'd be sure I wasn't cheating her, and that she could take some or all of that money whenever she wanted to, no questions asked. We talked about it a bit, so I figured we were all clear. Soon she started saving around 10% of her salary, so before long she had a decent little packet of money squirreled away.

One day she came to me and started asking for an advance on her salary, because she had this and that problem. I tried to stop her, and I repeated a few times that she could have the money she'd stored away, and she didn't need to give me any reason why —it was her money. After about three rounds of this she looked at me and said, "Ah, so *that's* the benefit." She'd been putting her money aside just because she thought I was asking her to do it.

The really unfortunate thing is how some Westerners who would be perfectly nice at home suddenly morph into really quite exploitative employers. I honestly think the power goes to their heads. They would never agree to work ten hours a day, six days a week, but think nothing of asking that of their employees.

It's not a question of what's legal, which can be pretty shocking in terms of lack of rights for house help, but silly me, I would rather not ask of someone what I wouldn't do myself. Of course some will prefer the long hours if it means making more money, and who am I to tell them they have to rest when they have mouths to feed. But I just don't get this attitude that it's normal to exploit people, as long as they get paid.

In Rwanda we had the (semi-)dynamic duo of Madeleine and Violette. Violette was a bit older and primarily did the housework, while Madeleine was really there to help with Marion, especially after I went to work at the embassy. They were both scrupulously honest, which is like winning the lottery.

One day, very close to New Year's Eve, Madeleine came to me and asked my forgiveness. OK, but, err, for what? I don't even remember most of what she said, but I know she said that sometimes she'd taken change from the little dish we kept by the front door, for example if she didn't have the right change for the bus. She always meant to give it back, she said, but there were times when she hadn't.

She was crying, telling me all of alleged sins, most of which were so grave I promptly forgot them. But *would I forgive her*? As it turned out, in her church she needed that forgiveness in order to be forgiven by God, and it was important that it happen by the end of the year. So I said the magic words, and she was OK after that. Hugely relieved, actually. In a way I was, too. If she was crying over a few stolen coins then I figured there wasn't anything truly awful lurking behind Curtain #2.

Madeleine was Adventist, which is not a religion I know much about, but in Rwanda at least they had a good reputation for being honest and hard-working. It's actually one of the biggest churches in Rwanda. Most of the time it was totally irrelevant, but every once in a while religion would poke its head up. At one point Eddie and I decided to start having more regular date nights, never a forte of ours. So we asked Madeleine to work a number of Saturday evenings, for which she would be paid overtime.

One day, when she came for one such sitting appointment, she asked that we not pay her. Huh? She'd do the work, she said,

but could we please not pay her? Hmmm… *suspicious face*
"So, why can't we pay you if you're doing the work?" we asked.

"Saturday is the Sabbath," she replied. "I can't work on the Sabbath, and if you pay me, it means I'm working. This way I am just doing you a favor."

In the end we settled on raising her regular pay and getting a certain number of evenings included in her regular work hours, to weaken the relationship between her working evenings and her pay.

Marion went through a phase of crying when Madeleine left at the end of the day. Madeleine would hand Marion to me and waaaaaaaa! Thankfully, I was able to see it as a good sign, that she'd really bonded with the person who was taking care of her. One day she asked me why Madeleine had to go home. I told her that Madeleine had her own family waiting for her at home, and she needed to take the bus. Why not a bicycle? No bicycle. Why not a car? No car.

"But Mommy, why don't we buy Madeleine a car, then?"

Actually, they got on very well, those two. I can definitely say that well before the end of the five years we were in Rwanda, Madeleine had come to love Marion as her own child. They'd take the big spare mattress out and put it on the lawn, and just sing and play games. She taught Marion the French version of "head, shoulders, knees and toes", which was super cute. Madeleine is not a "cute" woman, but I did think it was cute that she consistently jumped between "vous" and "tu" when talking to Marion. The "vous" always made me think she was putting Marion on a pedestal somehow, like "My lady, wouldst thou care for some banana?"

(Aside: I loved that mattress. It was a big, foam thing, probably king-sized, that had been on one of the beds until it was disposed of. We stashed it in the garage and asked the guard to bring it when the kids wanted to play on it, or if the grownups fancied a lie down outside. We spent countless afternoons watching the sky start to pale and then darken, listening to the birds and watching them flit about, waiting for Eddie to get home. Those were some of the most magical moments I ever spent with my children.)

And then there's the time Madeleine called me at work to tell me that Eirwyn (aged maybe 3) had locked himself in the bathroom. I could see her dilemma, but also thought it was pretty hilarious. She was trying to explain through the door how to turn the key to open it again, but Eirwyn wasn't really understanding her and was starting to get frustrated. We were just making plans for me to cut my day short and come home, when he finally jiggled it the right way and was free.

The one thing about Violette I really remember is that she brought some maize to work for her lunch, and of course wee cheeky Marion asked if she could have some. So Violette broke off a maize kernel and gave it to her. Well, that was a mistake. I'm not sure how much of her cob she gave to Marion in the end, but they were out there a long time, and I have the feeling the situation repeated itself more than once.

One of the guards we had initially in Rwanda, before we had to go with agency guards, was a young man called Issa. Issa was Muslim and so spoke Swahili in addition to Kinyarwanda (Swahili having been the language of Arab traders), but no English. Suddenly, I wished I'd tried a lot harder with the Swahili when we were in Nairobi. But he would happily climb the guava tree to bring some ripe fruits down for the kids. We called him "Issa kabisa", *kabisa* meaning very much in Swahili. It was totally silly but he liked it.

And then one day Issa got married, and we were invited to go. Eddie couldn't go for some reason, but I was free, and pretty curious about what this wedding would look like. So on the day I put on my trusty jelabya, we dressed Marion in a yellow, meringue fluff ball of a dress that had been a gift, and we headed out to Mahmoud's place.

I'd love to be able to tell you about the marriage ceremony, but as a woman I spent the whole time in a little room with all the other women, including the bride. Apparently, they'd done the actual ceremony very early in the morning, but while the guests were there the men went off to the mosque for some additional prayers, and that was about it.

Issa was very pleased that I'd come, though, so I felt that it had been worth it. And then just sitting with all these women and not being able to say anything to them was awkward but not horribly so. Now that I know that people will sit in silence for the first hour of any party, I think it was probably much less awkward for the other women than for me.

At one point Marion started fussing, so I picked her up and said, mostly because it was something I actually could say in Swahili, "she wants to sleep." Oops. Suddenly there were several women offering to help me tie her on my back in the way that they carry their children when they sleep. Sadly, at that point I was too shy to give it a go (and convinced I would drop my child on the floor). If I had the same opportunity today, I'd take it in a heartbeat.

Then there was Clarisse, our cleaner in Zambia. I really don't like it when people grovel, but this woman went a bit the other way. We paid for the mealie meal (maize meal à la southern Africa) in the house so that she could cook lunch. She was allowed to use our fridge to keep her "relish", i.e., the vegetables and such that you make to go with the *sadza*, the thick paste of maize meal and water that is the staple of the Zambian diet. She always used huge amounts of the mealie meal, cooked for the guard as well, and often took more than her full hour's rest in the middle of the day. She'd get chatting with the guard and sometimes they'd sit there for an awfully long time. I hate to sound petty, but dude, that's not what we're paying you for.

We've generally stuck with house help and lived with their various eccentricities, but in Ouaga we changed people twice. The Burkinabès generally don't stay silent the way folks will in eastern and southern Africa. West Africa is a little more confident and in your face. I took over our first house help from my predecessor, who loved her. Well, maybe it was because they weren't actually around during the day. This woman had attitude and then some. She'd argue with Eddie about how things should be done in the house, or just not do what she was asked.

Ouaga was the first place where the house help also received social security and unemployment insurance, so it was also where I became an official employer and had to pay money into the system for her. When we finally let her go, there was a whole bunch of malarkey because I'd miscalculated my payments to the social-security office, so I had to "regulate" that (i.e., pay more money), and then she tried to get me for wrongful dismissal. Thankfully, this was not one of those cases when being white also means being automatically at fault.

The next person we had, we shared with another family. This was a good arrangement for us because now that the children were older, there really wasn't enough to keep someone busy for a whole day. But you don't want to hire someone part-time because other part-time jobs are so rare that in essence you're just denying them half a paycheck.

So we thought we were in like Flynn, but this one turned out to be one of those people who just sucks the energy out of a room. She also started complaining about our arrangement, despite having known about it from the beginning. Eddie, who had to deal with her all the time, finally lost it and we had to let her go.

And then we got the wonderful Mr. Pibi (real name:

Edouard). He sort of bounced around the house and had the perfect amount of assertiveness: he said what he thought and wanted, without making unrealistic demands. He was someone you could have a normal conversation with. We brought him t-shirts back from our travels abroad, also for "the Madam", and they were thrilled.

Our luck with guards in Ouaga was pretty miserable. There was one who was irritating but at least seemed to have a kind of logic that we appreciated, and wouldn't let people into our compound just because they were white. We had constant guard rotation, making it nearly impossible to train any of them in things like not touching the generator and *under no circumstances* opening the gate when the dog was in the compound outside the house.

We were also pretty sure that one of the guards was stealing kerosene out of the generator; another guard pointed out the jerrycan under some bushes out in front of the house. They're little irritations but they can become bigger when they happen every day, like coming outside in the morning to find that the guard has chosen this moment, when you leave for work at the same time every day, to go have a shower. And he's got the key for the gate, so you're stuffed until he decides to show up again.

90

THE BREAK-IN

December, 2016

We were sleeping one night at maybe 2:30 a.m. and I heard a sound, something that half woke me up. I looked into the little room at the center of all the bedrooms, and saw a dark figure moving around. Thinking it was Eirwyn doing his usual thing of going to bed late, I rolled over and went back to sleep—sort of. Something was nagging me, and it was that I knew Eirwyn didn't move the way this figure was moving. And then I heard a door. I turned around and saw a silhouetted figure holding a carry-on suitcase from our closet, tiptoeing out of our room.

My voice didn't cooperate for me to scream or shout, but I rasped as loudly as I could to Eddie, "There's someone in the house!" He quickly leapt up and ran after the guy, who deposited the suitcase outside on his way out of the property. What a relief. The case had a number of valuable things in it, some money but all our important papers, so losing it would have been a minor catastrophe.

Maybe the guard was sleeping, maybe (as he said) he was

pretending to be asleep because there were two intruders; either way, we were somewhat bemused to find that the guard was sitting out front, in fine fiddle, for all the time that the intruder(s) were in the house. Soon after Eddie ran out, the guard left as well. It turned out later that he'd gone to find someone with a phone in order to call his company, and he did eventually come back, but his lack of action earlier made us suspicious. And also, since when does any self-respecting Burkinabè not have his phone on him?

The horrible thing (besides waking up to find a strange man in your bedroom, which is pretty horrible) was knowing that the thieves had probably received information from one of our guards. They knew how to break in, and they showed some signs of knowing where the valuables were. This is such a creepy feeling, knowing that someone who works in or close to your house doesn't have your best interests at heart.

In the living room, all of our bags were lined up on the couch and showed signs of having been systematically gone through. Thankfully, they were obviously only interested in cash or what they could easily sell for cash, so although they took our home laptop and my work one (skewer me now) and the cash from our wallets, they didn't take any credit cards or even my passport. Now, my passport does look like the creature from the black lagoon, but still. They'd even gone into the bedroom and grabbed Eddie's shorts so they could go through his wallet at their leisure. That was the second big shock of the evening, seeing for how long they'd probably been in the house before we heard anything.

After some minutes, the police "anti-crime forces" arrived, dressed to the nines with Kevlar vests, helmets (think WWII) and rifles. One of them fired into the air to try to flush the guys out if they were still in the house or close by, and they checked around the whole house to make sure no one was lurking in the compound. It was very strange to have these people on our premises. We asked only that they be super quiet going around the house, because we didn't want the kids to wake up to some dudes with guns going past their window.

At this moment Eirwyn emerged to take the dog out, and was nearly brained by Eddie, who was standing in the kitchen with a flip flop at the ready. At least then Eirwyn was warned so that when he did go out and see a man in full gear, he wasn't too shocked.

This one took Eddie and me both a little while to come down from. Knowing they'd been in our room just a few feet from the bed, and seeing our bags all lined up like that, it was just creepy. We did that thing of waking at the slightest noise, heart racing, for some weeks before it eventually subsided.

91

IN WHICH WE EAT

O ur family being our family, I can't let these stories go by without talking about food (cue the kids to say "You're talking about food—*again*?"). It's such an expression of the different climes and cultures we've been in, and in each place we've lived there have been different foods that caught our spirit.

Rwanda, for example, has the best potatoes I've ever eaten. It must be the volcanic soil up north, perhaps also the variety, I really don't know. But just a plate of fries is so flavorful, it's crazy. And you can get the "local" eggs, which are smaller than the commercially produced ones but with a super yellow yolk, and you put those with some potatoes, and, well. Heaven.

The peas are commonly a bit bigger than our peas, but otherwise similar in shape and color. This leads many a newbie to thing that they will taste like "European" peas, but no! The African peas are not sweet and very starchy, and take a long time to cook. Madeleine used to prepare half a potato with a sauce made of peas in tomato sauce. I can still hear my kids shouting for "potatoes and peas"!

And I have to say that all the fruit and veg we got there was pretty darned tasty. When we first arrived in Nairobi, I was impressed (if that's the right word) by how simple the cooking is —the African cooking, at least. Since the cuisine in Nairobi was an amalgam of British, Indian and African, you don't want to make too many sweeping statements. But when we moved to Rwanda, it was kind of the same thing. Fairly monotonous, mostly single-ingredient dishes.

With time, though, I came to appreciate that you don't need fancy preparation and sauces if the basic ingredients of your cooking are so full of flavor on their own. And this stuff was, and how. A plate of beans, amaranth leaves and rice was pretty much my go-to when in the field, and it was great for me that beans are the national staple in Rwanda and so are generally available for any non-breakfast meal. And there were these tiny little eggplant doodads, pale green or slightly yellow, extremely bitter but an excellent complement to beans.

Another thing was that fruit was less expensive than sugar, so the locally made jams were killer. There was a strawberry jam that would have been considered super gourmet in the developed world: almost entirely strawberries and very little sugar. It was like spreading concentrated strawberry on your toast. And cheaper than the "cheap" supermarket own brands from Belgium.

Something it took me a long time to get used to was that some people preferred their beer or Fanta (the collective name for soft drinks—in Lusaka it was "softies") at room temperature rather than chilled. So you'd order a beer, and they'd ask "warm or cold"? Generally speaking, one of the first things outsiders would learn to say is "ikonje cyane"! to have any hope of getting their beer properly cold.

When all the power cuts happened toward the end of our stay, though, we got used to drinking everything lukewarm, and I even started to get the appeal of the room-temperature soft drink.

I know. Stockholm syndrome? But the kids got so used to everything being warmer that when we went on vacation and everything came super chilled with ice, they couldn't handle it. It hurt their mouths or gave them stomach cramps. Makes you think.

As a vegetarian, I do appreciate having tofu around as a change-up from beans and lentils. We always had tubs of Thai curry paste in the fridge, and it was always better if you could add some tofu to a nice Thai curry. In Rwanda, you couldn't find tofu in the supermarket, so I went without for a long time, until someone showed me the little, non-descript shop where I could get it. This particular shop was Chinese, but I also noticed signs in most towns we passed through advertising tofu produced by Adventists. I asked around and was told that most Adventists were vegetarian, and so the tofu industry was sustained by Adventist weddings.

We had the most wonderful little garden out back of the house in Kigali. Not to undermine my husband's prodigious gardening skills, but I do think Rwanda is one of those places where you throw a seed down, you look sideways at it for a moment, and you'll have a beautiful plant. It's that volcanic soil again.

We grew all sorts of herbs and vegetables, so half the time when making dinner I'd head out back to the garden with a pair of scissors and just take the herbs I wanted for the dish. Sometimes we'd just take masses of chives, parsley, mint, dill, and whatever other herb tickled our fancy, mix it with a little oil and vinegar, and use it as a salad dressing.

One of the things we grew was cherry tomatoes. I made the mistake once of giving one to Marion when she was about two. Well, all she wanted after that was "maytoms"! She'd positively strip the bush, to the point that she got a rash around her mouth from the acid, but nothing would stop her.

And one more thing we grew, which we were told was difficult to grow but always produced more than we knew what to do with, was *akabanga*, aka habanero, aka Scotch bonnet peppers. Hot little suckers. But Madeleine had this way of cooking them with onion and garlic to make a kind of chili condiment, which was completely wonderful. We'd take ages to go through one jar, but we gave some to some Rwandan friends once, and the family used the whole jar in one evening!

And now I have to tell you about the fruit salad. There is some magical chemistry involved here, so bear with me. Now as I said, I am not a huge fan of the banana, so number one is not to put any banana in my fruit salad. Just a nice base of mango, papaya and pineapple, even if Rwanda is too wet to produce really good papayas.

Then you add the insides of a couple of *maracujas* (passion fruit), of which the Rwandan variety is nice and sweet. And then, the *ibinyomoro*. I have seen this fruit variously referred to as tree tomato, Japanese plum and tamarillo. Reddish gold on the outside and shaped like an American football, the flesh looks yellow-orange but the seeds are dark red, and the juice looks like blood.

The taste on its own is kind of musty, not something I really care for, but: put it in a fruit salad where it can interact with the maracuja and the pineapple, and something magical happens. It just puts a taste in the salad that a) binds the whole thing together and b) lifts the flavor to another dimension. (Speaking of wacky things that lift flavors, try putting basil in with your chopped pineapple one time. It's unintuitive but very yummy.) I confess that ever since Rwanda, anything labelled "fruit salad" is a royal disappointment to me. I am, sadly, a fruit-salad snob.

Sarajevo (and the Balkans generally) has some pretty awesome food. I won't bore you with all of it, but I have to talk about what the Serbs call *burek* (based on the Turkish *börek*) and the Bosnians call *pita*. This is filo dough wrapped around a filling, and traditionally cooked in a great iron dish suspended over a coal fire by a couple of chains, with a lid on top also covered in hot coals, so it cooks evenly from top and bottom. Traditionally the filo dough would be made by hand, and if you ever get a chance to see a grandmother work the great sheets, by all means do so.

Serbia tends to have mostly just cheese or meat as fillings, at least commercially available, but in Bosnia you can also get spinach, squash and potato. Generous amounts of butter have been known to go into the making of the *burek/pita*, so it's not exactly diet food, but there is nothing better when you've been out in the cold for a few hours.

To go with it, one would traditionally drink yoghurt, creamy and tangy but obviously not set or how could you drink it? You can also buy drinking yoghurt in liter bottles like you might find milk in. We could buy only two at a time for home because of fridge space, so we'd always have to buy some more later to get us through the week. We had to limit the kids to one glass of it every evening or they would have filled up on that and been too full to eat dinner.

Once we had a regional adviser for security visiting the office, who was a friend of mine, so I invited him to dinner. I'd explained to the kids that he was there to make sure our house was as safe as it could be. Over dinner, they informed him that "The drinking yoghurt is the most dangerous thing in the house!"

When I first arrived in Sarajevo and the family was still back in Kigali, a colleague of mine needed a place to stay so I invited her to come stay in the downstairs bedroom. It was a good arrangement and helped me feel less lonely, there without the family. There was a tree out front positively bursting with sour cherries, a bit too sour to eat on their own, so we decided to make jam. The whole endeavor wound up taking pretty much all day, what with picking what cherries we could get to and pitting them all. But the jam turned out great and we ate from it for about a year. It had a slightly cinnamon taste, which I could never figure out.

Eddie also tried to garden in Sarajevo, but it was tough because we were on a pretty steep hill and so the light was very limited. He did get some beautiful sunflowers. We tried tomatoes but they were too young to do anything with before we went on our annual home leave in the summer, and when we got back they'd grown but not turned red, and the season was already turning. This is how our great green-tomato chutney adventure began. Eddie found a great recipe and then did the obligatory tweaking. We've always had it since, and I use it on lentil dishes, soups, even cheese on crackers.

One thing I do also have to mention in Sarajevo are the bakeries. In other cultures it might be French fries and a sausage, or a curry, but in Sarajevo it's the bakeries that are open 24 hours per day. There's *kifle*, soft little rolls that come in a crescent shape, little things made out of puff pastry, you name it. Somehow this always seemed very civilized to me. Is there ever a bad time for bread? Surely not in the middle of the night, when the blood sugar is low, or after a night of dancing and drinking, when perhaps a little something neutral is just the ticket to calm the stomach.

In Lusaka I discovered three foods. The first is mustard leaves, which we'd never heard of until someone pointed out that we had some growing in our garden. I eventually screwed up my courage to try them, and now they are one of my favorite leafy greens. Lusaka was not big on fruit & veg to begin with, but the leafy greens were varied and plentiful. This is how we discovered sweet-potato leaves. Clarisse made them with peanut sauce and *sadza* when I wanted a night off from cooking, and it quickly became one of our favorites.

Pumpkin was the other one. Of course I'd eaten pumpkin before, but I'd never really seen it as kind of a staple food. What I mean is, the pumpkins in Lusaka were not expensive, and you could easily get four family meals out of one. The southern African type I mean is a good foot and a half across, with a shape as though someone had pushed down on the stem and squashed the whole thing a bit, with pale, green-silvery skin but very orange flesh. I've never been a fan of sweet things in my savory cooking, but this one was great for soups and curries.

One year we were doing Thanksgiving dinner, and I decided to do a proper pumpkin pie. Pumpkin-pie filling being not exactly found on Zambian supermarket shelves, I whipped out my trusty 1980s' edition of the *Better Homes and Gardens* cookbook and followed the instructions to make everything from scratch. Of course I had to make my own crust, too. The first pie I made died a tragic death when the pie dish slipped from the board I was carrying it on, spilling pie filling everywhere. Sob. But the second one survived, and I have to say it tasted just like a pumpkin pie is supposed to. I admit to having been chuffed when it passed my own taste test.

Lusaka was also much better for cheese than Rwanda had been, seeing as how it was in the South African zone of influence. And there were all sorts of other foods I'd never thought I'd see: frozen shrimp, veggie burgers. The supermarket had that sanitized, hyper-clean thing going on, there was piped music following you around as you shopped, and the shopping carts worked. It all felt way too Western for my taste. If I wanted frozen shrimp and piped music, I could be in the US where the kids could be closer to grandparents.

Zambia was a great place to illustrate that development and being African can mix perfectly well. In fact, I wanted to take a series of photos with the subtitle "this is also Africa" just to illustrate my point: the shiny shopping malls with designer brands; the fancy, 3D movie theater; the streets they redid in our neighborhood complete with zebra crossings, lines at the edges of the road, and reflective lights down the middle so that arriving home at night I always felt as though I was on a runway about to take off; my boss in a thick sweater huddled over his cup of tea.

92

RWANDA

2002-2007

It's not my objective to give a full picture of life in Rwanda, but in addition to the stories I've shared here, for you to get a fuller picture of what the situation was like when we were there, here are a few tidbits:

- The infamous plastic-bag ban, which is truly a great thing to have done, was announced on a Wednesday and took effect that Saturday. Shops were threatened with being shut down if they didn't have alternative packaging available by that day.
- The government had shut down the central market in Kigali, judging it too big and unruly, and not "developed" enough. So merchants were all pushed out to smaller markets on the outskirts of town, which were at times far away from where they lived and not nearly as profitable as the old sites. And for all of the five years we were there, nothing was

touched in the old central market (though I understand it has been developed since).

- Street trading was forbidden.
- Toward the end of our stay, flipflops were also forbidden in town, apparently because they looked too poor. There were stories of even foreign visitors being fined.
- The government revived an old custom of mutual aid called *umuganda* and converted it to a day per month of compulsory community service. The work might be clearing rubbish from a section of streets or engaging in reforestation efforts. Foreigners knew to just not go out onto the street on *umuganda* mornings, for fear of being swept up and forced to pitch in. Supervisors kept track of who showed up and who didn't. There might not be an immediate punishment for non-attendance, but either way you'd find out about their record-keeping the next time you went to the county office to get a permission or permit.
- Open grazing was made illegal, and only zero grazing permitted. This meant everyone had to tie their goats to a post somewhere outside, and produce forage for their animals where they would otherwise produce food, and where previously the goats could just wander around and nibble on everything. (The rationale for this was as an anti-erosion measure.)
- The only time we saw a demonstration have an effect was when the government banned motorcycle taxis. The drivers were upset because many of them had been bicycle taxis before those had been banned. They had sunk a lot of investment into their mopeds,

which they'd now not be able to recover. The drivers took to the streets for several days, and finally the government had to back down.

93

DRIVING

One real gift of all the traveling around is that I have become a much better driver. I can honestly say that everywhere I've driven, I've learned something about driving.

In Southern California, where I went to college, it was merging into traffic going 70 mph and zooming along at that speed with maybe a foot of clearance between me and the next car. In Kosovo I learned about 4WD and how to drive in snow (which later helped me a lot to drive in mud). I also learned about stopping for cows. I didn't drive much in Belgrade, but the one time I did, it was a big van, so that was new.

In Nairobi, I learned how to use roundabouts and also to drive on the left side of the road. It was also the first place where I memorized where all the potholes were—which was annoying when you'd come back from a month abroad and find that some had been repaired and there were new ones!

Rwanda taught me to use my mirrors and be more aware of the traffic around me, and to assume that if there was something another driver could do to advance his position, whether legally or not, he would do it. That illegal left turn? Yup. Merge around where there isn't really room just to get one car-length ahead? You got it. I also got better at reversing, because so many people's driveways went up or down a hill and around a bend, and had no room to turn around.

Sarajevo was all about the parallel parking. Here I can say that I got better, but am still not that great at it. Part of it was that I was always given a Twigo to drive, which though small, didn't have power steering. So the whole parking thing took a lot of muscle and was perhaps less exact than if there'd been some help. My buddy Marc used to look down from the balcony of our 2nd-floor office in the morning, watch me trying to park, and laugh maliciously.

In Zambia it's apparently illegal to turn your head around when you're trying to drive backwards. You're supposed to use your mirrors. Well, I never quite took that entirely on board, but I did learn a lot about the virtues of using mirrors to back out of a tight spot.

And Ouaga was extra special. The roads are crowded and chaotic, with donkey carts in the way and potholes that are sometimes allowed to get so big they'll swallow your car if you stumble into them. But the big one is the mopeds, along with bicyclists, which really clog the roads. Don't get me wrong—if all those moped drivers got into a car, no one would ever get anywhere. So I'm not complaining!

Some roads have well-demarcated moped lanes (which also cater to bicycles and donkey carts), and sometimes even separate traffic-light cycles, but other roads are a free-for-all and you may have mopeds driving practically on top of you. And you can't do anything to assert your own space, because they'll just sidle up to you wherever you are.

The worst are the Apsonics, the motos with three wheels and a big bucket at the back for hauling goods—or animals, or people. A friend of mine saw a live camel being transported in the back of an Apsonic once. The problem is that they're really wide, so they impede the flow of traffic and are much more likely to run into a car.

When I first got to Ouaga, I honestly wasn't sure if I'd be able to drive there. But, like everything else, it's all about the practice and a little bit of patience.

94

ZAMBIA

2009-2014

E ddie and I always seem to do better in places where there are some layers to peel back on the ol' onion, and I think it's no coincidence that we lived in three or four conflict-affected countries. Zambia was a break from all that. On one hand it was great—almost-Western shopping, if you had the money, grocery stores with beautiful fruit & veg sections, not very decent coffee, but hey, you can't have everything. There were nice cafés and some pretty good restaurants. There was even a movie-rental place, so we didn't have to go buying cheap copies—wait, did I say that? Of course we never bought an illegally copied film in all our years abroad. That's my story, and I'm sticking to it.

And the weather was pleasant-ish, apart from when it was raining so much all your shoes would start to go moldy. Or when things got hot and muggy right before the rains started. Or in the winter, when temps would get down to 7° C or around 45° F, when your house has slat windows and covered-breezeblock walls and you have no heating. I used to put on pajamas, a bathrobe and then a great woolen sailors' coat, the thickest socks I had, and maybe a scarf to sit and watch TV in the evenings. It's not so bad when you're moving around, but once you sit still, you chill right down.

The problem was that I just couldn't care about the politics. They seemed too one-dimensional to me: different factions vaguely associated with certain ethnic groups, and everyone just looking for a chance to enjoy the spoils of power. It all seemed terribly predictable.

Zambia is technically a middle-income country, largely because of the income from the mining industry (primarily copper). It's also often cited as proof that economic growth doesn't equal poverty reduction. What does that mean? It means that you've got a capital and a few secondary cities that are doing very well for themselves thanks to the mines and government. There are some very wealthy folks, and just enough of a middle class to justify having all kinds of aspirational consumer goods.

The malls were popping up like mushrooms while we were in Lusaka, and they all seemed to have the same 10-15 stores. Manda Hill, which underwent extensive renovation and reopened in our second year or so, installed the first escalator in the country, and people came from far and wide just to go up and down on it. (There's a great Trevor Noah sketch about the first escalator in Zambia.)

What fascinated me were the grocery stores, which stocked even basic staples such as mealie meal. In Rwanda, the shops focused more on perishables or imported goods, because people largely went back to "the village" to pick up enough of what they could grow. So that, to me, was a sign that there is a middle class sufficiently cut off from their village that they relied on shops in the city for all of their food needs.

But go outside the cities, and the situation is just as bad as in any other poor country. It looks like there's a lot of free land in Zambia, but that's not really true. Huge swathes of the country are national park or otherwise owned by the government, and most people also don't want to farm too far from a road. So, in fact, subsistence farming is largely crowded around roads and secondary population centers.

The staple food is maize, which provides calories but very little else in the way of nutrition, and is subject to contamination by (at times very toxic) mycotoxins. Throw in protein and micronutrient deficiencies, along with poor sanitation, and you start to understand why child-stunting rates are as high as two-thirds. I could go on, but let's just say this population is not worried about a ride on an escalator or whether or not the latest movie release was in 3-D.

On the positive side, we did get a house with a swimming pool, our first and only time to do so. We'd actually been looking for a house without one, because we didn't want the stress of maintenance and such, but it transpired that pretty much every house in the areas we were allowed to look in had a swimming pool. So, reluctantly, we gave in.

And then we loved it. The kids played in that pool what seemed like every day. It was too small for laps, but to go in and horse around was also a good workout. We were saved the planning of many a birthday party just by having the pool, even in the rainy season.

The thing about pools was that they were semi-non-formally-and-yet-in-reality verboten, or at least frowned upon, in the CRS world. And I get it, I mean in the US a pool is a definite luxury that seems above the station of how we expats are supposed to be living. So people in Lusaka generally "got it", but the issue of HQ-based folks was quite sensitive. I remember when a very senior person from HQ visited, and the staff member who hosted a dinner with him had to put up a screen so he wouldn't see the pool on the way in.

At one point we were advised that we should ask internally

before having any donors over to our house, since of course we wouldn't want them to think we're spending US government funds on luxuries for the international staff. Being friends with donors happened pretty easily through the baby mafia, kids' school, exercise class, whatever. I had to laugh because we had really good friends whom we'd met in Rwanda and who wound up living two blocks away from us in Lusaka. Their pool was way bigger than ours. I kind of made a show of asking whether they could come to our house, but I knew they didn't care about our pool, so I didn't take it all that seriously.

The pool did claim one victim, though. We had a beautiful, absolutely enormous pink cedar tree in the garden just next to the pool. The tree was so big, though, that its roots were pushing up the path around the pool, and threatening to make cracks in the pool itself. So we had to have it chopped down. I was amazed to see that the tree-cutters used nothing so sophisticated as a chain saw; they whole thing was done with machetes, by hand, as they painstakingly cut off the branches and then the trunk. You could have had a picnic on the trunk, it was so big around.

It was terribly sad to have to do that, but we didn't see any other choice. And even worse, we displaced the pair of owls that often sat in that tree. A lot of African cultures see owls as a bad omen, but I loved these ones. They were very big, and nearly white. One early morning I was standing outside the house in the near-dark, waiting for a taxi to the airport, and suddenly—and very silently—this white owl flew by right in front of my face. It was magical.

Besides our dog, Seamus, whom we acquired in Lusaka, our kids bonded most with horses. There's a pretty significant horsey culture in the formerly British colonies of southern Africa, and riding lessons are comparatively inexpensive. The kids took riding from a man named James, who was, as far as I know, the only black African with his own stables in the Lusaka scene. There were plenty of black hands, but no one else in an ownership position.

James was magic. He had such a nice way with our kids, pushing them out of their comfort zone but always with lots of encouragement. They'd go on "hacks", or walks on the trails in the bush, and as they came back you'd see James emerging from the bushes, talking animatedly about a scene in a *Transformers* movie, practically rolling off his horse as he demonstrated a move. He really became like a big-brother figure to the kids, and sometimes I thought their main reason for going riding was just to hang out with him.

One Mother's Day, I suggested we go out to a small lodge with a baby-elephant sanctuary. When we got there, it was closed for a wedding. Trying to think what to do, I suggested that we go check out a place we'd passed that was sporting a huge "Polo" sign. (Later I learned that "polo" means "testicles" in Bemba, and immediately wondered how all the hands keep from making lewd jokes all the time—or maybe they do.) It had seemed to me that there were quite a number of horses there, so I thought if nothing else, the kids can have a little visit with the horses before we do find something else to do.

We walked in and nothing was happening on the field, but we quickly understood that we had found the tail end of a three-day competition that included teams from Zimbabwe. This made a lot of sense, since not only would there have been an originally Zambian crowd, a lot of white families had moved from Zim to Zambia as things went south down there. We bought a couple of drinks and received a little orientation from the man behind the bar. The games were played in chukkas, little chunks of time a bit like innings, I suppose. If people needed to change horses, they could do so in the breaks between chukkas.

So we went over and found ourselves some seats, and it wasn't long before we were completely captivated. You didn't really need to know the rules; it's enough to sit there and just feel the vibration of the earth in your chest as the assembled horses pound their way up and down the field. I was blown away. We wound up staying for quite some time, and after that if there was polo going and we could make it, we'd be sure to go.

The whole thing was also an introduction to one aspect, at least, of the white southern African culture. These were seriously horsey people. A lot of the men had a touch of the beer belly and face and neck reddened by the constant sun exposure. But the women—now they were something.

You know how you can tell who has a really expensive haircut even when it's just hanging in a simple ponytail? These ladies had the cut and the highlights, white blouse, khaki riding pants, boots, that perfect English countryside look. But they were no wallflowers. Imagine said elegant figure turning to the field and shouting to her daughter at the top of her lungs and with the poshest of Southern African accents, "*You get them, Bunty!*"

95

SARAJEVO

2007-2009

I'm not even quite sure where to begin about Sarajevo. Scenery-wise, it is just stunning. There's the fact that it really is a bowl within a bowl (hence its siegeability), so from essentially anywhere you can look down and find the river at the bottom. Church spires and minarets mingle all through the city, and there are the old and new synagogues in and near the town center. The city's name comes from *saraj*, a travelers' waystation on the old road to Istanbul. It is also well known as the site of the murder of Archduke Ferdinand, an event that is commemorated in a museum just next to the bridge where the incident took place.

Up on a hill about 20 minutes' drive from downtown there is a place called Barice, where you can sit with your picnic and look down on the whole city. Barice is high enough to be in pine forests, and the area is mine-free, so you can take walks through the forest and even stumble upon a village. In the right times of year, there are puddles full of tadpoles, great fun to explore with young kids.

Culture is plentiful and inexpensive. Eddie and I went to a

number of concerts and operas, for the equivalent of something like eight dollars. The symphony is, in all honesty, a bit ropey, despite their fame for having continued to rehearse and play during the war. Besides their own concerts, they also accompany the opera. As this goes, while the chorus is nothing to write home about, they always manage to get good ringers to sing the main parts, so the experience is still captivating. All those years in Africa, I'd forgotten the visceral pleasure of live music, especially opera. You know how you see people moved to tears by opera in the movies? That was me.

There are a lot of ethnic and cultural shifts going on since the war. Old-timers bemoan the influx of rural folks who don't have the same sophistication as the long-time city dwellers. There are also moves to assert the city's Muslim character, which is a little weird considering how cosmopolitan the city can still be. But it's true that certain more observant Muslims came to the country to help fight during the war, and some of them have stayed. Certain of them have taken to preaching a more hard-core type of Islam, and they definitely have a foothold now.

Traditionally, the religions that were practiced in Sarajevo (Catholicism, Orthodox Christianity and Islam, plus a small group of Jews) were observed pretty loosely, a formula that allowed everybody to live together and basically get along. People adopted each other's traditions and helped each other celebrate holidays and life events. On Christmas or Easter, the first people to text to wish me a happy holiday were always Muslims.

Holidays were always a little tricky because rather than make each religion's holy days a government holiday, and thereby certainly offend somebody, the government preferred to err on the side of making everything a work day. So our organization determined eight official holidays to do with state events and our own American holidays, and then our office put out a list of all different religious holidays so that people could choose their four additional vacation days per year. Well, funny how Christians suddenly because Muslim if Bajram (Eid) was on a Thursday or Friday; you get the idea. It was actually a great arrangement and I appreciated the flexibility.

One sign of the creeping Islamization of the culture in Sarajevo was the decision by the mayor to ban Santa Claus from all Muslim pre-schools, saying that it was not a part of Islam. Well, you should have seen my colleagues. Everyone was incensed, including the Muslims. No one could understand what value there was in banning a tradition that had been around for many decades, if not longer. Many Muslims felt it was part of their tradition as well, and they were very unhappy on behalf of their children, who wouldn't have the opportunity to partake in this tradition.

Despite CRS being a Catholic organization, they had a good reputation in Bosnia from the war because of having served the entire population no matter what ethnic group they belonged to. The Jews did much the same, running an ambulance service in the city because they were the only population bloc that wasn't considered an enemy by anyone else. In CRS' case, it meant that they could send Muslim staff to deal with the Serb city administration of towns like Srebrenica and know they would enjoy good relationships with local-government officials.

Even though the city never got enough snow to stick for a long time in the two winters we were there, something everyone attributed to global warming, we certainly did have several drops of a couple of feet. I kind of laughed as I got the opportunity to gain first-hand experience of the joys of shoveling snow.

The really scary thing was that once I drove the car out of the driveway, I had to turn to the right and drive up a pretty steep hill to get up to the ploughed road. The secondary road was often cleared, seemingly by people who remembered growing up in Yugoslavia when the communal clearing of roads was considered part of civic duty. Once I saw two older men shoveling snow up this road, and they were singing old patriotic songs that were giving them a rhythm to shovel by. I really hated that little jog up the hill and was convinced that one day I wouldn't make it, to the point of not being able to sleep sometimes because I was so worried about that crucial three seconds the following morning.

What was really funny, though, was the notices we'd get from HQ that they were shut for a snow day because there had been two inches of snow, so the going was treacherous. The Sarajevo gang would just glance out the window and laugh. Though in fact, HQ wasn't being wimpy, per se: the city of Baltimore had only two snow ploughs, and most people had neither snow tires nor experience driving in snow, so in fact the going *was* pretty unsafe. And yet.

One thing about the women in Bosnia is that about 90% of them seem to dye and/or highlight their hair. Most Balkan folks' hair is pretty dark, which looks fine to me, but there was this whole culture around making things lighter and tinting and whatnot.

They used to *love* Marion's hair. At that age it was still very light blond, lighter than most women would dare to dye their own hair. People used to reach out to touch her hair on the bus, and I bet you can imagine how much our 6-year-old liked that.

I always figured that my gray hairs were my natural highlights and never really worried about it, until the day one of my colleagues said to me flat out: "You should dye your hair." Not "oh, wouldn't it be fun if." Clearly, I was not on the Sarajevo fashion train. It's true no one approached me just to touch my hair. I guess I don't know what I was missing.

One of the most lovely things we did was drive down to Mostar, in Herzegovina, or all the way to Dubrovnik in Croatia. The drive was one lane in each direction, so if you got stuck behind a big lorry you were just not in luck. But for much of the drive you are moving alongside the Neretva river, whose color is a pale turquoise or even teal, a color I've never seen in a body of water before then or since.

One year we were driving down in the autumn, and we passed some mountains with a mixture of deciduous and pine trees. The deciduous trees were a flame of red, gold, orange and yellow, surrounded by a layer of dark green, with the river flowing in front. I admit to nearly crashing the car, but I figure it's not my fault. Who could drive by and not be completely captivated?

96

IN WHICH WE ROOT, ROOT ROOT FOR THE HOME TEAM

Ouagadougou 2014-2017

I f there's one thing that culturally defined the experience experience at the International School of Ouagadougou for us, it was the softball. There were other sports there, of course, and many kids even traveled to places like Nigeria, Ghana and Senegal to play in league games. Softball was a different animal: more casual, less fixated on winning, and a lot of fun for a group of kids who often knew each other pretty well anyway.

The school would host a number of tournaments every year, from one-day local competitions to the unfortunately named but very important SOFANWET. This is when the teams came from Niamey, and there were enough to run both a social and a competitive league. We also got two Burkinabè teams, usually a social and/or competitive team from the US embassy, and wonderfully spirited teams from Taiwan and Japan. The Japan team was usually put together pretty spontaneously, but the Taiwanese team practiced all year, and they were very serious about their softball.

Their fans were also great fun. Noisemakers, flags, you name it. The Japanese team tended to have a couple of people chanting encouraging slogans for all their batters, and one year someone wore a wig of curly white hair with a big red dot in the middle.

For the Niamey folks, SOFANWET weekend was not only the time to play softball against a bunch more teams than they had at home, it was also a chance to stay in a nice hotel and to *shop*. Now if you consider what the shopping was like in Ouaga, this is quite a commentary on what must have been available in Niamey. The Sahel boarding school in Niamey, a Christian school that catered to kids who couldn't afford the international schools or wanted a more explicitly Christian atmosphere, would often also bring a team. And since there were a few kids who'd moved from Ouaga to the Sahel Academy, SOFANWET was a chance to see old friends as well.

The Burkinabè national team was killer. Obviously they'd practiced together a lot, which many of the other teams hadn't, but they were serious about their softball. Matching uniforms, yes, but also the ability to play as a team at speed was impressive.

Really the only fly in the ointment were the enormous turtles that roam around the ISO property. Their shells are easily two feet in diameter, and when the afternoon shadows lengthen, they come out onto the field to munch. Which, obviously, presents a hazard to the players. One time one of the Japanese outfielders was going after a fly, so he backed up, and backed up…and went straight back over the turtle's shell, heels over head. Thankfully he was on the smaller side and well built, so he seemed to roll right over and then bounce up again no worse for wear.

One of the nice things about the tournament was how people from other teams would "pitch in" (sorry) to help if there weren't enough people for some roles. So someone might play a whole game and then go out to umpire or even pitch for another team. It was always good to see this display of sportsmanship and general mucking in so that the tournament could go on for everyone.

For me, as a spectator, it was a great opportunity to enjoy a few beers and cheer on the various teams. Of course it was extra fun embarrassing our kids and their friends, but we didn't care. It was just a lovely feeling to wander home at the end of the day, covered in dust, happily exhausted, and full of the sense of being part of a community.

ACKNOWLEDGMENTS

I must first acknowledge my husband, Eddie, and in particular my children, Eirwyn and Marion, for keeping me focused on making this book a reality. In recording a chunk of family history for them, I hope I have created something that will also please a wider audience. And, obviously, without them there would be nothing to write.

My thanks also go to Ahou, who gave me the final push I needed to start writing, and the encouragement to keep going once I had started. I would also like to thank the Sidewalk Café HTS in Altadena, California and Michal Dawson Connor for providing, in their own way, the spaces where I was able to write.

Lastly, my heartfelt thanks and love go to Bill (Tosh) McIntosh, who besides being my uncle and a fine author in his own right, has devoted innumerable hours to shepherding the publication process of this book. I could not have done this without him.

ABOUT THE AUTHOR

Carey McIntosh spent 25 years living, studying, traveling, working and parenting in eight countries across Europe and Africa. She has traveled to some 45 more. Her overseas career began with a stint as a volunteer for the Balkan Peace Team based in Belgrade, Serbia. She spent three years as the Ambassador's Special Self-Help Coordinator with the US Embassy in Kigali, Rwanda, and 11 years working with Catholic Relief Services doing development work in such areas as agriculture, health, water & sanitation, peace & justice, refugees, and capacity building.

She lives in Monrovia, California with her husband, Eddie, and two cats who have never been abroad.